DINOSAUR HUNTERS

DAVID A. E. SPALDING

DINOSAUR HUNTERS

Prima Publishing
P.O. Box 1260
Rocklin, CA 95677
(916) 786-0426

For
my mother, Elsa Maud Spalding,
who was interested in my fossils, even when
they made holes in my pockets,
and
my father, Charles William Spalding,
who always let me choose a book for myself—
but did not live to see this one completed.

Front cover: Illustration of *Tyrannosaurus & Edmontosaurus*, by Eleanor M. Kish. Repro-
duced with permission of the Canadian Museum of Nature, Ottawa, Canada.
Black and white photo by Glenbow Archives
Original cover design by Annabelle Stanley
Cover adaptation by The Dunlavey Studio, Sacramento
Endpapers: Iguanodon bones being prepared in Brussels
(Photograph courtesy Institut Royal des Sciences Naturelles de Belgique)

Library of Congress Cataloging-in-Publication Data
Spalding, David A. E.
　　Dinosaur hunters : eccentric amateurs and obsessed professionals /
　　David Spalding.
　　　　p.　cm.
　　Includes bibliographical references and index.
　　ISBN 1–55958–338–X : $24.95
　　1. Paleontologists—Biography.　2. Dinosaurs.　I. Title.
　QE707.A2S63　1993
　560.9—dc20　　　　　　　　　　　　　　　　　　　93–15319
　[B]　　　　　　　　　　　　　　　　　　　　　　　　　CIP

93　94　95　96　97　RRD　10　9　8　7　6　5　4　3　2　1
Printed in the United States of America

CONTENTS

PREFACE

IN 1841 AN ENGLISH ANATOMIST DESCRIBED A NEW GROUP OF extinct animals, the dinosaurs. They captured the imagination of people around the world. I saw their bones in the Natural History Museum in London on childhood trips, and was fascinated. Although I knew that dinosaurs were not the only kinds of fossils, they symbolized for me the wonder of life before man. In time, they led me to study geology (the science of the earth) and paleontology (the science of fossils), and to a new home in western Canada.

My first "real" dinosaur was concealed in three large packing cases in the then new Provincial Museum and Archives of Alberta in Edmonton, Alberta, Canada. It had been collected by the Geological Survey of Canada in the year I was born, and had remained unprepared for thirty years. I learned that its collector was Charles M. Sternberg, and it had been named *Lambeosaurus*, after one Canadian paleontologist, Lawrence Lambe, by another, William Parks.

I soon found that the people who collected and studied dinosaurs were as interesting as the fossils themselves. Parks and Lambe had died, but I eventually met Charles M. Sternberg, by then in his nineties. Son, brother, and father to other fossil collectors, Sternberg had an amazing career in paleontology, in which he was active in much of North America. I talked to him in his apartment in Ottawa, near the National Museum, which had been his base for some sixty years. He was small but energetic, and eager to talk about his beloved fossils. At that time I knew little about his family and their remarkable achievements, and had few specific questions. "I don't know what else I can tell you," he said as I left.

Many times I have wished that Charlie Sternberg was still with us. He would have been delighted by the amazing resurgence of interest in dinosaurs, and the discoveries that have been made in recent years. I know now what questions I would like to ask him.

Those who have succeeded at what paleontologist G.G. Simpson has called "the most fascinating of all sports" have always been dedicated, frequently original and idiosyncratic, sometimes more than a little eccentric, and almost invariably entertaining. They are not ordinary people. They have not, as a rule, looked to dinosaurs to help them to secure place or wealth. Some were adventurers into remote and often dangerous parts of the world, looking for an unusual souvenir. Others have found their fossils in places people passed every day. Some have been namers, eager for new fossils to carry their own names to posterity. Others have been theorizers, trying to solve a puzzle or looking for material to support their theories. Some were innocents whose minds were fired by the shape of a bone and whose feet skirted the edge of the giddy gulf of time, and became entrapped for a lifetime in a pursuit that fed the spirit if not always the body.

This book tells the story of some of the men (and, more recently, the women) who have devoted significant parts of their lives to the discovery and study of dinosaurs. It is no longer possible to write a complete single-volume history of what is now sometimes (logically but awkwardly) called dinosaurology. I have focused on some of the major dinosaur discoveries, from different periods and from all parts of the world. Each has increased our understanding of the animals we call dinosaurs, by adding a new and interesting species, or a whole fauna, and often in circumstances that provide a special insight into the ways dinosaurs lived and died.

Perhaps the cost of collecting large fossils has necessarily kept dinosaur specialists in close touch with the popular audience that ultimately supports their work. At any rate, many of them have written lucidly of their work in nontechnical terms, and I have tried to include passages in their own words where possible, hoping to convey their enthusiasm to the armchair dinosaur collector of today. Together we argue that science offers no quest more exciting than that of discovering the dinosaurs.

ACKNOWLEDGMENTS

IT IS HARD TO ACKNOWLEDGE ADEQUATELY THE HELP I HAVE HAD IN preparing this book, because it derives from many years of association with dinosaur enthusiasts, and is part of an ongoing study of the history of dinosaur discovery.

My first thanks are to the collectors and paleontologists who have found and studied dinosaurs. Their scientific work has provided the subject matter, and I am particularly grateful to those who have seen fit to enliven or supplement their scientific reports with personal information in the form of articles, autobiographies, letters, and diaries, for they make it possible for me to show the extent to which science is a human activity. My second acknowledgment is to the many writers who have provided volumes and articles of biography, obituary, scientific history, and science related in various ways to the dinosaur story. These secondary sources have been invaluable. Archivists who care for their papers have usually been more than patient with my questions, as have librarians who cheerfully obtained for me books and articles from obscure sources.

My personal interest in dinosaurs has been fostered by the museums that have presented their remains, and especially by colleagues at the Provincial Museum of Alberta and what is now the Royal Tyrrell Museum of Palæontology with whom I have dug bones and discussed ideas, particularly Philip Currie and Brian Noble. A special debt is owed to my lifelong friend William A.S. Sarjeant, who has (as always) provided access to his remarkable library; copies of information from many sources; and, most important, unfailing encouragement.

Correspondence and meetings with elder statesmen of the dinosaur world have been inspiring, and I would like to thank especially Edwin Colbert, Ray Martin, Loris Russell, the late Charles M. Sternberg, and William Swinton, for their patient responses to my letters and questions. I have also been helped by relatives of fossil hunters, including Hazel Bird and Frances Brown.

Contemporary scientists and other museum colleagues have given freely of their information and wisdom, and I particularly thank Donald Baird, Angela Milner, Monty Reid, Dale Russell, and Tim Tokaryk for special information for this and other dinosaur projects. As the project neared completion, Edwin Colbert kindly commented on one of the chapters, and Phil Currie and William Sarjeant attacked the entire manuscript with deep knowledge and great enthusiasm. Needless to say, responsibility for the errors that remain is mine.

Writing is a lonely experience, and I am grateful to fellow writers who have provided advice and encouragement in various ways, including Robert Kroetsch, George Melnyk, Birk Sproxton, and Aritha van Herk, and inspiring writing situations provided by Dennis Johnson of Red Deer College and Rudy and Tina Wiebe of Strawberry Creek. Funding from Alberta Culture and the Alberta Foundation for the Literary Arts has provided help on earlier dinosaur projects, which have yielded information for this book. My agent, Joanne Kellock, brought writer and publisher together. Editor Meg Taylor has made a major contribution to the finished product, tidying my punctuation, smoothing my prose, and challenging my logic with such success that (with luck) the reader will never guess she was there.

Words are not enough for Jane, Penny, and Lucy who have patiently shared their dad with dinosaurs for years. Andrea, so much more than a partner, has made this book—and many other endeavors—possible.

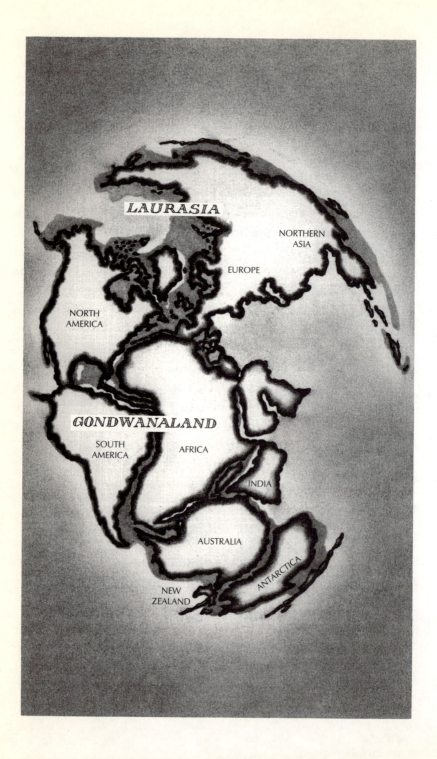

PANGAEA

When the first dinosaurs appeared, the earth had a single land mass, combining the ancient cores of all of today's continents. Although people never walked the plains and forests of this unbroken continent, its geography and history have been reconstructed in the minds of geologists. They call it Pangaea, the united earth.

The first age of the dinosaurs is called the Triassic period (lasting from approximately 248 million to 213 million years ago). During this period, the land masses were closely linked, though the first hint of the Atlantic was just beginning to appear, as a rift valley like that in East Africa today, between what is now North America and a combined Africa and South America.

The dinosaurs flowered in the Jurassic period (213 million to 144 million years ago), and the rift valley between North America and Africa, lengthened and eventually became the Atlantic. There were now two continents in close proximity. Geologists call the northern one Laurasia and the southern one Gondwanaland.

The dinosaurs flourished through the Cretaceous period (144 million to 65 million years ago), at the end of which the continents were much more distinct, though Laurasia was still connected across Greenland. The two ancient continents were linked between Europe and Africa, and perhaps North and South America, while Antarctica and Australia had not yet separated from other parts of Gondwanaland. Changes continued after the death of the dinosaurs, and the continents have continued to drift apart, to the familiar positions shown on today's map.

1

A WORLD OF DINOSAURS

PEOPLE HAVE A STRANGE LOVE AFFAIR WITH DINOSAURS. Over the centuries, increasing numbers of us have studied their remains, laboriously piecing together a world that vanished long before we came on the scene. The work of scientists has been introduced to the public through museum exhibits, publications, and documentaries. That information, in turn, has inspired the creation of fantasy worlds in novels and films, where people and dinosaurs coexist. A central part of our fascination with dinosaurs is the process of scientific discovery, by which bones and other remains have been found, collected, and interpreted. This book recounts some of the highlights of that story.

Dinosaurs saw the world long before we did, for they appeared around 230 million years ago, in the Triassic. Even so, they were relatively late in the geological story, and evolved from smaller, simpler reptiles that had already been developing for millions of years. The first dinosaurs were carnivores of small to medium size. Recent South American discoveries *Herrerasaurus* and *Staurikosaurus* seem to be closest to the ancestral dinosaurs, as they do not clearly fall into either of the two main groups of dinosaurs—the saurischians and the ornithischians.

The descendants of the first dinosaurs spread across the single continent that was then the land surface of the earth. As the pieces of Pangaea separated and slowly drifted apart, the dinosaurs were carried across the surface of the globe. Over millions of years, they evolved into at least 440 different kinds, and some of them grew to a remarkable size.

One group, the saurischians, had in common a reptilelike pelvis. Some of these remained two-legged forms, including the huge carnivores such as *Allosauros, Ceratosaurus, Tarbosaurus* and *Tyrannosaurus*, which may have run down their prey in a grim chase. Smaller and slimmer, relatively intelligent carnivores include *Ornithomimus*, which probably hunted small game, such as eggs and insects, or scavenged at the kills of larger relatives. Another, the long-clawed *Dromaeosaurus*, perhaps hunted in packs, which ran larger animals to ground and kicked them to death. Some of these small carnivores (and probably at least some other dinosaurs) were warm-blooded, and recent discoveries show that they were closely related to the ancestors of the birds.

Other saurischians were large two- or four-legged dinosaurs (prosauropods), which were probably ancestral to the huge four-legged forms with long necks and tails, known as sauropods, whose tiny heads reached browsing height on even the tallest trees. This group includes the huge *Brachiosaurus, Camarasaurus, Diplodocus*, and *Mamenchisaurus* and their more recently discovered relatives, including *Seismosaurus*, apparently the largest of all dinosaurs. The group includes *Saltasaurus* and its relatives, which recently have been shown to have had armored skin, and new Chinese forms that have tail clubs.

Another major group, the ornithischians, includes all the dinosaurs with birdlike pelvises (though, ironically, these are not the ones that actually evolved into birds). Four-legged ornithischians include several subgroups. The armored dinosaurs (ankylosaurs) such as *Ankylosaurus* shambled through the undergrowth like living tanks. Those with vertical bony plates on their backs (stegosaurs) are well known. The horned dinosaurs (ceratopsians) include "Centrosaurus" (now known as *Eucentrosaurus*), and *Triceratops*, which roamed the grassless plains in herds and whose eggs and nests were the first to be found.

Another group of ornithischians were two-legged and include *Iguanodon* and the many kinds of duck-billed dinosaurs (hadrosaurs) such as *Corythosaurus, Lambeosaurus*, and *Maiasaura*. The last named is known to have nested in colonies.

Dinosaurs shared the world with swimming reptiles (including crocodiles, turtles, ichthyosaurs, and plesiosaurs) and with pterosaurs, flying reptiles. Before long they also shared with their direct descendants, the birds, which are so closely related that some scientists now consider them to be dinosaurs. They preyed on tiny marsupials, and later shrewlike mammals that were our own remote ancestors. During their 165-million-year career, dinosaurs roamed and roared, mated and fought, laid their eggs, and (at least some of them) cared for their young. After a relatively sudden decline, for reasons that are now being intensely debated, they all died, leaving their feathered descendants in a world that was at last safe for mammals. It is reasonable to suppose that, if the dinosaurs had not disappeared, we would never have come along to wonder at their bones.

During the millions of years that they inhabited the earth, millions of dinosaurs were killed by predators or died as a result of accident or disease. Their flesh was eaten by beasts and bacteria, their bones were crunched and eroded, and all trace of most of them was lost. Only a small number of individual dinosaurs have left bones or other traces, saved by geological accidents that preserved them before they could be destroyed. Multitudes of dinosaur fossils are still buried in the ground, and those that are exposed by earth movements and erosion are slowly weathered away into dust. The only ones that become scientific evidence are those that chance to reach the surface of the ground in places where they were not covered by ice or jungle, and are seen by understanding people, or are excavated by chance or design. Of the many that have been exposed by erosion, only relatively few have been found, collected, preserved, and studied. Nevertheless, evidence of an amazing number of dinosaurs has been gathered from the rocks. Teeth, bones, and footprints, as well as gizzard stones, eggs, nests, and even excrement (fossilized into coprolites) and traces of skin, have survived the death of the dinosaurs. Those remains tell a wonderful tale of long ago, of amazing animals that haunt our dreams and inspire our imaginations, and whose lives and fate may help to shape our own future.

The first people evolved around two million years ago, more than sixty million years after the dinosaurs had disappeared. They had no reason to suspect that the world had ever been inhabited by animals other than those they saw around them. However, as human curiosity and intellectual capacity developed, people must sooner or later have found dinosaur remains (and other fossils), particularly in instances where fossil bones are large and conspicuous. Although there is no record of these early discoveries, we have hints that they were not uncommon.

In July 1923, Roy Chapman Andrews and his party from the American Museum of Natural History made a major dinosaur discovery at a site they called the "Flaming Cliffs," in the Gobi Desert. A nest of thirteen eggs was associated with bones of what was thought to be a primitive horned dinosaur, *Protoceratops*. In 1925, the collectors returned to the location to make further studies. Near the fossils they found sites containing remains of Stone Age man. In one place, bits of dinosaur eggshell had been worked into squares. "Then we realized," said Andrews, "that these people were the original discoverers of the dinosaur eggs."

In the state of Paraíba, Brazil, symbols have been found carved beside dinosaur tracks dating from the Lower Cretaceous period. The drawings, of crosses inside circles, do not resemble the tracks, but they are of similar size and are positioned so close to the tracks that they obviously relate to them. Clearly the drawings indicate an interest in the tracks taken by paleo-Americans at an unknown date.

It is impossible to tell how prehistoric people explained bones, tracks, and egg fragments. Although many of these must have gone unrecognized as remains of animals, in some documented instances quite astute guesses about the origins of these findings were made.

One such interpretation has been recorded from the prairies of Alberta in western Canada, where dinosaur fossils are abundant and conspicuous. A French Canadian, Jean-Baptiste L'Heureux, who was living with the Peigan (one of the three divisions of the Blackfoot), records being shown dinosaur bones in an area which can only be what is now Dinosaur Provincial Park, at a date before 1871. He writes that the Indians described them as remains of "the grandfather of the buffalo"—a remarkably scientific explanation by a people familiar with only one really large animal. Although the date of the report falls after the scientific discovery of dinosaurs, we can assume that the Blackfoot traditional explanation reflects a much earlier discovery of the fossil bones.

Written history has recorded speculations about fossils from the times of the ancient Greeks, who were aware of fossil vertebrates as early as the sixth century B.C., but whose speculative explanations were more imaginative and less realistic than that of the Blackfoot. The Greeks did not have dinosaur bones in their country, but the ancient Chinese did, and some of their accounts of dragon bones probably refer to dinosaurs. One such account is found in a book entitled *Hua Yang Guo Zhi*, written by Chang Qu. It refers to bones from Wucheng, Sichuan, in the southern Qinling Mountains, recorded during the western Jin dynasty (A.D. 265–317).

European folklore also has dragons in abundance—a recent book documents hundreds of different dragons reported in folklore from different regions of Britain alone. Although Europe has since yielded many dinosaurs to science, the most conspicuous bones found in the Middle Ages were those of Ice Age mammals. Most early fossil records are of mammoths and rhinoceroses in river gravels, and bears in cave deposits. Many were described as the bones of dragons or unicorns, but the Bible as chief authority also provided a variety of explanations for fossil finds. Thus, the early European history of vertebrate fossils is full of accounts of pre-Adamite giants ("there were giants in those days"), the behemoth, men drowned in the flood, and the bones of saints.

At the beginning of the nineteenth century, the educated community in Europe and America (mostly comprising ministers of religion) still tended to use the religious authority of the Bible to explain discoveries. In 1802, a farm boy named Pliny Moody was plowing near South Hadley in Massachusetts. Under the shallow soil, he found huge tracks, like those of three-toed birds. The local Congregationalist minister was probably asked what these might be. Noah's flood from the Bible had already been used to explain stratified rocks, the fossils found in them, and the great rocks called erratics (which were later shown to have been moved by glaciers). What could be more natural then, than that the raven — the last of the birds Noah sent out to find land in the flood story — should leave his footprints behind. The tracks were duly declared to be those of Noah's raven and, although they were known to the local people, no attempt to find a more scientific explanation was made for another thirty years.

Meanwhile, the methods of science were being developed. At first, the only people with scientific training were generally doctors, who had to study anatomy and herbs in order to be qualified. During the nineteenth century, clergymen and doctors often studied fossils as they broadened their interest in all aspects of nature, and gradually other people joined in the search. Their cumulative efforts led to a new understanding of the natural world. As geology and biological evolution were established as scientific disciplines, the dinosaurs found a place in the natural world. A growing number of people came to collect the remains of dinosaurs, which after so many millions of years could now be studied by a creature able to understand their significance.

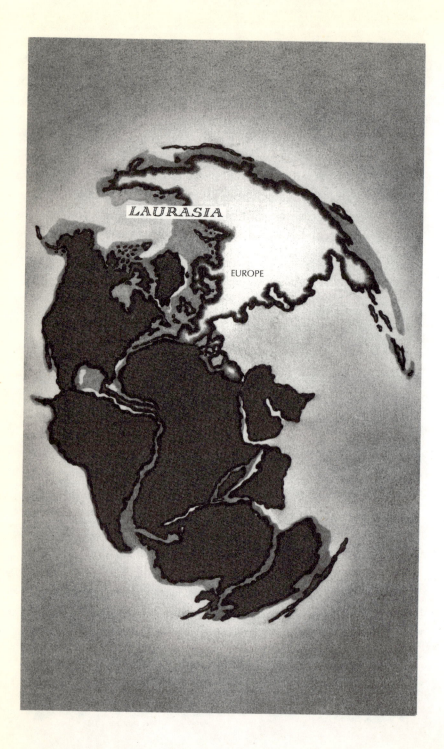

LAURASIA/EUROPE

FOR A WHILE, THE NORTHERN CONTINENTS WERE UNITED AS A single land mass, known to geologists as Laurasia. This supercontinent included the cores of modern Europe, North America, and Northern Asia.

The central part of that ancient continent is now Europe. Dinosaurs lived there in the Triassic and left many footprints and some bones. For much of the Jurassic and Cretaceous, Europe was submerged under shallow seas; therefore, dinosaurs are found only in occasional terrestrial and estuarine deposits.

As the mines and quarries, canals, and railways of the industrial revolution opened up the ground, many fossils were discovered. In more recent years, finds have lessened as exposures are grown or built over, but strong amateur and some professional interest continues to produce new discoveries.

In Europe, the first dinosaurs were scientifically described, and their name was invented. European-born collectors and trained scientists hunted dinosaurs on every continent, and colonial discoverers sent fossils from other continents to be described in European museums.

Many European dinosaur finds were fragmentary, but dinosaur remains have now been found in Europe, from Portugal to Spitzbergen (Norway), to Romania, and from the earliest to the latest times.

2

A DISTINCT TRIBE
OF SAURIAN REPTILES

SOUTHERN ENGLAND IS CLASSIC COUNTRY FOR GEOLOGISTS. Its geology is tidily laid out, almost like an English garden, as a succession of musically named ridges (the Cotswolds, the Chilterns, the Downs, the Weald) expose one layer after another of different rocks, each with its characteristic fossils. It is little wonder that some of the principles of geology were first understood in England—the evidence is so conveniently provided, it seems that they should have been obvious for centuries. However, the muddled mysticism of the Middle Ages was still strong when the first dinosaur bones were documented.

In the seventeenth century, some of Britain's most capable scientists felt that fossils were somehow created in the earth, by petrifying juices and other mystic means. One of these, Robert Plot (1640–96), an antiquary and naturalist, was secretary and editor for the Royal Society, first curator of the Ashmolean Museum in Oxford, and a professor of "chymistry." Plot came up with the whimsical idea that fossils might have been created as ornaments for the inside of the earth, just as flowers had been made to adorn the surface—after all, both seemed quite useless. Plot provided the first published record of a dinosaur bone that can be verified, because he also illustrated it. In his book, *The Natural History of Oxfordshire* (1677), he included a dinosaur bone in his section on stones: "I have one dug out of a quarry in the parish of *Cornwell*, and given me by the ingenious *Sir Thomas Pennyston*, that has exactly the Figure of the lowermost part of the *Thigh-bone* of a *Man* or at least of some other *Animal . . .* "

Plot describes the bone using anatomical terms, and comments on its size: "In Compass near the *capita Femoris*, just two Foot, and at the top above the *Sinus* (where the *Thigh-bone* is as small as any where) about 15 inches: in weight, though representing so short a part of the Thigh bone, almost 20 Pounds. Which are *dimensions*, and a *weight*, so much exceeding the ordinary course of Nature, that . . . such *Stones* have been rather thought to be Formed either in hollows of Rocks . . . or by some other sportive plastic power of the Earth."

It would have been easy for Plot to conclude that this, like so many strange finds, was an illusion, but he had the courage to suggest that this was "a real bone now petrified" and recognized that it "must have belonged to some greater *animal* than either an *Ox* or *Horse* and if so it must have been the *Bone* of some *Elephant*, brought hither during the Government of the Romans in Britain." After a living elephant was brought to Oxford and "shewn publickly," Plot changed his mind, and suggested the bone might have belonged to a giant man or woman. Although the bone is lost, it is clear from the illustration that it is a dinosaur bone, probably of the carnivorous *Megalosaurus*, and is the first dinosaur bone to be given any sort of scientific description.

Ironically enough, after Plot's courageous identification, his find was later the subject of a ludicrous chain of circumstances. In 1763, *The Natural History of Waters, Earths, Stones, Fossils and Minerals* by Richard Brookes was published. The author copied Plot's illustration and described it as *Scrotum humanum*—it is not known whether this was a serious attempt at identification, or a bizarre joke. Whichever it was, it was taken seriously when the French philosopher J.B. Robinet (1735–1820) described the same fossil as a "stony scrotum" in a book published in 1768, and explained that such objects were nature's attempts to form human organs, in an effort to create a perfect human type. In this century, paleontologist Beverly Halstead has pointed out light-heartedly that since *Scrotum humanum* is in the correct Latin form and was created after the agreed starting date for scientific names, it could be taken as a formal Latin scientific name having priority over any other scientific name for a dinosaur. This piece of valuable historic information was published in a less-than-serious periodical entitled *Journal for Insignificant Research*.

From the end of the seventeenth century, other kinds of vertebrate fossils were collected and described. A lizardlike reptile from Germany (older than the dinosaurs) was described by French anatomist Georges Cuvier (1769-1832) and was given the name *Proterosaurus*. The latter part of the name, "saurus," is the Greek word for a lizard, and was to become a common element in names of dinosaurs and other fossil reptiles. Cuvier also established that many species of animals were no longer alive, introducing the concept of extinction to science. In 1719 the Yorkshire clergyman and antiquary William Stukeley (1687–1765) described a fossil now known to be an ichthyosaur ("fish lizard"), publishing the first paper in the literature of British geology devoted entirely to vertebrate paleontology, the name now used for the study of fossils of vertebrates.

Despite Plot's published illustration, more dinosaurs were not recorded for some time. However, scientific treatment of fossils was advanced by one of Plot's protégés, John Woodward (1665–1728), a Derbyshire doctor who became a professor of "physick" at Gresham College, London. Woodward became fascinated by fossils after a visit to the fossiliferous Jurassic rocks of the Cotswolds, and was intrigued by the question of their origin. This was, he wrote, "a Speculation new to me; and what I judg'd of so great a moment, that I resolv'd to pursue it through the other remoter parts of the Kingdom, which I afterwards did." This search led, in 1695, to the publication of his *Essay towards a Natural History of the Earth*. He examined the arguments of his predecessors and recognized that fossils were the remains of animals, and then explained fossil vertebrates by the effects of the Deluge—the flood described in the Bible. His book was translated into several languages, and followed by a printed set of instructions on collecting specimens, a by-product of the collection he assembled at the college. The controversial Woodward (one of his contemporaries called him an "egregious coxcomb") was involved in pamphleteering and even a duel relating to his scientific opinions, but he undoubtedly created a climate in which serious investigation of fossils became a meaningful activity. Woodward later put his money where his pen was, and left a bequest to create the first chair in geology at Cambridge University, where his collection of fossils is still preserved.

The rival Oxford was not far behind, as Edward Lhwyd (1660–1709), second keeper of the Ashmolean Museum, as early as 1699 tore himself away from the study of Celtic languages for long enough to illustrate a tooth of a flesh-eating dinosaur and bones of fossil marine reptiles.

In 1728, the year of his death, Woodward's catalogue of his fossil collection was published under the title *A Catalogue of the Extraneous English Fossils*. Specimen A1, first in the list, was a dinosaur limb bone, broken into a number of pieces. Still at Cambridge University, it is the first dinosaur bone to be discovered that can still be seen in a collection.

A collector and dealer in natural history specimens, Joshua Platt (1669–1773) is responsible for the next recorded find. In 1755 he found three large vertebrae at Stonesfield, near Oxford, and sent them to botanist Peter Collinson in the Lake District. It seems that Collinson was not very responsive, but in 1757 Platt wrote with further information: "About three years ago I sent you some vertebrae of enormous size found in the slate-stone pit at Stonesfield, near Woodstock in this county. I have lately been so lucky as to find a thigh bone."

This bone would have been a challenge to send, as it was about 32 inches (81 cm) long and weighed (with the rock that enclosed it) about 200 pounds (90 kg). Collinson was a member of the Royal Society, and perhaps it was through him that the letter was published. With a drawing of the bone, "An Account of the Fossile Thigh-bone of a Large Animal, dug up at Stonesfield, near Woodstock, in Oxfordshire" appeared in the society's *Philosophical Transactions*. A catalogue of Platt's collection was prepared in 1772 for Sir Christopher Sykes (1749–1801) of Wheldrake, in Yorkshire, presumably for an intended sale. The catalogue has survived, and lists the thighbone for four shillings. (If shillings still existed, one would today be worth about ten cents, but it would have been worth much more in the eighteenth century.) The specimen is unfortunately lost, but is clearly a femur, probably of a *Megalosaurus*.

In 1784 a Dr. Watson gave another bone to the Woodwardian Museum at Cambridge, where it still remains in the Sedgwick Museum. No eighteenth-century Sherlock Holmes was available to identify it as part of the shoulder blade of a *Megalosaurus*.

In the nineteenth century, the pace of fossil discovery heated up in Britain. A geological society, the first in the world, was formed in 1807, and serious work was done by a number of earnest amateurs that laid the foundations of geology for the next century. Fossil hunters began to pry seriously into cliffs and excavations, hoping to find fossils for sale and for science. By 1811, Britain's first female fossil hunter, Mary Anning (1799–1847), was beginning her remarkable series of new discoveries at Lyme Regis. About this time Lyme was becoming a fashionable resort, and was featured by Jane Austen in her 1815 novel *Persuasion*. James Parkinson (1755–1824) was a founder of the Geological Society, but is also the doctor whose name was given to the disease he discovered. Between 1804 and 1811 he published *Organic Remains of a Former World*, a three-volume work in which he described all the fossil reptiles known up to that time.

As attention has increasingly turned to the discovery of dinosaurs, references to forgotten finds from this period have been located in obscure publications, and a number of dinosaur bones, their discoveries long unpublished, have been unearthed again in the basements of museums. William Smith (1769–1839) is well known as one of the first to relate fossils to the rocks in which they were found. He made the first good geological maps, and in his travels found a tibia and other bones at Cuckfield, in Sussex, as early as 1807–09. These ended up in the collections of the British Museum (Natural History) in London, but have only recently been identified and published.

In 1809 a vertebra was found in the gravels at Dorchester-on-Thames, Oxfordshire, which was added to the Woodwardian collection at Cambridge. It had probably been removed from its original deposit and washed into gravels of the much later glacial period before being found. The vertebra was later identified as being from a cetiosaur ("whale reptile") and is the first known bone of a sauropod dinosaur. About 1812 other dinosaur bones were found at East Cliff, near Hastings, Sussex, by the geologist Thomas Webster (1773–1844), a Scottish-born architect who later became professor of geology at the University of London. The bones are lost, but in more recent years these cliffs have yielded abundant *Iguanodon* bones.

By this time the science of fossils had moved beyond the casual illustration and vague description of previous centuries. During the eighteenth century, pioneers had developed systematic methods of describing and naming living plants and animals. Now that fossils were understood to be the remains of once-living animals and plants, the same methods were extended to them. It had become the practice to publish a complete scientific description each time a new kind of fossil was found, with illustrations whenever possible, and give the new fossil a name. Names had to be in two parts, both of which were from Latin or Greek (a hangover from the medieval period, when the classical tongues were the international language of scholarship). The first name represented the genus (Latin for "kind" or "sort"), the second became known as the trivial name, and the two together defined the species. For example, let us examine the well-known North American dinosaur *Tyrannosaurus rex* Osborn 1905. Its generic name is *Tyrannosaurus*, its trivial name *rex*, the two together defining the species. As some names have been used by more than one scientist, the namer (and often the date) are added for clarification. In our example, the dinosaur was named by American paleontologist Henry Fairfield Osborn in 1905. To be totally clear what species is referred to, it became customary to tie a name to a single "type specimen" so that, in case of dispute, the specimen could be looked at again. The type specimen of *Tyrannosaurus rex* was collected in Montana and is in the American Museum of Natural History in New York. This system generally works smoothly when complete specimens are available, but causes problems when incomplete specimens have to be identified or named, or when type specimens become lost or are accidentally destroyed.

The first dinosaurs to be described scientifically were *Megalosaurus* and *Iguanodon*. As we have seen, bones of both had been found from time to time in England, but no one had yet made any real effort to understand them, describe them, or name them. The first description of *Megalosaurus* was published in 1824, and of *Iguanodon* in 1825, but historians of the dinosaurs long thought that *Iguanodon* was the first to be found. The detailed story of the discovery of these two dinosaurs and the remarkable men who achieved it is complex but intriguing, and it now seems that the priority of discovery, as well as description, goes to *Megalosaurus*.

If William Buckland (1784–1856) did not keep very good records of his dinosaur discoveries, he had good reasons—William Buckland was extremely busy. He was not only a student of geology, but a clergyman, and he was very successful in both areas. He also had a remarkable range of other interests. He had been born in Devon, studied at Oxford, and been ordained in the Church of England. He traveled widely in his researches, and corresponded with scientific colleagues, some of whom fortunately left better information about his dinosaur discoveries than Buckland did.

In about 1815, Buckland found (or perhaps obtained from quarrymen) a remarkable fossil from the quarry at Stonesfield that supplied Oxford with most of its roofing material. There were several vertebrae, hind limbs, and parts of a pelvis. Most striking was a piece of jaw with teeth in place. Although most of these had not fully emerged from the jaw, one formidable fang, stuck up in the center, had jagged edges, like a steak knife. No doubt Buckland showed this fragment to fellow paleontologists, and then put it aside until he had time to work on it. He was already teaching geology at Oxford, and in a few years became canon of Christ Church.

The leading expert on vertebrate fossils in Europe was Georges Cuvier, who had been professor of comparative anatomy at the Botanical Garden (an institution that included the national natural history museum) in Paris since 1802. He commenced to publish his *Recherches sur les ossements fossiles* (Studies on Fossil Bones) from 1812 onwards. In the 1824 volume a reference is made to a visit with Buckland in Oxford in 1818, where he saw "cette belle découverte" (that wonderful discovery) that Buckland had made "depuis plusiers années" (several years ago).

This reference, ambiguous at best, was strikingly confirmed when a collection of old letters was advertised for sale in England in 1970 and came into the hands of then British (now Canadian) paleontologist William Sarjeant. They proved to be written by a little-known figure in nineteenth-century science, the Irishman Joseph Pentland (1797–1873), who had studied with Cuvier for at least four years and had corresponded with Buckland and other English paleontologists. The letters gave new clues about the dinosaur, for one written to Buckland on September 20, 1820, asked, "Will you send your Stonesfield reptile or will you publish it yourself?"

At this time in his early thirties, Buckland had become the first reader of mineralogy at Oxford University in 1813, and the world's first professor of geology in 1819. His flamboyant lectures attracted much attention to his subject, for he "would keep his audience in roars of laughter, as he imitated what he thought to be the movements of the Iguanodon or Megatherium, or, seizing the ends of his long clerical coat tails, would leap about to show us how the pterodactyl flew." His reputation increased steadily, helped not a little by his eccentricities. Buckland thought nothing of allowing his son to keep a bear (known as "Tiglath-pileser" after an ancient Assyrian monarch) and dressing it up in cap and gown to enliven solemn Oxford occasions. One startled visitor to the Buckland home reported sitting on the sofa, drinking afternoon tea, while a hyena crunched guinea pigs underneath. Those who stayed for dinner might find themselves dining on crocodile or ostrich.

One of Buckland's friends was William Conybeare (1787–1857), another clergyman (later Dean of Llandaff) who was also a geologist and took considerable interest in fossil marine reptiles. In 1821 he published, with Henry Thomas de la Beche, an account of a fossil marine reptile, and mentioned in passing the "Huge Lizard" of Stonesfield. Sometime between 1821 and 1822, Conybeare suggested the name *Megalosaurus* to Buckland, for the next reference to it had that name. James Parkinson published another book, *Outlines of Oryctology: An Introduction to the Study of Fossil Organic Remains,* in 1822. In it he illustrated a tooth, and gave a brief account of a remarkable fossil: "Megalosaurus (Megalos great, saurus a lizard). An animal apparently approaching the Monitor [lizard] in its mode of dentition, and not yet described . . . It is found in the calcareous slate of Stonesfield . . . Drawings have been made of the most essential parts of the animals and it is hoped a description may shortly be given to the public. The animal must in some instances have attained a length of forty feet, and stood eight feet high."

On the strength of this account, Parkinson is sometimes credited with the authorship of the genus *Megalosaurus*. However, this hardly qualifies as a scientific description, and it seems clear that he is just referring in passing to a fossil that has not yet been officially named.

Two years later, the eminent Cuvier (who was still writing his comprehensive and systematic study of fossils) was getting a little impatient for information, and his assistant Pentland wrote to Buckland: "Our friend Cuvier has this moment requested me to write to you on the subject of the paper which you proposed publishing on the Stonesfield reptile the Megalosaurus. He is now at that part of the work where he intends speaking of your reptile, and wishes to know if your paper has yet been published."

This inquiry perhaps spurred Buckland to finish his writing, and his paper finally appeared in 1824. "Notice on the Megalosaurus, or Great Fossil Lizard of Stonesfield" appeared in the *Geological Society Journal,* and is the first published description of any kind of dinosaur. In a later publication, Buckland wrote enthusiastically about his find.

> Although no skeleton has been found entire, so many perfect bones and teeth have been discovered in the same quarries, that we are nearly as well acquainted with the form and dimension of its limbs, as if they had been found together in a single block of stone . . . As the femur and tibia measure nearly three feet each, the entire hind leg must have attained a length of nearly two yards . . . The most important part of the Megalosaurus yet found consists of a fragment of the lower jaw, containing many teeth.

When Buckland first described *Megalosaurus,* he referred to a thighbone and teeth of the same kind of dinosaur found at Tilgate Forest, in Sussex, by another paleontologist, Dr. Gideon Mantell (1790–1852). Mantell was, like Buckland, an extremely busy man, but dinosaurs were closer to the center of his life than anything else, and he left better records of his discoveries than Buckland did. Mantell was professionally a surgeon, but he had been encouraged by James Parkinson in his avocation to study rocks and fossils, and he would clearly have loved to devote his life to them. He lived in Lewes, but as a rural doctor he was able to travel and collect as well as earn a living, and his enormous energy and low sleep needs (he is reputed to have slept only four hours a night) enabled him to make the best of his busy schedule. In addition to the work of his practice he wrote twelve books, mainly on geology; gave many public lectures; and created his own museum of rocks and fossils in his house. In 1816, Mantell married Mary Ann Woodhouse, daughter of one of his patients, who shared his interest in geology and engraved drawings for his books.

One of Mantell's favorite areas was known as the Tilgate Forest. Bones had been collected from this region by William Smith in the first decade of the century, but there is no indication that Mantell knew of these finds. Mantell was interested in the Cuckfield quarries as early as 1818, and had hired a quarryman named Leney to collect fossils for him there. Over the next few years Mantell gradually acquired more teeth and bones from the quarry. To keep his source secret he never named it in print, but it was known to later geologists, such as Horace B. Woodward (1848–1914) who identified it as a quarry near Wightman's Green, Sussex.

In 1819 shipments to Mantell included teeth and bones, and in June 1820, Leney supplied "a fine fragment of an enormous bone, and some teeth of the Proteo-saurus." In August 1820, Mantell visited the Tilgate Forest with his wife and brother, but found nothing of importance. In September 1821, he made two trips to the quarry, finding parts of an enormous bone, and by November when he wrote the Tilgate Forest section for his book, *The Fossils of the South Downs* (1822), he had six teeth and many bone fragments. "The teeth, vertebrae, bones and other remains of an animal of the lizard tribe, of enormous magnitude, are perhaps the most intriguing fossils that have been discovered in the county of Sussex," he noted.

At least some of these bones were later realized to be *Megalosaurus*, so Mantell had an opportunity to anticipate Buckland. On the other hand, Buckland had also found large bones around Christmas 1821 in beds of the same age in the Isle of Wight, which were reported as whales but which he later described as *Iguanodon*. It seems to be almost chance that Buckland did not name *Iguanodon*, and Mantell *Megalosaurus*.

A charming story of the discovery of *Iguanodon*, derived from Mantell's own reminiscences in later life, has been retold in almost every book on dinosaurs. Early in 1822, he visited a patient in the Cuckfield region of Sussex. The story goes that Mrs. Mantell rode in the carriage, but, instead of attending the doctor on his case, took a walk outside. In a pile of road metal (stone broken for road mending), she saw some fossil teeth, and later showed them to her husband. This may well have happened, for Mantell is known to have had teeth found by Mary Ann by November 1821, but it is abundantly clear from his own detailed records that this was not the first to be found, and was only one of many *Iguanodon* fossils in his collection. In later years he confused matters by issuing a number of accounts of the first discovery, some crediting Mary Ann and some himself and some dates later than those his own records of the time indicate.

"It was fortunate that the ardent and intelligent mind of Mr. M, enlightened by anatomical and physiological science, connected with his professional pursuits, perceived the true value of his discoveries," said a contemporary, and indeed Mantell (in his early thirties) now embarked on an effort to collect and interpret remains of this dinosaur that was to last for around thirty years.

The largest tooth intrigued Mantell, for it was like none other he knew of. It was large and worn, and thus seemed to belong to a plant-eating mammal, but at that time no mammals were known from rocks of the Cretaceous period. Yet, if it was a reptile, no such reptile was known from any age. Mantell showed his tooth at a meeting of the Geological Society in 1822, but most of the comments made by his fellow geologists suggested it was from a mammal of much more recent date, or that it belonged to a fish. Dr. Buckland suggested the teeth were of no particular interest, but the chemist and mineralogist Dr. William Wollaston supported his idea about a herbivorous reptile.

In 1823, Mantell's friend Charles Lyell took the tooth to Paris, to Cuvier, who was by this time not only a professor of anatomy, but also chief of a department in the Home Office and a baron. Cuvier identified it (not unreasonably) as a rhinoceros tooth, and a bone from the same quarry was identified as a rhinoceros horn. Some toe bones were identified by Cuvier as hippopotamus, and Mantell was at first prepared to accept the identifications. Lyell later told Buckland about Mantell's "rhinoceros tooth of the Tilgate beds. He seemed as much inclined to believe it as if we had asserted that a child had been found there," and advised Mantell not to be so sure that they were not a recent find, as they had been discovered loose, at the very top of the quarry.

In February 1824, Buckland presented his *Megalosaurus* paper to the Geological Society. Mantell was present, and spoke informally of his own discoveries. In June, Cuvier wrote to Mantell about a fuller series of teeth that had been sent to him. "Might we not," he asked, "have here a new animal, a herbivorous reptile?" Mantell continued to study his finds, and in the summer went to London, to the Hunterian Museum at the Royal College of Surgeons. While examining the teeth of a variety of living reptiles, the assistant curator, a naturalist named Samuel Stutchbury (1798–1859), showed Mantell an iguana skeleton that he had prepared from a pickled specimen. (Iguanas today grow up to about 5 feet [1.5 m] in length.) The iguana's teeth were remarkably similar to the much-larger fossil teeth, so it was clearly possible that the fossils could have come from a giant reptile. Mantell planned to call it *Iguanosaurus*, but the Rev. William Conybeare suggested *Iguanodon* ("iguana tooth").

Mantell first illustrated a tooth the same year, and the following year wrote "Notice on the Iguanodon, a Newly-Discovered Fossil Reptile, from the Sandstone of the Tilgate Forest, in Sussex." It was presented to the Royal Society by the treasurer, as Mantell was not a member; the account was published in the Society's *Transactions* later in the year, and Mantell was elected to membership in November. By comparing the size of fossil bones with the living iguana, he initially estimated the whole animal could have been 200 feet (61 m) long, but later modified his estimate to 60 feet (18 m).

In August 1829, the bones were displayed in Mantell's museum. The following month, visiting geologist Robert Bakewell (1768–1843) noted, "The room in which the objects were placed has been recently erected by Mr. Mantell for the purpose, and is well lighted from above; the larger specimens are arranged in glass cases and the smaller ones in drawers below." The museum was not as readily accessible as those of today, for "Mr. M. with much liberality, allows the museum to be seen on the first and third Tuesdays of every month, from one till three, application having been previously made by letter." Bakewell commented with interest that the fossils included "bones of verte-brated animals, some of which were of enormous magnitude" and that "it is the remains of large animals evidently formed for walking on land, that renders the museum of Mr. Mantell so unique." He was particularly interested in Iguanodon, which "is justly regarded by Mr. M. as the most gratifying result of his labours . . . It is indeed most extraordinary, not only from being the largest amphibious or terres-trial animal known, but from its peculiar structure, as an herbivorous masticating reptile."

In 1832 (the year Cuvier died) Mantell moved to Brighton, hop-ing to acquire a more fashionable connection for his practice and per-haps to interest influential people in his collection. He also found a new kind of dinosaur. In 1833, he described it as *Hylaeosaurus* ("woodland lizard or forest reptile"), also from the Tilgate Forest. Mantell obtained the front half of a skeleton embedded in a block of lime-stone, and remarkably, it was still embedded in its matrix 150 years later. Enough could be seen to show that it was an armored dinosaur, with bony plates embedded in the skin and spikes along the hips.

Meanwhile, in 1834 a more complete skeleton of *Iguanodon* had been discovered. While blasting in a quarry in Kent, workmen had found pieces of a substance they thought looked like petrified wood. The quar-ry owner, William Bensted (1802–1873), was himself an amateur geologist. He recognized the material as bone, arranged for the pieces to be collected together, chiseled some of them free of the rock that sur-rounded them, and published an account of his find. Bensted invited Mantell to see them, and recognized they were "the lower extremities of the iguanodon, a magnificent group." He offered £10 for them, but Bensted asked £25. Some of Mantell's friends clubbed together to purchase the block, and the delighted doctor worked in his Brighton house every night for three months, excavating the bones, and later illus-trated them in his book, *Wonders of Geology*. In a punning reference to

Mantell, a locally published poem referred to the "monstrous bones" as a potential "Mantel-piece"—a decoration for a fireplace.

It was some time after this that he drew the first restoration of a dinosaur. He had learned of a living iguana that had a horn on its nose, and placed the bony spike he had found in the same position in his drawing of the fossil.

His preparation and display of the "Mantel-piece" was perhaps the high point of Mantell's life, as increasing numbers of the eminent came to see his collection. Unfortunately, they did not stay to become his patients, and in 1835 he moved back to Lewes. His devotion to his collection of fossils had clearly become a strain on his marriage, for he separated from Mrs. Mantell around this time. In 1838 he moved to London, and arranged to sell his collection to the British Museum for £4,000 in 1839. The separation perhaps strained Mantell's relationship with his son Walter, who in 1840 left for New Zealand. Ironically, once away from his father, Walter played an important role in fossil discoveries in his new home, sending back to Britain remains of a giant fossil bird, the moa, which, as we shall see, has an indirect place in the dinosaur story.

❖ ❖ ❖

It was one thing to discover bones, but quite another to get them to a museum in one piece. Some fossil bones are hard and strong, and may be easily picked up intact from soft clay. Bones found on the surface have often been fragmented by erosion, and the pieces may be scattered down a slope. Bones that are enclosed in hard rock usually have to be laboriously extracted by hammer and chisel. The shocks of hammer blows, transmitted through the rock, can break up even hard fossils into pieces, and weaker ones may totally fragment as they are being extracted. The finders of fossils faced a problem that has been simply and independently solved a number of times and in various places, and yet the solution eluded some collectors until well into this century. It is therefore remarkable that the solution was first described in print even before the dinosaurs were named.

Despite his name, Sir Henry Thomas de la Beche (1796–1855) was English. He was thrown out of Military College in 1812, and moved to Lyme Regis, where he collected fossil marine vertebrates. Later, he started using the Ordnance Survey maps as a basis for geological maps. This led to his developing and becoming the first director of the Geological Survey in 1832, and later the founder of the Museum of Practical Geology and the School of Mines and Science.

De la Beche naturally found himself instructing geologists, and in 1836 published a book, *How to Observe—Geology,* in which he describes a novel collecting technique: "it may even be desirable to go to the expense of preparing plaster of Paris on the spot, and cover the fossil . . . By this process the exposed part of the skeleton becomes set in a block . . . so that by working carefully beneath it and the fossil in the friable rock, the skeleton is eventually on the surface of plaster of Paris, from which it may eventually be freed."

De la Beche had probably developed this technique at Lyme Regis. It is in essence the technique used by most vertebrate paleontologists for collecting crumbling and related bones. It was certainly used in Britain for a while, for William Davies of the British Museum was using essentially modern plastering techniques on a fossil elephant in 1863. Yet it was apparently not used in the Americas until the 1870s, when it seems to have been independently rediscovered.

The various finds of Buckland and Mantell (and, by this time, a few others) seemed to be quite different from each other, apparently having little in common except that they represented extinct reptiles of various kinds. On August 2, 1841, a common identity was recognized, when the anatomist and paleontologist Richard Owen (1804–92) delivered a report on British fossil reptiles at a conference of the British Association for the Advancement of Science in Plymouth. This report has been widely regarded as the "birth" of the dinosaurs, but it now seems that Owen only added the name "dinosaur" before the publication of the report the following year.

Owen was only thirty-eight, but was already known as the "English Cuvier" and regarded as a worthy successor to the great French anatomist. He had been born in Lancaster, and became a surgeon's apprentice, learning human anatomy by doing autopsies on prisoners. He had become Hunterian Professor of the Royal College of Surgeons in 1836 at the age of thirty-two (with access to the museum in which Mantell had made the connection between his fossil teeth and the modern iguana). Although respected for his knowledge, he was not liked. "It is deeply to be deplored that this highly eminent and gifted man can never act with candour and liberality," said Mantell.

Owen noted that the fossil reptiles all had five fused vertebrae welded to the pelvic girdle and that they were all terrestrial, of large size, and had resemblances to large living mammals such as the elephants. They had pillarlike legs under the body instead of the angled legs characteristic of familiar sprawling reptiles. Owen felt that these characters "will . . . be deemed sufficient ground for establishing a distinct tribe or suborder of Saurian Reptiles, for which I would propose the name Dinosauria." With an eye to dramatic effect, Owen explained that his name meant "fearfully great lizard." He pointed out resemblances between the dinosaurs and the elephants, and showed that Buckland's and Mantell's methods of calculating the size of their finds by comparison with lizards gave greatly exaggerated results.

Owen regarded the dinosaurs as very advanced animals: "The Megalosaurs and the Iguanodons, rejoicing in those undeniably most perfect modifications of the Reptilian type, attained the greatest bulk, and must have played the most conspicuous parts, in their respective characters as devourers of animals and feeders upon vegetables, that this earth has ever witnessed in . . . cold-blooded creatures."

He compared them with living crocodiles, and suggested they had "a four chambered heart; and from their superior adaptation to terrestrial life, to have enjoyed the function of such a highly organized centre of circulation in a degree more nearly approaching that which now characterizes the warm-blooded vertebrata."

It has been suggested that Owen's motives in naming the dinosaurs were not objectively scientific. He was, in fact, a staunch anti-evolutionist, and may have been attempting to discourage evolutionary ideas (which were current before Darwin provided them with a comprehensible mechanism) by drawing attention to these very advanced animals that seemed to have left no more highly evolved descendants.

3

ELEGANT JAWS
AND ANCIENT WINGS

SOMETIME IN THE LATE NINETEENTH CENTURY, A drawing of the skeleton of a tiny dinosaur was made on the smooth surface of a block of lithographic limestone. The stone came into the collections of Yale's Peabody Museum of Natural History, where it was preserved until rediscovered by paleontologist John Ostrom in 1961. It was not until 1977 that the stone was used to print the picture of the elegant little skeleton. Almost every detail can be seen: the strong hind legs, the long tail, the smaller forelimbs with claw-tipped "hands," the long neck bent backwards by contraction of the ligaments after death so that the delicately boned skull is inverted. In among the ribs can be seen another, much tinier skeleton, that of a lizard which must have been caught and eaten a short time before the dinosaur died.

Both skeleton and stone come from the same place, the area around Solnhofen in the German province of Bavaria. It is no accident that the drawing is made on the same kind of rock that the original fossil was found in, for the art of drawing on stone and the discovery of fossils in that region are intimately related.

The fine-grained, yellowish Upper Jurassic limestone has been quarried in the Solnhofen area since Roman invaders used it to floor their baths. During the Middle Ages it was extensively quarried as paving stone for the region. We cannot guess what the medieval quarrymen thought of the strange shapes that sometimes turned up in the rocks, but they were known as fossils by the eighteenth century, when a regular trade developed in them. By 1781 there was serious inflation in prices, and J.B. Fischer complained that, "in recent times the price of these rarities has soared and it is not unusual to find that a fine, well preserved piece with both the concave and convex sides would fetch one, two or perhaps even four ducats." In 1784, a crumpled skeleton reached the French paleontologist Georges Cuvier, which he described as the first known flying reptile, or pterodactyl, a group related to dinosaurs but distinct from them.

In 1793, a local man, Alois Senefelder, discovered that it was possible to print pictures from slabs of stone, a process that became known as lithography, which involves taking ink impressions from drawings on stone. In those days before photography, such a technique was invaluable for providing pictures for books and magazines, and the stone was quarried and exported around Europe. In 1828, Weitenhüller, an Eichstätt glassmaker, also discovered how to make roofing tiles from the rocks. Both purposes needed flat, clean slabs, and it was necessary for the quarrymen to examine each piece with care. They were well aware that the fine-grained stone had preserved delicate fossils, such as the wings of dragonflies, the shells of crabs, and the skeletons of small fish. As word of the fossils continued to spread, the quarrymen found a steadily expanding market for their discoveries, among learned and educated men who paid handsomely for the finds to add to their collections. As the years went by, more and more remarkable discoveries were made, and the site became famous around the world. The best-known find has been described as "the most famous fossil in the world," and has been compared to the Rosetta Stone, the bilingual inscribed stone which made possible translation of Ancient Egyptian hieroglyphics.

The delicately boned skeleton drawn on the limestone slab was a specimen of a dinosaur that had firs been found in the Solnhofen area in the late 1850s. It was found by a man named Oberndorfer, and came into the hands of Johann Andreas Wagner (1797–1861), a German zoologist and vertebrate paleontologist who was a professor at the University of Munich. In 1861 he named it *Compsognathus* ("elegant jaw"), but perhaps because of its small size did not recognize it as a relative of the huge dinosaurs known from Britain. When the relationship was realized, its 24-inch (60-cm) length and estimated live weight of 6 pounds (3 kg) meant it became known as the smallest dinosaur, but it did not attract much interest. Wagner did not have any theoretical difficulty with *Compsognathus*, but he was to find other fossils from Solnhofen much more difficult to swallow.

Compsognathus was not the only dinosaur to have been found in Germany during the early nineteenth century. The existence of much larger animals was suggested by some big bones found in Triassic rocks and described by Christian Erich Hermann von Meyer (1801–69) of Frankfurt, who is known as the founder of vertebrate paleontology in Germany. Meyer had the misfortune to be clubfooted, which made it difficult for him to do fieldwork. However, it did not stop him from being active in both politics and science. He studied all the fossils that came his way, and over the years he published five volumes of his *Fauna of the Ancient World*, in which many new kinds of fossil vertebrates were described, including a number of pterodactyls from Solnhofen. In 1837, before Owen had established the concept of the dinosaurs, Meyer described some fragments of a skeleton as *Plateosaurus*, or "flat lizard." Meyer was also one of the first to recognize that similarities between animals did not necessarily mean close relationships. "I have found," he said, "that in one or several parts a creature could have correspondences bordering on similarity with another creature, without being related to it." This is the recognition of the scientific principle of convergence: that animals from quite different origins may be similar in appearance. An example familiar to Meyer included bats (mammals), pterosaurs (reptiles), and birds, all of which fly by means of wings but have different origins.

Just before the discovery of *Compsognathus*, Darwin published *The Origin of Species by Means of Natural Selection*, in 1859. Late in the twentieth century it is difficult to envisage what an intellectual bombshell this book was. Yet, at the time the dinosaurs were named in England, Church and State were closely integrated, and science was so generally regarded as an extension of theology that many of the pioneer naturalists were clergymen. Facts about natural science had been considered to offer no threat to the theological status quo, as they could be fitted into the neat schemes that had been developed to rationalize the relationship of the visible evidence of the natural world with a more or less literal reading of the biblical account.

True, some ideas (such as evolution) were floating around that were incompatible with a literal interpretation of the Bible, but they were not well supported or widely accepted. Darwin's crime was to support a previously nebulous theory with a mechanism that could be seen to work, and to support it with such an apparently thorough and logical argument that, to the open mind, it was hard not to regard the theory as proven. This intellectual assault on theology could not be ignored by the churches. Thomas Henry Huxley (1825–95), (the scientist who invented the concept of agnosticism) said that "extinguished theologians lie about the cradle of every science as the strangled snakes beside that of Hercules," and later bestowed upon himself the title of Episcophagous, or "bishop eating." Scientists like Huxley who were open to new ideas were thrilled and delighted by what became known as Darwinism, and the fact that evolution had taken place was soon established. Arguments about the exact course it has taken, and the detailed mechanisms responsible for it continue today. Those for whom religious faith took precedence over logical argument were able to dismiss the fact of evolution as still unproved (as their philosophical descendants continue to do). Next to the theologians, the most threatened were the establishment scientists who had made their reputations in the natural sciences before evolution was established, and were either genuinely not convinced or unable to adjust their thinking to the new arguments.

Darwin had anticipated much of the debate, and personally dreaded getting involved in it, hoping that his ideas would speak for themselves. In *The Origin*, Darwin had been his own devil's advocate, for he wrote whole chapters dealing with the various possible objections to his argument. The chapter "On the Imperfections of the Geological Record" pointed out that the absence of fossil intermediate forms was "probably the gravest and most obvious of the many objections which may be urged against my views." Light-hearted critics suggested it was necessary to locate a mermaid as the missing link between man and fish, and the public seized on the term "missing link."

Recognizing the weakness of this area of Darwin's argument, supporters of evolution began to look for fossils that might fill gaps between major groups, such as reptiles and birds, while their opponents prepared to use their scientific weight to cast doubt on every example that was brought forward.

In Germany, the debate was even less courteous, and rationalist church-baiting materialists such as the Swiss zoologist Karl Vogt (1817–95) aroused vigorous controversy. The fires of debate were fanned when, two years after publication of *The Origin*, a fossil feather was found at Solnhofen!

There had been a number of hints of fossil birds at Solnhofen since the early nineteenth century. Fragments of feathers were mentioned in a book in 1820; in 1827 the head of a bird was reported, but it was never described and was lost. It is now known that a genuine bird fossil was found north of Eichstätt in 1855, but von Meyer failed to recognize its true identity, and described it as a new kind of pterodactyl, *Pterodactylus crassipes*. It was not recognized as a bird for more than a century.

However, it was von Meyer who reported in 1861 that a fossil feather had been discovered. His letter to editor Heinrich Bronn was published in August in the *Neues Jahrbuch für Mineralogie* (New Yearbook for Mineralogy). The single feather was blackish in color, 2.4 inches (60 mm) long and 0.5 inches (11 mm) wide. The vane on one side was half the width of the vane on the other, so that it appeared more like a flight feather of a modern bird that had dropped onto the rock than a fossil from the remote past. At that time, no birds were known before the Tertiary, so von Meyer, remembering his generalization about convergence, was duly cautious. The feather, he said, "need not necessarily be derived from a bird," and could be from a "feathered animal differing essentially from our birds." He gave it the neutral name of *Archaeopteryx lithographica* ("ancient wing from the lithographic stone"). The main slab went to the Academy of Sciences in Munich, while the counterslab was placed in the Humboldt Museum für Naturkunde, in Berlin. Better material would clearly be needed before the feather could be shown with certainty to belong to a bird.

Before the scientific world had a chance to react, von Meyer published in the same journal, on September 30, 1861, another letter announcing the discovery of a headless skeleton, with a long tail decorated with short feathers, and impressions of feathered wings. Von Meyer suggested that this new find should be given the same name as his feather. It had been reported by O.J. Witte, a lawyer, and was found in a quarry belonging to Herr Ottmann near Langenaltheimer Haardt, close to Solnhofen. Clearly, the specimen was of enormous scientific value; but, before it could take its place in the scientific literature, its value was to be measured in another way.

The new fossil had come into the hands of Dr. Karl Häberlein, who was medical officer for the district and based at nearby Pappenheim. Häberlein was an enthusiastic collector who took fossils in exchange for his services, which is presumably how he acquired the feathered skeleton. Häberlein knew enough about fossils to understand the potential importance of his acquisition, and he happened to be in need of cash for a dowry for his daughter. After letting the scientific world simmer for three months, he offered his feathered skeleton for sale. He allowed a few people to see it so that no one would think it was a fake, but did not allow anyone to draw it. One scientist, Albert Oppel (1831–65), outsmarted Häberlein. After looking intently at the fossil for several hours, he went home and was able to draw a fairly accurate picture from memory.

There was some interest at court in obtaining the new fossil for the Natural History Museum in Munich. However, not all scientists were enthusiastic. Andreas Wagner (who had described *Compsognathus*) was a scientist at the museum. He did not believe that birds could be as old as the new fossil suggested, and was an opponent of Darwin's views. Most scientists today would feel that direct access to the fossil would be necessary for any serious work, but with no more information than Oppel's sketch, Wagner not only wrote a paper about it, but gave it a new name. His paper appeared in the publications of the Munich Academy of Science under the title "A New Reptile Supposedly Furnished with Bird Feathers." He noted that its long tail was composed of separate bones, unlike that of any bird, and named it *Griphosaurus problematicus* ("puzzling mythical lizard"). Wagner then spelled out his views very clearly: "I must add a few words to ward off Darwinian misinterpretation of our new Saurian. At first glance of the *Griphosaurus* we might certainly form the notion that we had before us an intermediate creature, engaged in the transformation from the Saurian to the bird. Darwin and his adherents will probably employ the new discovery as an exceedingly welcome occurrence for the justification of their strange views upon the transformation of animals. But in this they will be wrong."

While the German establishment prevaricated, word of the fossil had reached England. George Robert Waterhouse, Keeper of the Department of Geology at the British Museum, consulted with his chief, Richard Owen. The namer of the dinosaurs was unsympathetic to evolution, and perhaps felt that this threatening fossil should be in his care, where he could make sure it was interpreted properly. Waterhouse wrote to Germany in February 1862, asking to buy the fossil for the museum. On March 21, Häberlein invited Waterhouse to come to Germany and select the best pieces from his collection. He described the fossil, with the wing feathers arranged as in flight, the leg bones well preserved, and the clawed legs and long tail present. Häberlein suggested (wrongly) that the head was present but covered with rock. He heated the pot by referring to expressions of interest from other scientists and collectors, such as Swiss-American scientist Louis Agassiz, the Duke of Buckingham, and Lord Eniskillen. Waterhouse replied on March 29, and asked the key question: how much did Häberlein want? Häberlein offered the whole collection for a price of £750, but expressed willingness to sell part of the collection for less. On June 14, the British Museum trustees approved a recommendation by Waterhouse and Owen to pay up to £500 for part of the collection. Waterhouse travelled to Häberlein's home at Pappenheim, and convinced himself of the "true ornithic nature" of the fossil, but could not convince Häberlein to accept the lower price for what he wanted and so returned empty-handed.

Häberlein probably waited for a German offer, then got cold feet and wrote Waterhouse again on July 10. This time he offered the whole collection for £700 or a part for £650. The British Museum trustees met on July 26, and one of their number, Roderick Murchison, director of the Geological Survey, added his support. It was decided that £400 could be paid from the government grant for that year, and a further £300 from endowments and the following year's grant. Waterhouse wrote and asked for all the 1,703 specimens in the collection, offering £450 for the first part (including the feathered skeleton) and agreeing to take the rest the following year. On August 26, Häberlein accepted the offer. By September 13, Häberlein had the first part packed in chests and sent to London. He perhaps suffered regrets as he saw his prize specimen leave the country, but was no doubt delighted to be able to promise his daughter a £700 dowry. The eagerly awaited shipment arrived in London on November 1 without any damage.

We can only guess at Owen's excitement as the feathered creature was unpacked. Wagner's and von Meyer's articles had been translated and published in England earlier in the year, so public interest had already been aroused. As early as November 20, Owen reported to the Royal Society that the fossil was unequivocally a bird, though one of a primitive kind. The fossil "as preserved in the present split slab of lithographic stone recalled to mind the condition in which I had seen the carcass of a Gull or other seabird left on estuary sand after having been a prey to some carnivorous assailant."

In December 1862, a junior assistant in the museum, Henry Woodward (1832–1921), described *Archaeopteryx* as a "wonderful discovery" in the *Intellectual Observer*, and accompanied his article with a colored plate. Back in Germany, with the specimen no longer available, Christof Giebel (1820–81) examined Woodward's drawing and was the first of many to suggest in 1863 that the fossil was a fake that had been drawn on the lithographic stone. He wrote an article, "The Lithograph of the Lithographic Pterosaur," which was published in Berlin. In England, S.J. Mackie published an article in 1863, "Aeronauts of the Solenhofen Age," referring to the new find as a "sensation" and noting that the geological and paleontological worlds were astonished.

Owen was not new to fossil birds; he had already studied the giant moas from New Zealand, found by Mantell's son Walter. He at first was inclined to call Häberlein's specimen *Griphornis longicaudatus* ("long-tailed mysterious bird"). In 1863, when his article appeared in the *Philosophical Transactions of the Royal Society*, he called it a real but primitive bird, used von Meyer's name, *Archaeopteryx*, but gave it a new trivial name, *macrura* ("long-tailed"). It had feathers and a wishbone—both characteristic of birds—but other features were very unbird-like. Not only was the tail reptilian, with a long string of individual vertebrae, but the strange bird had fingers with claws on its wings. A puzzling jawbone with four teeth was found with the fossil, but Owen dismissed it as part of a fish.

Owen's account was not able to dampen the evolutionists' interest. Sir John Evans (1823–1908), an industrialist and amateur archaeologist who had just published his classic work *The Coins of the Ancient Britons*, still had the energy to enliven "a Neolithic expedition to Aberdeen by going to an assembly ball and dancing till two." In 1865, the energetic Evans wrote that *Archaeopteryx* "seemed to link together the two great classes of Birds and Reptiles" so that "its extreme importance as bearing upon the great question of the Origin of Species must be evident to all." He also pointed out cranial bones and a brain cast that Owen had missed, and suggested that the toothed jaw belonged to the fossil. This view was supported by von Meyer and others. Hugh Falconer, one of Evans's friends, responded less seriously: "Hail, Prince of Audacious Palaeontologists! Tell me all about it. I hear that you have to-day discovered the *teeth* and jaws of the Archaeopteryx. To-morrow I expect to hear of your having found the liver and lights [lungs]! And who knows, but that in the long run, you may get hold of the fossil song of the same creature."

While the jokers laughed, the theorists were busy absorbing the implications of the new find. Thomas Henry Huxley, one of the most eminent biologists of the day, had become known as "Darwin's Bulldog" because of the enthusiasm with which he entered into controversy on the side of evolution. In 1867 Huxley published a paper showing fourteen features that birds and reptiles had in common and that were not shared with mammals, and suggesting a new high-level category—the Sauropsida—to include both of them. He also suggested that dinosaurs might have been hot-blooded, like birds.

In the following year, 1868, Huxley produced a popular article in which he explored the similarity between the tiny dinosaur *Compsognathus* and the dinosaurlike bird *Archaeopteryx:* "It is impossible to look at the conformation of this strange reptile and to doubt that it hopped or walked, in an erect or semi-erect position, after the manner of a bird, to which its long neck, slight head, and small anterior limbs must have given it an extraordinary resemblance."

In the same year, Huxley gave a popular lecture on evolution in which he cited *Archaeopteryx* as a missing link that had been found. He could not accept the teeth, however, and as late as 1868 wrote that the head was lost.

His American counterpart, Othniel Charles Marsh of Yale, also recognized *Archaeopteryx* as a missing link between two widely separated groups: "The classes of Birds and Reptiles, as now living, are separated by a gulf so profound that a few years since it was cited by the opponents of evolution as the most important break in the animal series, and one which that doctrine could not bridge over. Since then . . . this gap has been virtually filled . . . *Compsognathus* and *Archaeopteryx* . . . are the stepping stones by which the evolutionist of to-day leads the doubting brother across the shallow remnant of the gulf, once thought impassable."

Although the loss of the specimen rankled in Germany, the London *Archaeopteryx* was soon accepted by most scientists as an undisputed fossil bird. Though the specimen had been intensively studied and had found its place in the textbooks of the opposing sides, there was little agreement about the extent to which it provided proof of evolution. Evolutionists saw it as a stepping stone between reptiles and birds, and were fascinated by its similarity to *Compsognathus* —if the feather impressions had not survived, the fossil might well have been classed as a dinosaur. On the other hand, Owen and his followers had no problem fitting the remarkable intermediate specimen into a variety of intellectual structures, which still amounted to special creation of each different kind of creature. All except the followers of the theory that the fossil was a forgery thought that it was altogether a remarkable discovery, though there was regret at the absence of most of the skull. It was too much to expect that a better specimen would turn up; yet that is precisely what happened.

The new fossil came from a quarry on the Blumenberg River, near Eichstätt, about 10 miles (16 km) from the site of the original discoveries, and it had a head. Karl Häberlein had died in 1871, but history repeated itself when the specimen was bought by his son Ernst (1819–95), for 140 marks. Ernst Häberlein reported the discovery in the scientific journal *Leopoldina* in May 1877, and strongly hinted at the possibility it would be for sale. The German scientific establishment was determined to obtain this specimen, but even so it took four years.

O. Vogler was the founder and chairman of an endowment society in Frankfurt. As a first step, he arranged for the new fossil to be placed in the care of the society for six months, during which time arrangements could be made for its sale to the society or another appropriate organization. Häberlein agreed, but with the condition that no casts or copies should be made. He set the price at 36,000 marks for his complete collection—more than twice the price of the first specimen. Vogler was unable to raise this sum, even after a three-month extension, and so he had to return the specimen in December 1879. Häberlein started negotiating directly with museums, but was no more successful. The radical zoologist Karl Vogt had had to leave Germany, and was now professor of zoology at the University of Geneva, in Switzerland. After seeing the specimen, he told a naturalists' congress, "The Emperor Wilhelm I has money for soldiers and guns, but none for science."

Häberlein offered his entire collection to the Prussian Ministry of Culture for 26,000 marks. Professor August Beyrich (1815–96), director of the Mineralogy Museum at Berlin University, was sent to inspect the specimen, but despite his positive recommendations, no funds were available. In the spring of 1880, industrialist Werner von Siemens discussed the fossil with Wilhelm Barnim Dames (1843–98), who was the custodian of the Humboldt Museum für Naturkunde in Berlin. Siemens then purchased the collection directly from Häberlein, and gave the ministry an option to buy it from him for the same price within one year. With two installments of 10,000 marks in 1881 and 1882, raised from private endowments, scientists, and the German government, Siemens was paid, and the collection at last was secured for Germany.

The Berlin *Archaeopteryx*, as it soon became known, was finer than the London specimen. It was lying in a natural pose, with the wings outstretched, and had a skull with sharp reptilian teeth in the jaws. It has reasonably been hailed as the most famous fossil in the world. Dames at first called it *Archaeopteryx macrura*, like the London specimen, but when Owen pointed out it was a different species, Dames changed the name in 1897 to *Archaeopteryx siemensi,* honoring the generous bene-factor who had secured it for Germany.

It was not until the twentieth century that Germany's larger dinosaurs received much serious attention, but their chief researcher appeared in 1875, shortly before the discovery of the Berlin *Archaeopteryx.* Friedrich von Huene (1875–1969) was born in the picturesque town of Tübingen (southwest of Stuttgart, more than 60 miles (100 km) west of Solnhofen). He later followed a career in paleontology at the university there, but if this fact suggests an untraveled man content to stay close to home, it is misleading. As a baby, he moved with his family to Basel, Switzerland, where they stayed for ten years. He then was taken to Estonia, where he lived for a while on a huge estate and enjoyed riding his pony around the fields. In 1888 he returned to Basel to attend the gymnasium, and then went to the University of Lausanne. There he was torn between theology and science, and although he chose the latter, he retained a strong interest in religion throughout his life. He transferred to the University of Tübingen, where Professor Ernst Koken suggested to him that the Triassic dinosaurs of southern Germany would repay attention. He became a specialist in the earliest dinosaurs, those of the Triassic period, rather than those of one region, and his dedication took him to almost everywhere they could be found. In pursuit of his quarry, von Huene (unlike many students of the dinosaurs) worked on a number of continents, and will appear elsewhere in this story. He also did impor-tant work on a number of other groups of fossils.

About 1900, he began fieldwork in the valley of the River Neckar and other sites in Würtemburg, where Upper Triassic rocks are well exposed in the country between the Black Forest and the Swabian Alps. In 1908, he produced a monograph, *Triassic Dinosaurs of Europe,* in which he discussed what was known of *Plateosaurus.* In 1914 he published *Triassic Dinosaurs of the World.* These two monographs estab-lished von Huene as the authority on Triassic dinosaurs, though much of his work had been done on fragmentary remains first described by others.

After the First World War, von Huene returned to his beloved Neckar valley. There, in 1921, he opened a dinosaur quarry on a hillside in a wooded valley near Trossingen, 30 miles (48 km) south of Tübingen.

With the help of technicians from the Museum of Geology and students from his classes, Huene supervised the excavation of a remarkable collection of bones, some isolated and some articulated as partial or even complete skeletons. As the quarry was dug back with picks and shovels into more or less level strata, it became clear there were two bone beds, separated by about 9 feet (2.7 m) of boneless material. The cliff face grew higher and more material had to be removed, until a track was laid and mine cars were used to shift the rock. So successful was the operation that the quarry was continued for another two summers, during which more than 70,000 cubic feet (2000 m^3) of rock were moved, and thousands of bones were collected. Financial assistance was provided by the American Museum of Natural History in New York, in exchange for a complete skeleton. The best modern techniques were used: sites were carefully mapped, and the bones were hardened with shellac and then wrapped in plaster of Paris before being taken back to the University of Tübingen to be prepared.

All the bones belonged to *Plateosaurus*, the large prosauropod dinosaur first described by von Meyer nearly a century earlier. There were several complete skeletons, which were mounted at the university over the next few years. A find of this size should have been enough to provide most paleontologists with a lifetime of work, but von Huene was off to Argentina in 1923, South Africa in 1924, and Brazil in 1928.

For an early dinosaur, *Plateosaurus* was large, about 26 feet (8 m) long. It had a small head, connected by a short neck to a dumpy body and balanced by a long tail. It walked on four legs, and may have reared up on its hind legs to browse on leaves, which it tore with its leaf-shaped teeth. Its large size is an indication of things to come, for it was classified as a prosauropod, and is probably related to ancestors of the giant four-legged sauropods of the Jurassic.

Von Huene continued to work on Triassic dinosaurs, as well as other fossils, with remarkable energy into his old age, and even in his late eighties he startled colleagues by taking a 100-mile (160-km), three-day hike to attend a scientific meeting.

During most of von Huene's lifetime, there were no new *Archaeopteryx* finds, but the two known fossils continued to stimulate debate. As usual in science, a new piece of evidence is likely to provide as many questions as solutions. Though by the turn of the century it was clear to most scientists that *Archaeopteryx* was a stepping stone between reptiles and birds, almost every other detail was subject to debate. For nearly a century, this debate has continued, heating up from time to time as new discoveries or arguments shed light on the questions.

The first argument was about *Archaeopteryx* itself. As a bird, it had primitive features, such as teeth, claws on the wings, and a bony tail. Did this mean that it did not fly like a modern bird, but could only glide between tree branches? What did it eat, and why did its skeletons turn up in marine deposits? A second discussion was about the origin of bird flight, and the feathers that made it possible. Since feathers would have to be well developed before flight was possible, had they evolved to serve some other purpose? Had feathers developed on a primitive reptile to keep the creature warm, to assist it in gliding out of trees to the ground, to balance it while running, or even to help it catch insects?

Other arguments went on about the placing of the two specimens in the family tree of the birds. The two specimens had already been given a number of different names, but in the 1920s the Berlin specimen was considered to be less closely related to the London one and was placed in a new genus, *Archaeornis*. It was even suggested at one point that modern flying birds had evolved from the Berlin specimen, whereas more primitive, flightless birds, such as ostriches, had as their ancestor the London specimen.

Yet another debate was about the kind of reptiles that had given rise to the birds. Some said they were little running dinosaurs like *Compsognathus*, but others pointed to much more primitive, predinosaurian reptiles that were discovered in later years. Although one school of thought felt that *Archaeopteryx* was close to the dinosaurs, Huxley's suggestion that dinosaurs may be hot-blooded was quietly forgotten, and no one even dreamed of suggesting that *Archaeopteryx* itself was a dinosaur, feathers and all.

In 1925, Danish amateur ornithologist and anatomist Gerhard Heilmann published an important theoretical study, *The Origin of Birds*. He showed that the stumbling block to the dinosaur-origin theory was a critical bird characteristic: the large collarbones that are fused together in modern birds to form what is commonly called the wishbone. Indeed, the wishbone is essential to flying birds because it braces the shoulders against the strains of flying, and its presence in *Archaeopteryx* is one of the best arguments that it was a bird capable of powerful flight. Unfortunately for those arguing for a dinosaur origin for birds, *Compsognathus* and other dinosaurs did not show more than the tiniest fragment of a wishbone. This seemed to show that the bird ancestor had to be farther back in reptile ancestry than the dinosaurs, as a bone that has once been lost in evolutionary development cannot normally be regained. Based on this evidence, dinosaurs and birds could be no closer than cousins in the evolutionary family tree. The many similarities between them could only be a result of convergence, like those of birds and pterodactyls, which used totally different anatomical structures for flight.

It was not until 1956 that another *Archaeopteryx* was found. The badly decomposed specimen was noticed in a quarry shed by a student, and proved to have come from a site only 275 yards (250 m) from the London specimen, but 20 feet (6 m) higher in the sequence of the rocks.

Two more specimens turned up in the 1970s, but both had been collected in the previous century, before von Meyer's feather and the London specimen, but had been misidentified. The first found had originally turned up in 1850 a few miles north of Eichstätt. Slight feather impressions went unnoticed, and because no wishbone was present, it was identified as *Compsognathus*—a striking support for the similarity between *Archaeopteryx* and this little dinosaur. It was not recognized as a bird until 1973.

John Ostrom, whose unearthing of the lithographed drawing of *Compsognathus* began this chapter, discovered another *Archaeopteryx* in 1970 in the Teyler Museum in Haarlem. It was the one that von Meyer had found in 1855 and described as a pterodactyl. Ostrom was able to borrow the fossil, and took it away in a shoebox (insured for $1 million) for further study. It proved to have a horny sheath on the claw of one of the wing "fingers," showing that *Archaeopteryx* had claws like a modern bird. "My find," said Ostrom, "is a classic example of why a paleontologist or museum should not throw things away that can't be absolutely classified as worthless."

The discovery naturally interested Ostrom in looking closely at *Archaeopteryx*, and he found it compared remarkably closely to *Deinonychus*, a dinosaur he had recently found in the United States (see Chapter 10). According to classic views, birds were warm blooded and dinosaurs cold, yet these examples were remarkably similar. This comparison coincided with a revival of Huxley's idea of hot-blooded dinosaurs, with implications that the two were physiologically similar, and hot-blooded physiology and perhaps even feathers had evolved in dinosaurs before birds appeared. The apparent absence of a wishbone in dinosaurs was countered by the reasonable suggestion that dinosaurs may have had cartilaginous wishbones that were not fossilized (an idea now supported by the discovery of a wishbone in a Mongolian dinosaur, *Oviraptor*). In 1974, these anatomical and physiological ideas led two scientists, Robert Bakker and Peter Galton, to suggest a new way of classifying the vertebrates. To replace the traditional classes of Reptiles and Birds, they suggested that dinosaurs and birds should be brought together in a new class, the Dinosauria, leaving crocodiles, snakes, turtles, and their allies to bear the name "reptile." While there sometimes seems to be more heat in the "hot-blooded debate" than in the physiology of any dinosaur, there is growing acceptance among scientists of the idea that at least some of the dinosaurs may have been hot-blooded. Many recent books include among the small running dinosaurs not only *Compsognathus*, but *Archaeopteryx*. Bird watchers and dinosaur enthusiasts alike are still getting used to the idea that dinosaurs may not be extinct, but live on in the sparrows and hummingbirds at their feeders—and the chickens and turkeys on their dinner plates.

In 1984, a conference was devoted entirely to the *Archaeopteryx*, bringing together much of the new research. In 1985, an old controversy was reignited when a serious suggestion was again made that both the London and the Berlin specimens were forgeries. This time the suggestion came from a scientist of great eminence, Sir Fred Hoyle, who had previously advanced alternative theories of the origin of life and attempted to discredit evolution. Hoyle is not a paleontologist, or even a biologist, but an astronomer, one of the originators of the steady-state theory of the origin of the universe. He is also a well-known writer of science fiction, and some readers must have wondered in which capacity he approached *Archaeopteryx*. Others involved were Lee Spetner, an American-Israeli physicist, who claimed that a genuine reptile fossil had been faked by putting cement on the rock and adding impressions of feathers. Another was astrophysicist N.C. Wickramasinghe, who had formerly testified on behalf of "creation science" at a 1981 Arkansas trial protesting the teaching of evolution.

The accusers produced photographs of the London specimen that, they suggested, showed blurring of the feather impressions, a gap between slab and counterslab, and different grain size for the sediments surrounding bones and feathers. This evidence was alleged to show that the fossil was a fake. As the Häberleins (father and son) had been involved with both fossils, it was easy to suggest that they were perhaps responsible, and it was hypothesized that the unpopular anti-evolutionist Owen knew about, and perhaps even commissioned, the forgery.

The technical questions raised by the accusers were easily answered in geological terms, and they failed to explain the discovery of new specimens, long after Owen and the Häberleins were dead, or the rediscovery of old specimens collected before *The Origin of Species* was published. Although Owen was unpopular with many of his contemporaries, there is no evidence that he stooped to forgery to prove his anti-evolutionary agendas.

However, the British Museum was still sensitive after the Piltdown forgery—a faked human skull—had fooled one of its keepers thirty years before, and felt it necessary to take the accusation seriously. The museum embarked on yet another thorough study of the fossil, published the following year. "Archaeopteryx Is Not a Forgery" claimed the title of the paper by five eminent paleontologists. Whatever puzzles *Archaeopteryx* may still pose, it seems clear that authenticity is not one of them.

4

THE IGUANODONS OF BERNISSART

ÉDOUARD DUPONT (1841–1911), DIRECTOR OF THE Royal Natural History Museum in Brussels, was not accustomed to being hurried. It was April 12, 1878, and the telegram was imperative: "Discovered important bones in fault Bernissart coal mine that are decomposing with pyrite. Send Depauw tomorrow can arrive at Mons at eight in the morning. Urgent—Gustave."

Gustave Arnould was chief mining engineer of the province of Hainaut in southwestern Belgium, where the little town of Bernissart lay. He was a man to be reckoned with, and if he said he had found important fossil bones, then perhaps he was right. Yet, what would bones be doing down a coal mine, where fossil plants were far more likely? Dupont sent for L. De Pauw, director of the museum laboratory, and told him to be ready to leave early in the morning to investigate.

On the train, De Pauw perhaps ruminated upon the technical problems before him. Iron pyrite is a brassy-looking mineral that is often called fool's gold because of the number of times it has misled greenhorn prospectors. It is very unstable, decomposing readily into a gray powder, which damages any fossils partly composed of pyrite. "Pyrite disease," as this condition is called, was known to be hard to treat, and the fossils—whatever they were—would probably not survive long.

At the Fosse Sainte-Barbe (Saint Barbara Mine), De Pauw was briefed. A new gallery was being opened up in the mine, at the level of the

Luronne coal seam, 1,056 feet (322 m) underground. On February 28, the gallery had left the regular Carboniferous strata and passed into broken blocks of coal and limestone in a smelly black clay, which leaked water, and then into bedded sands. In the dim light the miners had dug on for some 33 feet (10 m), hoping to find the coal again, when miner Jules Créteur noticed something unusual. "What we had in front of us," he later explained, "was something too black to be stone and yet too hard to be wood. The pieces that we pulled out looked like the broken ends of pit props." Inside, they glistened with pyrite, and some of the miners thought they had found tree trunks full of gold. After mine manager Gustave Fagès had seen them, he had sent miners back to the gallery to collect more pieces. Fagès had sent specimens to François Léopold Cornet (1834–87), a local geologist, who had sent them on to Pierre Joseph van Beneden (1809–93), a comparative anatomist at the University of Louvain. Van Beneden specialized in fossil mammals and birds, but knew enough to realize he now had bones of a fossil reptile to deal with, and started searching his museum and library to try and identify the discovery.

Arnould had come across the fossils later, while working on a detailed report on the Mons coalfield, and had lost no time notifying the museum. After visiting the coal face, De Pauw recognized that something special had been found. He went back to the museum, planning techniques for dealing with the pyritized bone.

On May 7, van Beneden reported the finds to the Royal Academy of Science. He had found some teeth among the bones, and suggested (as it turned out, correctly) that they belonged to the dinosaur *Iguanodon*. This famous dinosaur was known from Mantell's and Owen's work in England half a century earlier, so clearly the rocks in which the remains had been found were not from the coal age, dating from long before the dinosaurs. They also contained fish and plant remains that could be dated.

The matter was discussed by the board of directors of the mine, who not only offered to give the dinosaur bones to the state, but were willing to provide facilities and miners to help. This was just as well, as no one in the world had experience in mining for dinosaurs. The miners knew how to dig and manhandle heavy materials in the wet, narrow mine galleries, but had no idea how to recognize the fossil bones and take them out without damage. The Royal Museum staff had experience in handling delicate materials and protecting them from harm. The supervisory responsibility was assigned to L. De Pauw, who was, like all the best museum technicians, an ingenious and practical man, and equal to the task.

On May 15, De Pauw became a dinosaur miner; with the help of the mine staff he began the excavations. Day after day, the men put on their work clothes, took their lamps and gear, and descended the shaft. At the end of the new gallery they put in a hard day, picking at the roof or the floor, finding and tracing the bones by the light of their dim lamps. It became clear that the miners had already dug through an entire fossil skeleton and destroyed most of it before they realized what they were doing. Had it been the only skeleton, it would have been disastrous. Fortunately, there were many more.

Gradually, a method emerged. Each bone was given a letter for identification, and, by careful surveys and measurements, its position was recorded. As they were traced, the bones and their surrounding rock were cut into blocks small enough to be manhandled through the narrow passages. Each block was covered with plaster and strengthened with bands of iron. When the plaster was dry, the blocks were taken along the gallery and up the shaft to the pithead, to be transported by train to the Royal Museum.

Excavation was not without incident. In August an earth tremor caused a roof collapse, which trapped De Pauw and his team underground for several hours before they could be rescued. Soon afterwards, flood water seeped into the galleries, filling them by October 22, when work had to stop. They were reopened in May of the following year, and excavations continued to 1881. Meanwhile, miners had opened a second gallery at 1,167 feet (356 m), which produced similar skeletons from a smaller fissure.

Gradually, the large scale of the deposit became clear. The bones extended in all directions from the two galleries, beginning at the point where they left the coal-bearing rocks. The two mine galleries had cut into a deep hole in the coal-bearing sediments, which had been filled with the same Lower Cretaceous sediments that lay above the coal.

The upper surface of the Carboniferous (Pennsylvanian) beds had been eroded when the later Cretaceous rocks had been deposited, and the bones were at the bottom of what must once have been a steep-sided valley, part of a "fossil landscape" buried by the later rocks. As the mine workings extended, the dimensions of the hole were defined, and it became known as the "Cran du midi," using the miners' term for a buried ravine. The dinosaur bones were articulated— still arranged as they had been when the dinosaurs were alive—so the deposit was of more or less complete skeletons. It gradually became clear that the team was excavating fossil dinosaurs buried in an ancient ravine.

No one had envisaged the scale of the deposit when work had originally begun. But, for month after month, year after year, De Pauw continued his excavations, and still there were more bones. Eventually, he had taken out 600 blocks, weighing a total of 120 tons (108 t). These represented around 40 complete or partial skeletons of dinosaurs, as well as other reptiles, 3,000 fish, and 4,000 plant fossils. Excavation stopped in 1881, not because there were no more bones, but because the Royal Museum had run out of space to store the fossils. The mine management maintained water pumps and ventilators in the gallery so that work could resume when new buildings were made available. Although a new building was built for the museum in 1902, there were no more excavations before the First World War.

As he watched these startling developments over the three years of excavation, perhaps Gustav Fagès had time for a wry smile, as he saw his busy coal mine (designed to excavate the fossil remains of ancient forests) take on a new identity, and become a dinosaur mine. He probably did not foresee the day when his little town would become known around the world as the source of what was perhaps the first herd of dinosaurs ever to be recognized, and there would even be centenary celebrations of that occasion.

For the other staff of the Royal Museum, 120 tons (108 t) of bones and rock were not the most convenient addition to the collection, nor were the years 1878 to 1881 the most convenient time to acquire them. Belgium did not have a long-established national museum; indeed, Belgium was not a long-established nation, as the region had spent most of its history governed by other countries. Its national natural history collection began with the cabinet of curiosities gathered by Charles of Lorraine when he was governor of the Austrian Netherlands. It was not until 1880, two years after the first finds, that, in celebration of the fiftieth anniversary of Belgian independence, the Royal Museum of Natural History had a building of its own erected in Leopold Park, Brussels. Meanwhile, the boxes had been arriving by train, to be placed in temporary quarters. There was no staff member experienced in dealing with fossil bones, and, worst of all, any that were unpacked were found to be crumbling to powder soon after being exposed to the air.

The phenomenon is now well understood. The glittering specks of iron pyrite that deceived the miners are subject to chemical decay when the humidity falls. As the bones dry out, the pyrite penetrating them turns to a powdery iron sulfate, which leaves the bones fragile. There was no known "cure" for the mysterious ailment called "pyrite disease." With considerable ingenuity, the technicians developed a method to counteract its effects. As one side of the bones was cleared of the rock, it was chemically treated in a large tank under a fume hood. The bones were soaked in a mixture of alcohol, saturated with arsenic and shellac. This inflammable and poisonous mixture had to be handled with care, but in the short term it did the trick. The alcohol was able to penetrate the bones, carrying the arsenic (supposed to kill the mysterious "germ" causing the problem), and the shellac successfully hardened the weaker parts. After an hour, the fossil was removed, the rock matrix taken off the other side, and the treatment repeated. Badly pyritized fragments were then chiseled away, to be replaced by *carton pierre*, a mixture of shellac and talc.

As the bones accumulated, the director had to decide who would be responsible for cataloguing, storage, and study of the tons of bones received by the museum. G.A. Boulenger, vertebrate zoologist at the museum, was the first assigned to the task. In 1881, he presented a paper to the Royal Academy that described the anatomy of the fossil pelvis. He noted that there were six sacral vertebrae (in the hip region), whereas Owen had shown only five in the English discoveries. Boulenger considered that this justified naming a new species, *Iguanodon bernissartensis*. The Academy paper was refused, perhaps for reasons not unrelated to a brief critical review of it published by van Beneden in the same year. It may have been for this reason that Boulenger left Belgium and took a position at the British Museum (Natural History). A new paleontologist was needed in Brussels to take charge of the *Iguanodon*.

The task of mounting the skeletons for exhibition may have been uppermost in the director's mind when he hired a mining engineer, Louis Dollo, to replace Boulenger, but his choice proved excellent in many ways. Dollo had been born in 1857 in nearby Lille, across the border in northern France. He took a degree in civil and mining engineering in 1877 (the year before the Bernissart discovery), but he had also studied zoology. Five years later, in 1882, he came to Brussels to be an engineer in a gas plant. By this time, the fossils had been brought to the Royal Museum and the excavation was complete. Dollo joined the museum as assistant naturalist to work on the fossil reptiles.

It was a formidable task that awaited him. With the help of the technical staff, he had the remains of forty iguanodons to extract from the rock that encased them. He had to reconstruct the skeletons and prepare some of them for exhibition, working out in the process the positions in which they stood and moved. He had to describe this richness of material for the benefit of other scientists. And, most difficult of all, he had to try to understand what this new wealth of fossils could tell the world about *Iguanodon*. Using the other fossils and the information he could glean from the coal mine, he had to find out how they related to the other living creatures of the time, and the landscape they lived in, and where they fitted into the wider story of dinosaur evolution. Like a detective, he needed to reconstruct the appearance of the victims from their bones, and then find out how they died.

Louis Dollo superficially resembled that well-known fictional Belgian detective, Hercule Poirot. Round-faced, he cultivated a bushy mustache and a dedicated expression. He took himself and his task seriously, so seriously that he labored for twenty-two years before he took a holiday. Clearly recognizing that he had found his life's work, he became a Belgian citizen in 1886.

With such dedication, it is not surprising that he neglected relations with his colleagues. The space required for his iguanodons, the public interest they aroused, and Dollo's scientific success provoked a lot of resentment and jealousy. He soon found himself working in a small, cold room in the basement, but seemed unconcerned, and continued to work long hours, writing notes and preparing scientific papers. In 1891, he was made conservator of the museum, but in 1895 found himself transferred from the reptiles to the fossil fish, apparently as a result of the jealousy of the director. His successor with the dinosaurs was incompetent, and Dollo was soon switched back again.

Since the Bernissart iguanodons were the first complete dinosaur skeletons discovered, Dollo gave his early attention to mounting a complete skeleton, and had one on display by 1883. In preparing the mount, he had to consider how the animals had appeared when they were alive. There were some previous suggestions to go on. The original discoverer, Gideon Mantell, had envisaged *Iguanodon* (on very fragmentary remains) as a kind of giant lizard, and Richard Owen (the anatomist and namer of the dinosaurs) had seen it as a sort of reptilian rhinoceros. American Joseph Leidy had described a partial skeleton of *Hadrosaurus*, a related duckbill in 1858, and suggested that it had a kangaroolike posture. Meanwhile, Darwin's supporter Thomas Henry Huxley had pointed out the anatomical similarities between dinosaurs and birds, which provided further clues. With his new skeletons, Dollo had enough information to see that Mantell and Owen were mistaken, and so he turned to the ideas of Leidy and Huxley as his starting point. Contemporary photographs of the *Iguanodon* being constructed show that he used skeletons of an emu and a wallaby for reference.

The only place available for preparation of the skeletons was the fifteenth-century Chapelle Saint-Georges, once used as an oratory by the Princes of Nassau, and appropriately dedicated to the saint who is famous for vanquishing a dragon. Dollo and his team of six technicians worked in this unusual museum laboratory. It made a bizarre setting for the dragon skeletons that slowly took shape under its gothic arches; a scene more reminiscent of the fantastic paintings of Bosch and Pieter Bruegel than of a modern scientific laboratory.

With reference to the careful drawings made in the mine, the lettered blocks representing each skeleton were selected and opened. The bones were freed from the rock and given their chemical treatment, after which they were laid out in order on the floor. Then the laborious work of constructing a standing skeleton began. To support the bones, a crude wooden scaffolding was erected between the stone pillars of the chapel. The individual bones were suspended by ropes from the wooden framework until Dollo was satisfied that the complete skeleton could be seen in the position it assumed when the dinosaur was alive. Once the skeleton was satisfactorily arranged, an iron framework was constructed to hold each of the bones in place. Later restorations were backed by elaborate life-size drawings made by the artist Lavalette.

Preparation of all the skeletons took twenty-five years, and long before they were all finished it was found that the bones that had already been prepared were still decaying and had to be returned to the lab for more treatment. The planned building of the Royal Museum was completed near the end of the century, and five skeletons were then displayed. Public interest in the wonderful fossil material led to a new wing being constructed in 1902. The Royal Museum display now contains eleven standing skeletons, the largest of which is 32 feet (10 m) long from nose tip to tail, and stands 16 feet (5 m) high. Another twenty complete and partial skeletons lie in the positions in which they were found. Despite the treatments, there was an ongoing problem with pyrite, and all the fossils had to be treated again with shellac in the 1930s, when huge glass cases were built around them to control the temperature and humidity. The whole exhibit makes a unique group of the same kind of dinosaurs.

Dollo's training in engineering led him to take a precise, almost mathematical, approach to his fossils. In those days when printing and paper were relatively inexpensive, and many scientists published copious and detailed partial conclusions, Dollo instead waited until he had concentrated his thoughts as much as possible. He once said, "I am not yet close to the end of my work; it is not yet sufficiently brief." His many scientific papers were concise, with numbered paragraphs. His first paper on *Iguanodon* was published in 1882, the year he started work on the fossils, and showed the differences between the two species. A second paper later the same year described the pectoral girdle. A third note in 1883 gave an analysis of the pelvis and hind limb, as a contribution to the debate about the posture of dinosaurs. The structure of the hand and backbone, and some bipedal dinosaur trackways found in England led him to conclude it walked on its hind legs. In 1883 he described the skull, and in 1884 published a study of the possible structure of the jaw muscles in relation to the diet. Many short notes appeared on the anatomy and postulated physiology of *Iguanodon*. In 1923, Dollo commemorated the centenary of Mantell's original discovery of *Iguanodon* with a review paper. Although later work on other elements of the fauna and flora were published by other scientists, Dollo's flood of research was the richest, and at its peak saw ninety-four papers on *Iguanodon* and other topics published in one year (1887). Up to the end of the century, Dollo published a total of twenty-seven papers on the Bernissart fossils, including nineteen on *Iguanodon* alone. Yet he never did a comprehensive description of his remarkable herd.

One focus of his dinosaur work was the detailed anatomy of the skeleton. Dollo, working closely with the German anatomist Paul Albrecht, was the first scientist who had the chance to study the variation within one kind of dinosaur. Remains of dinosaurs of different ages make it possible to work out how dinosaurs grew. By comparing several skulls, Dollo was able to work out the succession of the teeth and show that new ones grew in the jaw as the others wore out, providing a continuously available grinding surface for mashing vegetation.

He described the complex structure of ossified tendons that supported the bones of the tail like the girders of a bridge. He was able to identify the places where the muscles were attached to the bones. And he was finally able to solve the problem of the bony spike that Mantell had found as a separate bone, and had placed tentatively on the skeleton's nose. Dollo showed that the spike was in fact the end of the thumb. The rock surrounding the skeletons even had skin impressions, showing that the reptile's outer surface had a regular pattern of bumps. Dollo also drew attention to the small and primitive brain, a mere twenty-thousandths of the weight of the body (compared with the human brain, which is a sixtieth of the body weight). He was the first to suggest that the low intelligence implied by these statistics may have been one of the reasons for dinosaur extinction.

Dollo attempted to interpret the lifestyle of the *Iguanodon*, whose big bodies may have weighed as much as 4.5 tons (4 t). The flattened tail might have been used as a crocodile uses its tail for swimming, or as a weapon of defense against fierce carnivorous dinosaurs. His reconstruction of the skeleton suggested that, on land, the animal walked on its hind legs, keeping the kangaroo position. This posture would also bring its head high enough to enable it to strip leaves from trees. Dollo suggested it may have had a long tongue like that of a cow or a giraffe, which could hook around a bunch of leaves and pull them into its mouth, where they would be clipped off and pulped by the flattened grinding teeth before being swallowed. The spiked thumbs might have been used to grip the trees, or even tear the bark. (An alternative suggestion was that they may have belonged to males only, and were used to hold females during mating.)

These details intrigued Leopold II, king of Belgium from 1865 to 1909 and the proprietor of vast estates in the Congo. Leopold's mind naturally ran to comparisons with African animals. "I would like to tell you what I think," he said to Dollo during a museum visit, "and if it is something foolish, please forgive it. I think that the iguanodons were some sort of giraffes." As *Iguanodon* was regarded as a reptile, and not a mammal, there was certainly a measure of foolishness in the royal suggestion, but Dollo was equal to the occasion.

"Yes, Sire," he explained tactfully, "but they were *reptilian* giraffes, because they were scaled animals as were typically all reptiles, and not furred animals as were the mammals. Moreover, like the giraffes they searched for their food among the leaves of trees."

Although all the specimens of *Iguanodon* were very like each other, one of the skeletons was significantly smaller and more slender than the rest. It was only about 18 feet (5.5 m) long and the animal would have been less than 1 ton (900 kg) in weight when it was alive. It was very like Mantell's *Iguanodon*, which had been named *Iguanodon mantelli* by Owen in 1832, and Dollo decided it belonged to the same species. After much thought, Dollo decided the larger skeletons were a different species, and named them *Iguanodon bernissartensis*. Later workers, such as the eccentric Baron von Nopcsa in 1918, have suggested that the large and small *Iguanodon*s actually represent different sexes of the same species. He thought that the larger skeletons represented the female, as is true in modern crocodiles. However, male turtles are often larger than females, and so other scientists have suggested that *Iguanodon bernissartensis* was the male.

Another of Dollo's innovations was what he called ethological paleontology, or the study of the relation of fossil animals to their environment. He studied the rock in which the bones were found, and also the other animals associated with the *Iguanodon*, to see what clues they gave to the landscape and environment of the time. The existence of a group of fossils of the same kind of dinosaurs suggested the possibility that they had traveled in herds, yet the absence of any young ones suggested that this was not a family group. For this reason Dollo at first thought the skeletons represented a kind of "elephants' graveyard" where the old had gone to die. Another theory was based on the excavation of a single tooth from a carnivorous dinosaur, suggesting that a *Megalosaurus* had driven the *Iguanodon*s over a cliff. The presence of fossils of five kinds of crocodilians suggested the *Iguanodon*s fell into water in which crocodiles might have scavenged on their remains. The presence of five turtles, a salamander, and sixteen species of fish also supports the idea that there was water in the gorge, at least from time to time. Later students studied the plants and insects and gathered more information.

The reconstructed geological picture shows a shallow ocean across what is now southern France and Italy, while land joined northern Belgium and Britain. Rivers flowing over this land mass had created a large delta, which had gradually filled, forming a deep bay. The remains of this delta now extend across southern Belgium and into southern Britain. The fragmentary *Iguanodon* fossils from Britain came from farther out in the delta, from skeletons that had been broken up and washed out to sea. The Bernissart fossils were from deposits of the same age, but from a gorge near the edge of the land. With this information it was possible to reconstruct the "scene of the crime" in some detail as Dollo and some later paleontologists imagined it.

Picture a broad flat delta, bounded by an area of somewhat rougher topography threaded by ravines and valleys. The higher ground was well wooded, with tropical forest containing cycads and pines, and a ground cover of ferns. Crocodile-haunted rivers flowed through some of the valleys, while others were filled with stagnant ponds where turtles basked on logs. On the higher ground moved herds of *Iguanodons*, bending to munch the ferns, or rearing up to pull down leaves from the trees. From time to time they were stalked by carnivorous dinosaurs such as the terrible *Megalosaurus*. One day, an astute *Megalosaurus* or two cut off a herd of *Iguanodons* against the cliff edge. Some of the victims may have tried to fight, flailing their long tails to drive away the attackers, while the younger and more agile members of the herd escaped. The others panicked, and in struggling to flee, they plunged over the edge, piling up at the bottom, in the water. Although the crocodiles feasted for a day or two, a flood brought down fresh sediments which buried the corpses before they had time to decay and fall apart. Their remains were buried ever deeper, until in our own time the coal miners' picks brought them to light again. Unless more evidence is found, "who done it" will never be known for certain, but Dollo felt the finger of suspicion pointed at *Megalosaurus*.

Dollo's scholarship was not limited to the dinosaurs themselves. The late nineteenth century was a period of intense interest in evolutionary theory, as the implications of Darwin's brilliant generalizations were slowly worked out in many different animal groups. Dollo's interests in evolutionary theory had been strongly influenced by the Russian paleontologist Vladimir Kovalevsky (1843-83). Kovalevsky had started out as a social revolutionary, but later became interested in paleontology and did extensive work on fossil mammals in Paris, tracing the development of different groups. Dollo did similar work with fish as well as dinosaurs, and developed the important generalization that has become known as Dollo's Law. Like all scientific laws, this generalization embodies an interpretation of many facts. Dollo's Law is often summarized by the words "Evolution is never reversible." In practice, it means that a major evolutionary change (such as adaptation to a new habitat or loss of particular bones) is never reversed by return to the original habitat or regrowth of the missing bones. Modern scientists have pointed out some apparent exceptions to this rule, so that it is now often called "Dollo's principle," but it generally holds true.

This idea had important implications for the politics of nineteenth-century science. The anti-evolutionary Richard Owen, the leading fig-

Dr. Gideon Mantell, discoverer of Iguanodon

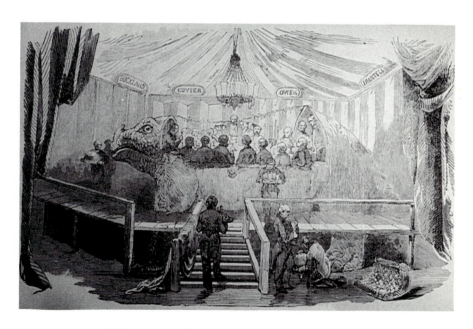

Dinner in a dinosaur at the Crystal Palace

ILLUSTRATED LONDON NEWS

A skeleton of Iguanodon being mounted

INSTITUT ROYAL DES SCIENCES NATURELLES DE BELGIQUE

Edward Drinker Cope

Left: Osborn and Brown collecting fossils at Como Bluff

NEG. NO. 17808, COURTESY OF LIBRARY SERVICES, AMERICAN MUSEUM OF NATURAL HISTORY

Below: American Museum of Natural History party at Bone Cabin

NEG. NO. 17905, COURTESY OF LIBRARY SERVICES, AMERICAN MUSEUM OF NATURAL HISTORY

Above: Diplodocus carnegii at the British Museum (Natural History)

Right: Earl Douglass happy with his Diplodocus

George Dawson, discoverer of Canadian dinosaurs

Right: Roy Chapman Andrews — or is it Indiana Jones?

Below: George Sternberg with the jaw of a carnivorous dinosaur

Tarbosaurus, a Mongolian carnosaur

WOJCIECH SKARZYNSKI

Phil Currie at work in Dinosaur Provincial Park

TOM WALKER/CALGARY

ure of British science and the man who first named the dinosaurs, tried in his earlier interpretation of *Iguanodon* to show that it was more advanced than the living reptiles, which he assumed had descended from dinosaurs, thus providing evidence against evolution. It is possible that Dollo (focusing on the primitive aspects of his dinosaurs) was articulating the support *Iguanodon* offered for evolutionary ideas. Dollo's Law also has important consequences for our modern understanding of the relation of dinosaurs and birds, and will appear again in a later chapter.

In 1904, on the strength of his important scientific work, Dollo became director of the Royal Museum, but stayed only a few more years. In 1909, he became a professor of paleontology at the University of Brussels, culminating a notable scientific career for a man trained as an engineer. In his years at the museum, he had made known to the scientific world what is still one of the most important dinosaur finds, and had worked toward a definitive scientific explanation of the discoveries, while also pursuing a wealth of other scientific interests. He had also prepared a major exhibit, which is still a place of pilgrimage for dinosaur enthusiasts. Although not all his work has stood the test of time, he is an important figure in the history of dinosaurs.

As the results of *Iguanodon* studies were released to the scientific world, and the increasing number of skeletons on display excited public interest, *Iguanodon* aroused great excitement outside Belgium. A number of other museums became anxious to obtain skeletons and approached the Royal Museum to see if any of the fossil herd could be spared. When Albert Gaudry (1827–1908) of the Jardin des Plantes in Paris attempted to obtain a specimen, he was opposed by a vigorous campaign in the Belgian press, and Paris (as well as London and other museums) had to be content with a plaster cast.

The German museums attempted a more direct approach. During the First World War, the German troops occupied Belgium, marching into Brussels on August 20, 1914. Rather than pillage the Royal Museum of its collections, the Germans sent paleontologist Otto Jaeckel (1863–1929), a distinguished scientist in his forties from the University of Greifswald, to supervise the reopening of the mine. Jaeckel started a new gallery between the existing 1,056- and 1,167-foot (322- and 356-m) ones. Before he reached the first fossil layer, however, the Allies retook Bernissart, and no more skeletons were recovered. Later attempts were planned to work the fossiliferous beds again, but lack of money was always an obstacle. In 1921, the mine was abandoned, and it soon became flooded and inaccessible.

Dollo died in 1931 after studying other dinosaurs, but leaving his long-promised monograph on *Iguanodon* unwritten. For a century or so, Dollo's interpretations of the *Iguanodon* skeletons, and the life and death of their owners were more or less accepted, with minor uneasiness as work on other dinosaurs began to suggest some problems with his interpretations. Successful attempts were made to relate the skeletal *Iguanodon* feet to fossil tracks found first in Britain and later in Spitzbergen, and fossils believed to be *Iguanodon* have been reported from every continent, though only the European finds remain entirely undisputed. In Europe, more fossil material has been discovered, including baby specimens from a site in Nehden, Germany, where Karl-Heinz Hilpert of the University Museum of Münster excavated between 1980 and 1982.

The most critical look at *Iguanodon* since Dollo's time has been taken by David Norman, then of the Department of Zoology and Comparative Physiology, Queen Mary College, London, subsequently of the Department of Zoology at Oxford University, and now director of the Sedgwick Museum at Cambridge. As the centennial of the mine discovery approached in the late 1970s, he critically restudied the Bernissart *Iguanodon* material, which is now known to be over 100 million years old. His results show up some weaknesses in Dollo's work, resulting partly from the limited experience available in Dollo's day of the complex business of restoring dinosaur skeletons and lifestyles, and partly from the new information available from related dinosaurs found in abundance since. Dollo's descriptions were not done in enough detail to allow comparison with the many related dinosaurs discovered subsequently, so Norman set out to systematically redescribe *Iguanodon*.

Norman was able to study the twenty-four complete and several partial skeletons of the original collection, and had to get special scaffolding constructed so that he could study the skeletons as they are mounted in the Salle de l'ère secondaire of the Museum. The original matrix had been left inside the skulls, and he found that the decay had continued, leaving many of the skulls too delicate to be handled easily.

As Norman says, "The majority of the specimens are . . . in such a fragile state that they are almost impossible to study. It is clear that a long term, very careful programme of conservation needs to be undertaken so that the collections can be of use scientifically, and also to prevent a gradual process of decay which appears at the present time to be destroying the skulls of many of the better preserved specimens."

In his restudy Norman concluded that *Iguanodon* had definitely had a horny beak, which was sharp-edged and irregular at the front and thus formed an efficient cropping device, allowing it to eat a wide range of plant food. Previous interpretations had suggested that its main food was soft aquatic plants, but the presence of conifer needles in the stomachs of hadrosaurs, and the strong jaw muscles and battery of efficient grinding teeth supported feeding on relatively tough land plants. Dollo had suggested that *Iguanodon* had had a giraffe-like tongue, but Norman found that the hole in the skull Dollo had cited as evidence was accidentally produced by fracturing, and although the herbivore no doubt had a strong tongue to move food around in its mouth, there was no need for it to be long. The plant material *Iguanodon* ate would have been bitten off by the horny beak at the front of the mouth, and the upper jaws could move so that the herbivorous dinosaur could actually "chew its cud," with the same effect as (but in a quite different way than) a modern sheep or cow.

The posture and movement of *Iguanodon* had been particularly difficult problems. Mantell and Owen had used lizards as models, while American paleontologist Leidy had compared *Hadrosaurus* to a kangaroo. Leidy and his successor, Cope, had shown affinities between the pelvis and hind limbs of birds and dinosaurs, suggesting some similarities in position. The German Heilmann in 1926 was the first to suggest a running position, with neck and tail horizontal, but backed off from it later. British paleontologist Peter Galton reevaluated the evidence in 1970 and showed that a horizontal running position was more usual for hadrosaurs and carnivorous dinosaurs. One of Norman's most striking discoveries is that Dollo had to bend the *Iguanodon's* tail to mount it in the upright position he selected, and this bend is clearly visible even in pictures of Dollo's restorations. The rigid structure formed by the bony tendons actually made it possible for the tail to be held out rigidly, and because it is so long, the dinosaur could not have easily sat upright in the way it is shown in Dollo's restorations. The curved neck does not fit the bones either.

If the tail was held out horizontally, balanced about the pelvis, in a straight line with the spine, the short forelegs would have come nearer to the ground and could have sometimes been used for walking, rather than being held out of the way like those of a kangaroo. The middle three fingers of the hand have small hooves, and the upper arm and shoulder girdle are rigid and strong, also suggesting that the animal walked on its forelegs at least part of the time. Trackways in Britain have small oval impressions beside the larger prints of hind legs, which probably represent the marks of front feet. Norman notes that younger and therefore smaller individuals had shorter front legs and were light enough to run away from enemies on their back legs alone. The older and larger individuals used four legs, were slower, and probably therefore used the sharp thumb as a defense. All of them could rear up to about forty to fifty degrees for feeding or resting.

The forelimb was therefore carried closer to the ground than in Dollo's restorations. The wrist of the forelimb seemed designed to carry weight, yet the outside finger of the hand (the fifth) seemed to be able to be opposed, like the thumb of the human hand, so that its hand could have been used for grasping vegetation. Although Mantell had placed the "horn" on the nose, Owen had recognized that it might be a toe bone by 1858, though he at first assigned it to the hind foot. Dollo had shown that it belonged to the hand. The English paleontologist Richard Lydekker (1849–1915) had found a scapula of *Iguanodon* from Wadhurst in southern England with a large lesion, representing a partially healed wound which could have resulted from fighting with the claw.

Norman regards the two forms as different species, not different sexes. Restudy of the careful drawings made in the mine has made possible a new interpretation of the manner of their death. The *Iguanodon* skeletons were lying more or less flat, but one above another, with as much as 110 feet (33.5 m) between the highest and lowest. Clearly, the animals did not stampede over the hill in a single herd, but dropped into the ravine from time to time, where their remains would have been covered and preserved. While evidence elsewhere in the world suggests that at least some dinosaurs may have lived in herds, the Bernissart find cannot now be used to confirm that idea.

Nor have all Dollo's theoretical ideas stood the test of time. One concept he developed was that groups of animals can die out from "over-specialization," the development of specific characteristics adapting them to a highly specialized way of life. This idea was for a while seized upon with enthusiasm by those trying to explain the extinction of the dinosaurs and other groups. They pointed to what appeared to be the more bizarre features of dinosaurs and other extinct groups, and felt that great size and elaborate development of horns and scales were enough to explain why they had disappeared. We now know that many of these creatures survived perfectly well for many millions of years before they became extinct, and were clearly well adapted to the world they lived in, however odd these special features may appear today.

From a single find of over a century ago, a remarkable picture of a past world has developed. As our understanding of the dinosaurs continues to increase, the dinosaur detectives of tomorrow will probably have new questions to ask of the *Iguanodon* of Bernissart, and they will perhaps have new clues for us to unravel.

5

FROM WHALE LIZARD
TO SUPERCLAW

SUPPOSE A JIGSAW ENTHUSIAST RECEIVED A BOX containing all the pieces of two—or even half a dozen—different puzzles. Before any one puzzle could be completed, it would be necessary to distinguish (without any pictures to provide guidance) between the pieces of each puzzle, not an easy task if they all include gray castle walls or multicolored flower beds. This complex task provides a crude analogy to the problem of sorting out the dinosaurs of Britain. The analogy can be improved if we envisage pieces of the puzzle arriving singly or in small numbers, selected from more than forty different puzzles, and rarely adding up to more than half of a single puzzle. If the pieces then arrive at irregular intervals over the next 150 years, so that some are dealt with by the original puzzler and the rest by the next three or four generations of his family, the analogy becomes even more precise.

Megalosaurus, *Iguanodon*, and *Hylaeosaurus*, the first three dinosaurs to be recognized in Britain, were initially described from fairly fragmentary remains, though there was enough of each for Owen to recognize that they were related to each other. Since then, Britain has yielded remains of more than forty other dinosaurs. Most of these are hardly known beyond the narrow circles of science, because they are based on even less satisfactory evidence—a piece of a limb here, a fragment of skull there. In the patient way of scientists, each piece of bone that seemed to be new has been described and named. Attempts have been made to relate separate bones found in the same place to each other, and sometimes confusion has resulted when two different dinosaurs have been described under the same name. There is rarely enough information available to bring the dinosaur to life in the popular mind, though there have been tantalizing hints at greater completeness: such as a complete *Iguanodon* that was not recognized, or two separate halves of dinosaurs that may belong to the same species. Yet most finds remained unexplained until relatively complete skeletons of related dinosaurs turned up in some other country.

This kind of fragmentary fossil record carries its price in terms of the sorts of scientists a country can develop and support. Without a strong body of fossil evidence, it is hard for scientists to become motivated and trained to specialize in a particular group. Dinosaur specialists in Britain have always been few, and have been largely sustained by (and have made major contributions to) the study of dinosaurs in other parts of the world, at first in the countries of the British Empire, and later in such remote areas as China and Antarctica.

This situation is, in fact, typical of most areas of the world where dinosaurs are found. Most of this book deals with the exceptions—the dramatic discoveries, the complete skeletons—which have given us such a rich knowledge of the world of the dinosaurs. It is important to bear in mind that the romantic story of the great discoveries takes place against a background of careful study of the fragmentary evidence by a few scientists who are not able to work full-time on dinosaurs, or even on vertebrate fossils.

And yet, even Britain, whose well-known geological exposures have probably been hammered, probed, and crawled over by more professional and amateur fossil collectors than those in any other part of the world, has had another brief moment of glory, when it produced in the 1980s a virtually complete skeleton of a completely new kind of dinosaur.

The first three dinosaurs to be described had represented three distinct groups. *Megalosaurus* was a carnivore; *Iguanodon* was the first of the ornithopod dinosaurs; *Hylaeosaurus* represented the armored dinosaurs. Other British dinosaurs soon followed. In 1836 H. Riley and

Samuel Stutchbury described three new fossil reptiles from the Bristol area. Stutchbury (1798-1859) was a geologist and naturalist a few years younger than Mantell. He had an early interest in dinosaurs, for two decades earlier he had pointed out to Mantell the similarity between the teeth of the then-unnamed *Iguanodon* with the modern iguana lizard. Two of the fossils Riley and Stutchbury described are now regarded as dinosaurs. *Thecodontosaurus*, the "socket-toothed lizard," had serrated oval teeth. *Palaeosaurus*, the "ancient lizard," was described from a single tooth. These are now known to be very early prosauropods, belonging to a primitive group of dinosaurs ancestral to the great sauropods. Stutchbury later went to Australia and did important geological work in New South Wales.

In his original notice of *Megalosaurus*, Buckland also mentions bones of another large animal, which he describes as being either a cetacean (whale) or a crocodile. One large bone had been found in a railway cutting by geologist Hugh Edwin Strickland (1811-53) of Merton College, Oxford. Strickland was an earnest seeker after geological truth in the rock exposures opened up by the flurry of railway building of newly industrial Britain. (This passion was his undoing, for he went down in history as the first man ever killed by a train.) The bone, when cemented and bound with wire, was "long the object of admiration in the Oxford classroom for geology," for it was 4 feet, 3 inches (1.3 m) long, the longest single bone yet found.

This huge bone was merely the first piece of this large dinosaur to be discovered, and the struggles of successive scientists to name and connect a few bones nicely illustrates the complexity of dealing with single pieces of the jigsaw. The system of naming fossils, and using a type specimen to define the meaning of a name, was aimed at making science as objective as possible. Unfortunately, when a species name is based, for instance, on a skull instead of a complete skeleton, it is hard to look at a pelvis found somewhere else and decide if it belongs to the same species. Under such circumstances, the process of science becomes extremely subjective. This is abundantly illustrated by the discovery of the whale reptiles (cetiosaurs).

In 1825, more finds were made by John Kingdon in Jurassic beds near Chipping Camden, Oxfordshire, including pieces of backbone twice the size of those of *Iguanodon*. Other bones were acquired by Buckland for his museum from time to time, and in response to one correspondent, he wrote of "some yet undescribed reptile of enormous size, larger than the *Iguanodon*, and of which I am collecting scattered fragments into our museum, in hope ere long of being able to make of its history." Buckland then quotes Cuvier's opinion that it was a whale. Mantell had bones of this large species, but thought they all belonged to his *Iguanodon*.

In 1840, a number of gigantic bones were found in a railway cutting at Blisworth, Northamptonshire. Five vertebrae, limb bones, and a piece of rib were passed on to a Miss Baker of Northampton, who sent them to Richard Owen at the British Museum. In 1841 he gave the new reptile a name, calling it *Cetiosaurus*, the "whale lizard." Although this was the year in which he defined the dinosaurs, he thought *Cetiosaurus* was a kind of crocodile. Professor John Phillips (1800–74), who had succeeded Buckland at Oxford, reported a fairly complete skeleton in 1869, and Thomas Henry Huxley pointed out that it was clearly a dinosaur.

Two brothers were responsible for the next discoveries. The older brother, Charles Edward Leeds (1845–1912), was a lawyer in York, and began to collect fossils about 1867. His younger brother, Alfred Nicholson Leeds (1847–1917), was a farmer at Eyebury near Peterborough, Northamptonshire, and he continued to collect fossils after his brother emigrated to New Zealand in 1887. The clays of the region were used for making bricks, and the workmen digging out the clay often found bones. Alfred regularly rode around the district in his dogcart, persuading the men, with generous tips, to save the bones for him. His wife and five sons helped him to clean and repair the bones. Some time after 1917, the collection was shared between the British Museum and the University of Glasgow.

John Whitaker Hulke (1830–95), a surgeon and ophthalmologist, was an amateur student of botany and vertebrate fossils. In 1887, Hulke described some dinosaur remains from the Leeds collection as a new species and placed them in a genus, *Ornithopsis*, which he had named from fragmentary fossils of large dinosaurs from the Isle of Wight. In 1889, Harry Govier Seeley, an independent researcher, suggested that *Ornithopsis leedsi* really belonged with *Cetiosaurus*.

One of Owen's successors at the Natural History Museum, Arthur Smith Woodward (1864–1944), attributed a partial skeleton including a pelvis to what was now accepted as *Cetiosaurus leedsi* in 1905. By now, complete skeletons of American relatives were known. W.P. Pycraft, in his 1910 book *The Natural History Museum*, illustrated *Cetiosaurus* with a crude drawing of a sauropod almost entirely submerged in water, and referred to it as "an ancient British river dragon." Comparing it with the American *Diplodocus*, Pycraft commented, "it is difficult to imagine animals of this colossal size roaming about over what is now Great Britain."

When the new skeleton was examined by German paleontologist Friedrich von Huene in 1927, he decided it was different from *Cetiosaurus*, so named yet another new kind of dinosaur, which he called *Cetiosauriscus*, or "whale-like reptile." However, he accepted Woodward's attribution of the specimen to *Cetiosaurus leedsi* without seeing the type specimen. It was left to British Museum paleontologist Alan Charig to point out in the 1980s that, as the type specimen from which *Cetiosauriscus* was named could not be directly compared with *Cetiosaurus leedsi* (as the same bones were not present), the type species did not have a trivial name. He called it *Cetiosauriscus stewarti*, after Sir Ronald Stewart, then recently retired chairman of the London Brick Company, whose company had allowed the Natural History Museum continued access to the fossils in the clay pits first investigated by Alfred Leeds so many years before. Another partial skeleton was found in the Rutland area of Leicestershire in 1968, which was prepared for display in the Leicester Museum. This, and virtually complete skeletons of *Cetiosaurus* from Morocco, have finally provided a good picture of a short-necked, long-legged sauropod.

Charig pointed out that *Cetiosauriscus* had the double-chevron vertebrae that were characteristic of *Diplodocus* and its near relatives, and also described a single bone found by an amateur collector and off-duty policeman, Stephen Hutt, on May 21, 1975, in the Wealden (Lower

Cretaceous) near Grange Chine on the southwest coast of the Isle of Wight. Hutt repaired the fragments and later presented the bone to the British Museum. There, its chevron shape was recognized as characteristic of the "double beam" that gave *Diplodocus* its name, but it was still extremely difficult to decide what species it belonged to. Charig resisted the temptation to give it a new name, pointing out that, "to be blunt, it seems to me that the endless, frequently repeated discussion as to whether two similar fossils from different continents represent the same species, the same genus, . . . or merely members of the same family is, in most cases, a complete waste of time." The new bones could represent *Diplodocus*, but this is quite uncertain. They do show clearly that the range of such animals was not limited to the Jurassic, but extended well into the Cretaceous.

Despite his poor opinion of Owen, Mantell was no doubt gratified to find his *Iguanodon* made part of the basis of a new group of reptiles. In 1841, Mantell suffered a carriage accident which injured his back, and afterward his work as both a doctor and a paleontologist was increasingly handicapped by physical difficulties resulting from the accident. Although Mantell continued to publish papers on his fossils, he became embittered at not receiving the recognition he thought was due to him during the last decade of his life.

During the 1840s, Mantell continued to publish new papers on his earlier dinosaurs, *Iguanodon* and *Hylaeosaurus*, and discussed them in his popular books. He eventually claimed that he had studied the remains of seventy-one specimens of *Iguanodon*. In 1848, he described *Regnosaurus* from an incomplete lower jaw with teeth found in Lower Cretaceous rocks. The specimen is so incomplete that, though it has been placed with the armored dinosaurs, it is now thought to be a large sauropod.

In 1850, Mantell described another new genus, *Pelorosaurus*, or "monstrous lizard," which he summed up as "an undescribed gigantic terrestrial reptile whose remains are associated with the Iguanodon and other Saurians in the Strata of Tilgate Forest." This huge animal was represented by an incomplete leg bone and a few vertebrae. It clearly belongs to one of the large sauropods, but there is not enough evidence to be sure which. Mantell died in 1852 (perhaps as a result of suicide), and his second collection (made since he moved to London) was also sold to the British Museum in the following year.

Mantell was no doubt missed at a New Year's dinner party on December 31, 1853. The invitations were engraved on what seemed to be the wing of a pterosaur (a flying reptile), and the guests were twenty-one of the most eminent natural scientists of the day, along with directors of the Crystal Palace Company. Most unusual was the setting, for the banquet was held inside the bottom half of the body of a life-size *Iguanodon* model. Owen presided at the head of the table, which was appropriately located inside the head of the animal. Edward Forbes (1815–54; Professor of Natural History at the Museum of Practical Geology) wrote a song for the occasion, which the company sang with gusto.

> A thousand ages underground
>   His skeleton had lain;
> But now his body's big and round,
>   And he's himself again!
> His bones, like Adam's, wrapped in clay,
>   His ribs of iron stout,
> Where is the brute alive today
>   That dares to turn him out?
>   Beneath his hide he's got inside
>   The souls of living men;
>   Who dare our saurian now deride
>   With life in him again?

> *Chorus:*
> The jolly old beast
> Is not deceased
> There's life in him again (Roar)

Thus the eminent cavorted, joked, and sang, and newspapers reported that their noise could be heard across the park. The humorous magazine *Punch* commented solemnly, in an article called "Fun in a Fossil," that "if it had been an earlier geological period they might perhaps have occupied the *Iguanodon's* inside without having any dinner there."

Beyond the hilarity, the occasion marks the first time that dinosaurs were brought to the attention of a popular audience. Owen was close to the British royal family, and was frequently called in to lecture to the royal children. Prince Albert, who had had a major influence in developing the Great Exhibition of 1851, was interested in Owen's fossils. When its prefabricated building, the Crystal Palace, was moved in 1853 to a new site at Sydenham in South London, Prince Albert suggested that the grounds should include a lake, where the life of ancient times should be illustrated. A painter and sculptor named Benjamin Waterhouse Hawkins was determined to "summon from the abyss of time and from the depths of the earth, those vast forms and gigantic beasts which the Almighty Creator designed with fitness to inhabit and precede us in possession of this part of the earth called Great Britain." Hawkins began his task of "revivifying the ancient world" by making life-size models of *Iguanodon*, *Megalosaurus*, and other extinct creatures, and Owen was asked to provide the technical information. Queen Victoria and Prince Albert visited the studio to observe the work in progress. After they were completed, the models became popular attractions, and generations of schoolchildren were taken to see the antediluvian monsters. They survived after the Crystal Palace burned down in 1936, and can still be seen.

Naturally, the models showed Owen's vision of the dinosaurs: huge, mammal-like beasts with their scales and teeth alone suggesting reptilian relationships. *Iguanodon* still had a horn on its nose. Unfortunately for Owen, interpretations of *Iguanodon* changed and, half a century later, at least one scientist dared to deride his saurians. "So far as I can judge," said Othniel Marsh, "there is nothing like unto them in the heavens, or on the earth, or in the waters under the earth. The dinosaurs seem to have suffered much from both their enemies and their friends."

Like Mantell, Owen described other dinosaurs in later life. After Buckland died in 1856, Owen was the only one of the first three namers of the dinosaurs left, and from his position at the Natural History Museum he was well-placed to see new material. He described *Nuthetes* in 1854 from some small bones from Purbeck in southern England. It has been variously regarded since as a juvenile *Megalosaurus*, or another reptile that is not even a dinosaur.

In 1859, the year Darwin published *The Origin of Species*, more dinosaur bones, dating from the Early Jurassic of Charmouth, on the south coast, were found by James Harrison (1819–68), a physician. Owen referred to the remains under the name *Scelidosaurus*, or "limb lizard," in the same year. In 1861, Owen described some bones, and in 1863, an articulated, almost complete skeleton, missing only the forelegs and the tip of the snout. The heavy hind legs suggested at first that the animal was bipedal, but it is now thought to have walked on all fours. The teeth were leaf-shaped and not sharp, suggesting some sort of plant diet. It had a long slender neck, but had small plates (scutes) embedded in the skin along the neck, back, and tail. It was relatively small, about 13 feet (4 m) long. Most dinosaurs are found in deposits laid down on the land or in fresh water, but this carcass had clearly drifted down a river and out to sea, as it was found with remains of marine reptiles.

Most of the bones described as *Scelidosaurus* belong to what is probably an early ancestor of the later heavily armored dinosaurs. Owen had mixed up the bones, and the type specimen much later proved to be a knee joint of a carnivorous megalosaur. Since the international rules for naming animals specify that the name is defined by the type specimen, the familiar name for the armored dinosaur would have had to be replaced. However, exceptions are made, and the rules were suspended to allow the dinosaur to keep its familiar name. The original skeleton was reprepared in 1985. It has been supplemented with some fragments found in 1980, and another complete skeleton found in 1985 by three amateur collectors—David Costain, Peter Langham, and Simon Barnsley. This one has the front of the skull (which was missing from the older specimen), and a heavy bone from the upper foreleg. *Scelidosaurus* seems to have had a limited distribution in England (and perhaps Portugal), but occasional scutes of the same kind have been found in other parts of the world.

Jaw fragments from quarries in Upper Jurassic rocks of the Isle of Purbeck in Dorset were found by Samuel Beckles (d. 1890) an amateur collector of fossils. Owen described them in 1861 as *Echinodon becklesii*, or "Beckles's spiky tooth." Owen considered that the leaf-shaped, spiky-edged teeth belonged to a small herbivorous lizard, but they had long roots in deep sockets, so were definitely dinosaurlike and quite like those of *Scelidosaurus*. No similar material has since been found in Britain, but small dinosaurs now known from Africa called fabrosaurs seem to be related. Although relatively late in dinosaur history, this type of dinosaur seems quite primitive and was probably ancestral to later types.

Samuel Beckles contributed other material to Owen. In 1871, he discovered *Iguanodon* bones in the soft Wadhurst Clay which outcrops near the town of Hastings in Sussex. Owen made the classic museum curator's mistake and left the inexperienced Beckles to collect the bones. Although he described some of the bones which gave new information, he never realized that the fossil was actually a complete skeleton of *Iguanodon*. With more attention to fieldwork, he could have anticipated many of Dollo's discoveries in Belgium.

❖ ❖ ❖

Thomas Henry Huxley had many preoccupations in the 1860s. Employed at the School of Mines in research and teaching on fossils, he also lectured on other natural history topics and was secretary, and later president, of the Geological Society. In addition, he was occupied in leading the supporters of Darwin's new theory, demolishing the ideas of Bishop Wilberforce and Richard Owen in open debate, and writing an endless stream of papers and books. He reclassified the now relatively abundant group of dinosaurs, recognizing three groups (armored dinosaurs, iguanodonts, and carnivorous dinosaurs) within Owen's Dinosauria, and (recognizing its close relationship with birds discussed in Chapter 3) set up a separate class for the little *Compsognathus* from Bavaria. As new dinosaur fossils made their way to the Geological Museum, Huxley also described a number of new genera from Britain and overseas.

His first British dinosaur was *Acanthopholis*, or "thorn bearer," a new armored dinosaur, described in 1867 from scattered fragments of bones and armor plates from the Lower Cretaceous Chalk Marl of Folkestone and the Cambridge Greensand.

More interesting was *Hypsilophodon*, or "high ridge tooth," a bipedal dinosaur superficially similar to *Iguanodon*. A partial skeleton was found in a slab of sandstone from the southwest coast of the Isle of Wight as early as 1849. Mantell had described it as a juvenile *Iguanodon*, and this view was supported by Owen. By 1868, the Reverend William Fox (1813–81), an amateur collector, had found several skeletons from the same locality, and Owen described them as a new species of *Iguanodon, I. foxii*. In 1870, Huxley pointed out that there were distinct differences between the new species and *Iguanodon*, and named the new genus. This move resembles an intellectual version of croquet, the very Victorian game in which a player is allowed to drive his opponent's ball into the middle distance. Owen was probably bitter at the renaming of his discovery, but there was little he could do.

John Hulke provided a detailed description of *Hypsilophodon* in 1882. The little dinosaur was about 6 feet (2 m) long, and was more primitive than *Iguanodon*, having four toes on the hind feet (where *Iguanodon* had only three), and having only a limited number of tendons supporting the tail. Hulke noted its long toes and fingers, and thought it was adapted for climbing on rocks and trees. He misinterpreted the position of the first toe, suggesting that it was turned back to form a birdlike, grasping foot. These suggestions led to comparisons with the Australian tree kangaroos, supported by interpretations of the claws of the hind foot as too strongly arched to be comfortable on the ground, and the flexibility of the shoulder joint. For a while, restorations of this little dinosaur were drawn perched on branches. More recently, in 1974, British-born paleontologist Peter Galton has reviewed the evidence and revised the interpretation to that of an agile runner.

Another new discovery was made in 1874, when William Davies (1814–91), a Welsh naturalist and paleontologist who worked at the Natural History Museum from 1843 onward, was sent to collect "many large bones" from the Swindon Brick and Tile Company's Kimmeridge clay pits in Wiltshire. The bones of a "huge dragon" were enclosed in a large septarian nodule (divided by mineral veins), located

9 feet (2.7 m) below the edge of the pit. The nodule was "8 feet in its longest and 6 feet in its shortest diameter" and to "raise it entirely with such appliances as we had was impossible." Davies cut a trench around the nodule, and "a workman was then instructed to insert his pick beneath and try to slightly raise the mass." The block began to crack, so that Davies hoped that they could lift it in pieces. However, when a large piece was lifted, "it fell from our hands in many pieces by its own weight, and its enclosed bone was found to be wet, rotten and crumbling." Davies was undaunted, and "the exhumation being completed, the whole mass, packed in many cases . . . weighing nearly three tons, was forwarded to the British Museum." There, it was taken in hand by "Mr Barlow, the mason attached to the Geological Department." Caleb Barlow was employed for £101-14-6d a year (about one-eighth of Owen's salary as superintendent of the Natural History Department), and was responsible for developing (uncovering), modeling, casting, and mounting vertebrate fossils—perhaps the first professional technician so employed anywhere. Eventually the remains were described by Owen in 1875 as the sacral region of a new dinosaur, *Omosaurus armatus*, which must have been about 15 feet (4.5 m) long. Large spines of bone showed that it was armored in some way. *Omosaurus* is the first of the stegosaurid dinosaurs to be described, but only two years later, wonderful finds from Wyoming provided complete skeletons of *Stegosaurus*, with flat plates that seem to have been upright on the dinosaur's back. *Omosaurus* was clearly similar, but interest in it was eclipsed by the much finer specimens from the United States.

Later, the name *Omosaurus* was found to be already in use, so it was renamed *Dacentrurus* ("pointed tail") in 1902. It was interpreted as having erect paired spikes along its neck, back, and tail. The pelvis was shorter and deeper than that of *Stegosaurus*, and the suggestion was made that the difference between the two was a matter of gender. However, it seems improbable that males would be found mainly in the United States (though *Stegosaurus* has been reported from Gloucestershire), and the females from Britain, France, and Portugal.

Mantell's discovery of *Hylaeosaurus* on the Isle of Wight in 1833 has been discussed in Chapter 2. The front half of the 14-foot (4-m) armored dinosaur, encased in a block of stone, went from Mantell's collection to the British Museum, where the bones, covered by rows of curved plates along the back, could be admired. The fossil was left encased in the rock, and thus could not be studied closely.

Meanwhile, the Reverend Fox (whose later discovery of *Hypsilophodon* has been mentioned) found a dinosaur in 1865. It had weathered out of the cliffs of the Isle of Wight, and had spines, hip bones, hind legs, and the back and tail vertebrae, all from the rear half of the animal. Eventually in 1881 the fossil was named *Polacanthus* ("many spikes") by Hulke.

Intriguingly, *Polacanthus* lived about the same time as *Hylaeosaurus*, and is much the same kind of dinosaur. Since one is the front half of an animal and the other is the back half, it would be helpful if they could be related to each other. In 1979 William T. Blows, an amateur collector, discovered some more *Polacanthus* material which may prove to link the two. Although far from complete, there are nice pieces of armor-plated hide, and some bones from the back.

❖ ❖ ❖

Harry Govier Seeley (1839–1909) was one of Britain's leading vertebrate paleontologists in the later part of the century. He came from a cultured family, and became assistant to eminent geologist Adam Sedgwick (1785–1873) at the Woodwardian Museum, Cambridge, from 1860 to 1870, where he catalogued its fossil reptiles. Although he was offered positions at both the Natural History Museum and the Geological Survey, he preferred (and could afford) to remain independent. He was associated with the Natural History Museum for two decades, during which time he made important contributions to the study of dinosaurs, as well as flying reptiles and the mammal-like reptiles of South America. From 1890 to 1896 he taught at the Royal Indian Engineering College, in London, after which he transferred to King's College, London.

His first British dinosaur was a singularly unhelpful clump of bones from the Cambridge area. The bones of one foot, and forty tail vertebrae do not provide much evidence from which to reconstruct a dinosaur. Seeley named it *Macrurosaurus* ("long-tailed lizard") in 1869, but beyond the fact that it was probably a sauropod, little could be said. Not much more useful was a bone from Bedfordshire, which he named *Craterosaurus* in 1874. The name "bowl reptile" suggests his interpretation of the bone as part of a skull, but it is actually an incomplete arch from a vertebra, probably from some kind of stegosaur.

More important than Seeley's numerous other descriptions of fragmentary dinosaurs was his survey of the increasing body of information about the group. Owen had regarded them as a single order, the Dinosauria. After some forty years, Seeley was able to survey the far greater number of species that had been found, and in 1887 pointed out that there were two kinds of pelvis characteristic of all dinosaurs known, and made these the basis of two new orders, which replaced the Dinosauria. The dinosaur pelvis is made up of three bones, united around the socket for the upper leg bone. One, the ilium, is always linked with the vertebrae of the back. The second, the ischium, points backward in both groups. The third, the pubis, points forward in one group, and in the other at least one part points backward. The three-way pelvis resembles the pelvis of the more primitive reptiles, so he called the order the Saurischia ("reptile-hipped"). The one with the backward pubis was much more like that of living birds, so he called the order the Ornithischia ("bird-hipped"). The saurischians included both the small and large carnivorous dinosaurs, such as *Compsognathus* and *Megalosaurus*; the prosauropods, such as *Plateosaurus*; and the giant sauropods, such as *Cetiosaurus*. The ornithischians included the duck-bill relatives, such as *Iguanodon* and *Hypsilophodon*, as well as the armored dinosaurs *Scelidosaurus*, the plated *Dacentrurus* and *Stegosaurus*, and, when they were discovered, the horned dinosaurs. These two groups of dinosaurs were accepted by other scientists, and have been used without much disagreement until the last twenty years, when new views of dinosaur classification have been advanced.

Even in Britain, the source of frustratingly fragmentary dinosaurs, exciting discoveries continue to be made from time to time. In January 1983, London plumber and amateur fossil hunter William J. Walker explored a clay pit in Surrey where bones of *Iguanodon* and crocodiles had been found. In a concretion was a large claw, shaped like a sickle, which was broken into several pieces. When he restored it at home, Walker found the tip was missing. He returned to the site and amazingly found it. Similar long claws were known in a family of small running dinosaurs known as the dromaeosaurs, but this claw was almost one foot (30 cm) long—three times the size of that of the largest dromaeosaur yet described. Walker's son-in-law took it to the British Museum (Natural History). The press promptly dubbed it "Superclaw" or "Claws," and attracted much popular interest—it even starred in its own television show. The quarry was being worked for clay for bricks, and it is sheer chance that the quarrying had stopped at the level that it did. Any higher and the fossil would not have been found; any lower and it would have been destroyed.

The museum staff checked the site in February and found more bone. They returned for an excavation in the spring of 1983. Eight people worked for three weeks, and two tons of rock and fossil material were removed to the museum. These produced about half of the skeleton, the most complete carnivorous dinosaur ever found in England. The skeleton was partly enclosed in a hard ironstone nodule, which made its removal very difficult, taking thousands of hours.

In November 1986, it became known scientifically as *Baryonyx walkeri*, or "Walker's heavy claw," when it was described by Alan Charig and Angela Milner of the Natural History Museum. The dinosaur was about 30 feet long (9 m) and 10 feet (3 m) tall, and must have weighed more than 2 tons (1.8 t). Its long head was like that of a crocodile, and it had many more teeth than most similar dinosaurs. Its forelegs were long enough to have been used occasionally in walking, and the great claws were on the thumbs. It is thought that they may have been used to hook fish out of the water, as grizzly bears do, because partly digested scales and teeth of a large fish, about 3 feet (1 m) long, were found inside the rib cage. Or it may have caught them by swimming. *Baryonyx* was also of sufficient size to catch land animals as large as an *Iguanodon*, though its teeth were weak—a handicap in attacking such a large animal—and the suggestion has been made that it was a scavenger on dinosaur carcasses. *Baryonyx* became the basis of a new family, the Baronychidae, although it is now regarded as the earliest relative of a spine-backed dinosaur, *Spinosaurus*.

Superclaw provides a powerful reminder that no dinosaur story is complete. Even Britain, with its generally fragmentary dinosaur remains, may still produce surprises of great scientific importance.

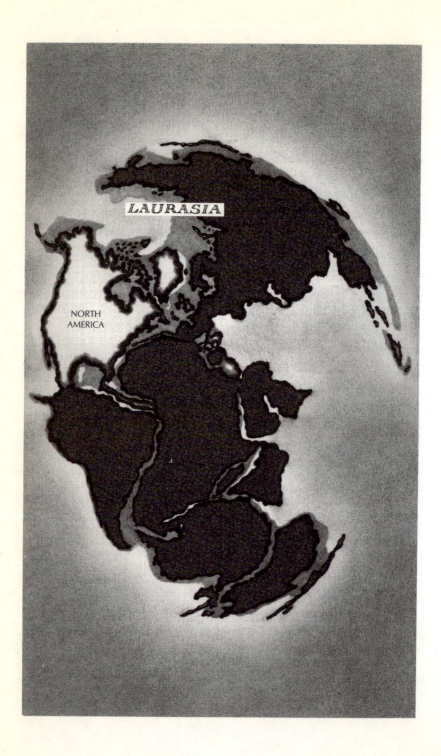

LAURASIA/
NORTH AMERICA

IN THE LATE TRIASSIC, NORTH AMERICA WAS STILL FAIRLY CLOSE TO all the other continents, though the North Atlantic seaway was beginning to open up. In the Jurassic there was a sea between North America and Asia/Europe, but by the Cretaceous there was a land connection across the North polar region. Intermittent seas or climatic barriers seem to have prevented some dinosaurs from migrating, while others managed to colonize several continental areas.

Abundant dinosaur remains have been found in many parts of North America. As the continent was settled by the time scientific discoveries of dinosaurs began in Europe, American finds also start in the early nineteenth century, and scientific treatment of them was not far behind Europe. Dinosaurs in the eastern part of the continent were infrequently found, as rich forests were only slowly cleared for farms and settlements. In the semi-deserts of the West, great expanses of bare country (badlands) provided a wealth of fossil material once discoveries had been made and expeditions were organized. The pattern of finds can be summarized:

- Triassic sites are clustered in the southwestern states of Arizona and New Mexico.
- Jurassic sites are most common in New England and adjacent Canada, and in the west-central states.
- Cretaceous sites are best exposed in the northwestern states and adjacent parts of Canada.

The remarkable abundance of fossils led to the rapid development of technical and scientific expertise, which, combined with the relative wealth of Americans (and to some extent Canadians), has led to the export of specialists to other continents. North American paleontologists appear in the stories of excavations around the world.

6

A MARVELOUS ABUNDANCE
OF FOOTPRINTS

ONE OF THE EARLIEST LARGE FOSSILS FOUND IN THE UNITED States, and apparently the first documented dinosaur find, was recorded by Dr. Caspar Wistar (1761-1818), whose name is now best known to gardeners because the flower *Wistaria* was named for him. Wistar was born in New Jersey, but went to Edinburgh for his medical training in 1785. On his return he settled in Philadelphia, became professor of anatomy at the University of Pennsylvania, and joined the American Philosophical Society. He soon had a chance to report to the society in 1787 on a thighbone found in Gloucester County, New Jersey. Although the description was not published and the specimen lost, the thighbone was from beds which later yielded dinosaurs, and so was probably from the first North American dinosaur to be scientifically noticed.

The dinosaur story in eastern North America continues with a footprint in a field and a bone in a well. Both were misunderstood at first, but European and North American scientists soon developed an approach to such discoveries. A wealth of fossils gradually emerged to challenge the intellects of the New World who (like their transatlantic colleagues) at first found the finds maddeningly difficult to interpret. Whereas Europe had produced many fossil bones and few footprints, so that attention could be focused on the familiar materials of the comparative anatomist, the eastern U.S. fossil fields produced what a later student called "the dearth of actual bones and the marvelous abundance of footprints."

By the nineteenth century, brownstones from the New England states were quarried for the famous houses of Manhattan, and yielded more than just building stone, for the quarries also produced remarkable quantities of dinosaur footprints. The period produced two major and a number of lesser students who worked out the significance of these discoveries. The leading figures, Joseph Leidy and Edward Hitchcock, were both American born (and, coincidentally, both the sons of hatters). Although scientists from Europe visited or corresponded with them, they were basically working on their own. Hitchcock devoted thirty years to a mistaken interpretation, but in the process founded almost single-handedly a new branch of science—the study of fossil footprints. Leidy not only described the first reasonably complete dinosaur skeleton found in the New World, but became North America's first great vertebrate paleontologist.

But the first fossils to be found did not receive the serious attention of capable specialists. Not only were the first footprints found in New England initially ascribed to Noah's Raven (see Chapter 1), but the first bones were blown up with gunpowder.

❖ ❖ ❖

When Solomon Ellsworth Jr. of East Windsor, Connecticut, uncovered dinosaur bone in 1818, his finds did not result from careful searching, for "they were discovered by blasting in a rock for a well; they were 23 feet below the surface of the earth, and 18 feet below the top of the rock. Unfortunately, before Mr. Ellsworth came to the knowledge of what was going on, the skeleton had been blown to pieces, with the rock which contained it, and several pieces of the bone had been picked up, and then lost."

No doubt the workmen pocketed some fragments before Ellsworth found out was going on, but Ellsworth managed to salvage some bones, and sent them off to Nathan Smith, organizer of the medical school at Yale, who in 1820 wrote a brief account of them for *The American Journal of Science*. These are the earliest discovered dinosaur bones from North America that are still preserved.

At first the bones were thought to be human; they were not identified until the early twentieth century, by which time some better dinosaur bones had been found from the area. However, before they were discovered, attention had largely shifted to footprints.

The abundance of dinosaur tracks in the Connecticut Valley suggests that Pliny Moody was not the only one to find them. But the scientific study of dinosaurs depends not only on discoveries, but also on scientists who have the temperament, opportunity, and motivation to collect, study, and try to make sense of the discoveries. In Connecticut, a ten-year-old boy named Edward Hitchcock had perhaps heard of Moody's find, but it was not until he was in his forties that the footprints seized his attention, becoming an obsession that dominated the rest of his life.

Hitchcock was born in 1793 in Deerfield, Massachusetts. His father was a hatter from an old New Haven family, and he had for an uncle General Epaphras Hoyt, who encouraged the child's interest in astronomy and military engineering. As a boy, Hitchcock suffered delicate health (perhaps attributable to his father's profession—Lewis Carroll's Mad Hatter was based on the real fate of the tradesmen at a time when arsenic was used freely in preparing hats). As a boy, he published astronomical observations on a comet in 1811, and his discovery of eighty errors in the mathematical tables of a locally published nautical almanac led the publisher to retract the reward he had promised for the discovery of errors. Hitchcock was also interested in botany and mineralogy; he was, in fact, well equipped with the sort of enquiring mind that would take an interest in anything odd that came along.

He soon became principal of the Deerfield Academy, but then studied theology at New Haven, getting to know leading scientists of the day before he became a Congregationalist minister in Conway, Massachusetts. In 1825, he became professor of chemistry and natural history at the newly established Amherst College, a struggling institution initially designed to provide a free training for the ministry. Though Hitchcock was to make important contributions to science, he continued to live in the Calvinist atmosphere of Amherst, holding revival meetings in his home and opposing "that *chef d'oeuvre* of licensed gluttony, a New England Thanksgiving." The college later remembered his passion for patent medicines and for renaming mountains. He remained at Amherst until his death in 1864, serving as president for ten years (1845–54), and then creating a chair of geology and natural theology for his declining years. He also headed the first state geological surveys of Massachusetts and Vermont, wrote a textbook of elementary geology that passed through thirty editions, and played a leading role in founding the American Association for the Advancement of Science.

Hitchcock's attention was directed to the tracks at Turners Falls by Dr. James Deane of Greenfield, Massachusetts, in 1835, and he began to collect and study examples. Students of fossil tracks—called ichnologists—know that fossil footprints are not easy to collect. The fossil itself is a hollow in the surrounding rock, which is only too inclined to break unless a lot of it is collected too. Then it becomes very heavy, and consequently difficult to transport. Nevertheless, in 1836 Hitchcock managed to make some collections and published his first scientific paper on the subject, in *The American Journal of Science*. As a classically trained scholar, Hitchcock was concerned with developing a correct terminology: "I include all the varieties of tracks under the term ornithichnites . . . signifying stony bird tracks: and if it be convenient to speak of the subject as a distinct branch of knowledge, I should call it Ornithichnology."

The seven kinds of tracks he describes are logically divided into thick-toed and thin-toed groups, and are all given descriptive Latin names in the same way as was customary for species of animals. In one brief paper, Hitchcock provides a valuable description of several kinds of tracks, devises an ingenious method of naming tracks distinctively from the unknown and unidentifiable species that made them, gives a name to a new subscience of ichnology—and makes what is apparently a colossal blunder of interpretation. One of his finds, *Ornithichnites giganteus*, was huge, yet at this point Hitchcock unhesitatingly attributed them all to birds. Human nature has determined that he is generally remembered for his apparent blunder, and not as the ingenious founder of a new scientific discipline with his very first contribution to the field.

In 1837, he introduced another fourteen kinds of "fossil footsteps" and was tempted by another explanation: "some of them bear so near a resemblance to the feet of living Saurians, that I have denominated them Sauroidichnites. I have sometimes thought that they might have been made by Pterodactyles."

In 1841 he described all the footprints he knew in his two volume, 831-page *Final Report on the Geology of Massachusetts*, with drawings by his wife.

The English geologist Charles Lyell developed important geological theories, which were not approved of by Hitchcock but led to Darwin's inspired explanation of evolution. When Lyell traveled in North America in 1841, he was greatly interested in the fossil footprints in Hitchcock's collection, and saw some tracks on the ground at Smith's Ferry near the Connecticut River. He noted their similarity to footprints of shorebirds in the tidal flats of the Bay of Fundy.

Hitchcock continued to find and describe new kinds of footprints, including one later described as "the gem of the collection at Amherst," which had a remarkable history. The type specimen of *Ornithoidichnites sillimani* had been used for sixty years as a flagstone in the streets of Middletown before it was collected and described.

While Hitchcock pursued his stony studies, Dr. James Deane (who had first brought the footprints to Hitchcock's attention) had continued his own researches. Deane (1801–58) had gained a medical degree through an apprenticeship in Deerfield and attendance at lectures in New York, before establishing a surgical practice in Greenfield, Massachusetts. In 1844, he published an account in which he claimed to have been the first to recognize the significance of the fossils. Hitchcock was incensed at this suggestion, and published later in 1844 an angry "Rejoinder to the 'discovery of fossil footmarks' by J. Deane." This led to a bitter controversy between the two. Deane continued his work, publishing an account of further tracks in 1849.

Hitchcock was trying to develop an explanation for his discoveries, and he turned to the world of birds. In 1848, he published a paper for the American Academy of Arts and Sciences entitled "An attempt to Discriminate and Describe the Animals that Made the Fossil Footmarks of the United States" in which he summarized his work.

> It is no idle boast to say, that I have devoted much time, and labor and thought, to these mementos of the races that, in the dawn of animal existence in the Connecticut valley, tenanted the shores of its rivers and estuaries. Whatever doubts we may enter-

tain as to the exact place on the zoological scale which these animals occupied, one feels sure that many of them were peculiar and gigantic: and I have experienced all the excitement of romance, as I have gone back into these immensely remote ages, and watched those shores along which these enormous and heteroclitic beings walked. Now I have seen, in scientific vision, an apterous [wingless] bird, some ten or twelve feet high,—nay, large flocks of them,—walking over the muddy surface, followed by many others of analogous character, but of smaller size. Next comes a biped animal, a bird perhaps, with a foot and heel generally two feet long. Then a host of lesser bipeds, formed on the same general type, and among them several quadrupeds with disproportioned feet. . . . Strange, indeed, is this menagerie of remote sandstone days; and the privilege of gazing upon it, and bringing into view one lost form after another, has been an ample recompense for my efforts, though they should be rewarded by no other fruit.

Despite some evidence of doubts, it is clear that by this time Hitchcock had formed a strong opinion that giant birds were responsible for the largest tracks, an opinion that he retained until his death. In the mid-nineteenth century, this was not the silly idea it appeared to later generations. The only dinosaurs which were well known were the duckbill *Iguanodon* and the carnivore *Megalosaurus* (both from incomplete skeletons), and these had been restored by one of the foremost scientists of the time as cumbersome quadrupeds quite unlike the elegant bipedal dinosaurs they are now known to be. Yet large living birds, such as the African ostrich and the South American rhea, were well known, and even larger fossil birds were being discovered. The giant moas of New Zealand were made known by American sealers from as early as 1823, and moa bones were being studied by Owen in Britain as early as 1839. Hitchcock's idea that large birds were responsible for the huge birdlike footprints was, at that time, the most reasonable interpretation.

Hitchcock's rival, Dr. Deane, not only described footprints, but supplied specimens to other medical men, including Gideon Mantell in

England—the doctor who had discovered *Iguanodon*—and Dr. John Collins Warren, who was professor of anatomy and surgery at Harvard University. Warren (1778–1856) was a son of the founder of Harvard Medical School and an innovative doctor in his own right. He had trained in London, Edinburgh, and Paris, and in Paris had studied comparative anatomy with Cuvier. He helped establish the Massachusetts General Hospital in 1821, published the first American book on comparative anatomy in 1822, and performed the first operation using ether anesthesia at the Massachusetts General Hospital in 1846. He was also interested in fossils, and established the Warren Anatomical Museum at Harvard, for which in 1846 he obtained a perfect mastodon skeleton and published a description of it.

In 1854, he published a paper, "Fossil Impressions from the Sandstone Rocks of the Connecticut River," which, although brief, uses the first photograph ever to appear in an American scientific publication. His colleague Deane was also using photographs, and prepared a publication, which appeared posthumously in 1861, featuring early photos of specimens tipped into each copy, with those of tracks of a living alligator for comparison.

Hitchcock was not just concerned with fossil footprints. As a clergyman he became deeply involved in the developing controversies over evolution, and was in the forefront of the attack on Darwin's predecessor Robert Chambers, whose anonymously published *Vestiges of the Natural History of Creation* appeared in New York in 1845. In 1851, Hitchcock published *The Religion of Geology and Its Connected Sciences*, attempting to reconcile science with religion. By careful analysis of the Hebrew word usually translated as "day," he interpreted the six days of creation as successive bursts of creative energy with pauses between, and argued against any evolutionary development of life, explaining that "advance has been by special creative acts and not by infinitesimal development." These relatively conventional sentiments were attacked by the more literal interpreters of the divine word.

By this time, Hitchcock had crowned his scientific career with a substantial museum and a definitive publication, both devoted to his beloved tracks. In 1855 his collection of "bird" tracks was gathered in the Appleton Cabinet at Amherst (named because it was funded by an endowment from Samuel Appleton of Boston). The churchlike building provided natural southern light to illuminate the 8,000 tracks on display. In his 220-page 1858 publication, *Ichnology of New England*, Hitchcock gathered the descriptions and explanations of his specimens. In his introduction, he regretted his inability to work with the large scientific collections of Europe, but reasonably summed up his own achievement. "Living in the midst of a region which has become classic ground for ichnology, I have done what I could in laying the foundations, and in gathering a storehouse of materials. Let others, with better light to guide them, carry up and complete the structure."

Hitchcock had by now developed the methods of ichnology by defining thirty characters to describe tracks, and proceeded to name and describe many tracks from thirty-eight different quarries. From one site at Turners Falls, for instance, Hitchcock named thirty-nine genera and eighty-two species.

Although he considered some of the tracks to be those of lizards, turtles, and even "marsupialoid animals," Hitchcock still felt most of the tracks were made by birds. By this time, there was more evidence to support his views. Stories of the elephant bird *Aepyornis* of Madagascar (which gave rise to Sindbad the Sailor's adventures with the Roc) had been reported from the thirteenth century (when it was probably already extinct) by Marco Polo, and elaborated by a French traveler in 1661. Now it passed from legend to science, as Mr. Joliffe, surgeon on a British naval vessel, gave vivid descriptions of giant eggs in 1849, which led to discoveries of the bones of these huge birds, some 13 feet (4 m) high. Before his death in 1864, Hitchcock continued to keep a close eye on new evidence. The discovery of *Archaeopteryx* in 1862 stimulated him to compare its feet with the tracks he called *Anomoepus*.

Hitchcock is in many ways the founder of the science of ichnology, but he never realized he was the first man to describe the remains of dinosaurs in North America. His scientific honesty shines through when he is able to say, "The real question is, not whether these hypotheses accord with our religious views, but whether they are true."

When Hitchcock started his studies, there were almost no fossil bones from the area for him to relate to his footprints. As settlement and civilization increased, there was more disturbance of the rocks, and more bones began to turn up. A jawbone with fierce teeth was found in a well in the red sandstones of Prince Edward Island in Canada about 1845. It passed through the hands of Canadian geologist John William Dawson and British geologist Charles Lyell to the Academy of Natural Sciences in Philadelphia, where it was eventually purchased in 1853 for thirty dollars by a group of members. One of them was Joseph Leidy, who was closely associated with the Academy for most of his life. At this time, Leidy was thirty, and on the threshold of a remarkable career as "the father of vertebrate paleontology in North America."

Born in Philadelphia in 1823, Leidy was the son of a German hatter who valued education, perhaps because he had had so little himself. Leidy's mother died when he was only young, but his stepmother was sympathetic, and the boy had a happy childhood. At school he studied Latin and Greek in the fashion of the day, but also roamed the countryside, sometimes playing truant from school to do so. He graduated in medicine at the University of Philadelphia at age twenty-one, and practiced unsuccessfully for two years before finding a good use for his skill in dissection. His first appointment as demonstrator at the Franklin Medical School led to a position as professor of anatomy at the University of Pennsylvania, then in 1854 he became professor of natural history at Swarthmore College.

It was in this year that the still young man described the Prince Edward Island fossil, in words that are enthusiastic as well as scientific: "The fossil has seven large teeth protruding beyond the . . . jaw; and it is hard, brittle and cream colored, and stands out in beautiful relief from its dark red matrix."

Leidy compared it to the carnivorous dinosaur *Megalosaurus* and to recent lizards, and gave it the name *Bathygnathus borealis*, or "northern deep jaw," from the extraordinary relative depth of the dental bone and its northern locality. Although he did not clearly identify it as a dinosaur, he was ready to speculate about its connection with Hitchcock's finds, and asked his readers, "Was this animal probably not one of the bipeds, which made the so-called bird tracks of the New Red Sandstone of the valley of the Connecticut?" The following year he compared it with other dinosaurs, and other scientists regarded it as a dinosaur for the rest of the century. It is now known to belong to an earlier group of reptiles, the pelycosaurs, and to be from the Permian (270 million to 220 million years ago), substantially older than the Connecticut rocks.

A few years later, Leidy was able to describe a better specimen. As early as about 1838, fossil bones had been found in a marl pit (now known to be Cretaceous) on the farm of John E. Hopkins at Haddonfield, New Jersey, just across the Delaware River from Philadelphia. Unfortunately, the workmen had carried off many of the bones, and the discovery was forgotten until a member of the Academy, William Parker Foulke of Philadelphia, spent the summer in the area twenty years later and heard of the find. Although the farmer had forgotten who had taken the bones, one workman remembered the location of the pit, and a new excavation was started. When a new bone deposit was found, Leidy was summoned, and the excavation was continued to October.

In 1858, the same year as Hitchcock published his *Ichnology,* Leidy named the Haddonfield dinosaur *Hadrosaurus foulkii* ("Foulke's big reptile"), and described it the following year. Although not complete, this skeleton was by far the best found so far in North America, and its 30 foot (9 m) length was impressive. The fore and hind limbs and pelvis were intact, there were twenty-eight vertebrae, fragments of the jaws, and nine teeth. Leidy recognized that the teeth of his new find resembled those of Mantell's *Iguanodon,* which at this time was still regarded as rhinoceros-like, but the completeness of the specimen forced him to look at proportions and posture with fresh eyes: "The great disproportion of size between the fore and back parts of the skeleton of *Hadrosaurus* leads me to suspect that this great extinct herbivorous lizard may have been in the habit of browsing, sustaining itself kangaroo-like in an erect position on its back extremities and tail."

Leidy must have felt uncertain about this bold statement, for he immediately backtracked and suggested that "it is not improbable that *Hadrosaurus* retained the ordinary prostrate condition." He also analyzed its way of life and death in a way that was to dominate dinosaur studies for many years: "*Hadrosaurus* was most probably amphibious; and though its remains were obtained from a marine deposit, the rarity of them in the latter leads us to suppose that those in our possession had been carried down the current of a river, upon whose banks the animals lived."

With the Haddonfield *Hadrosaurus*, the world's first reasonably complete dinosaur skeleton had fallen into the hands of one of the few men capable of dealing with it, and it was capably restored and imaginatively brought to life.

Hadrosaurus was from more recent rocks than the New England footprints, and Hitchcock must have longed for more bones from his area, so that he could relate his footprint finds to the fossils from the rest of the world. About 1856, a few years before the start of the Civil War and shortly before Hitchcock's *Ichnology* was published, another find emerged explosively in Springfield, Massachusetts. Hitchcock described its discovery in *Ichnology*: "The Springfield bones were discovered by William Smith, Esq., while engaged in superintending some improvements at the water shops of the United States Armory, which required blasting. He did not discover them until a large part had been taken away by the workmen. General Whitney, superintendent of the armory, very kindly ordered a re-examination of these fragments, and Mr. Smith obligingly presented me with whatever pieces could be found."

Hitchcock had the bones—a few vertebrae and limb bones—reviewed by Professor Jeffries Wyman (1814–74), an anatomist who did some work on paleontology "just before he started for Surinam in February 1857." Wyman reported that the bones were reptilian, though many were hollow. Oddly enough, considering how zealous Hitchcock was in naming footprints, the bones were left without a name until Hitchcock's son, Edward, Jr., prepared a supplement to his father's work in 1865. By this time, Edward, Jr., had shown the bones to Richard Owen, "who very kindly gave his attention to the fossils during the limited time I was in London. . . . They are regarded by him as belonging to a Saurian reptile with an unusually compact wall of bone in the limb bones, which . . . if they were filled with oil or light marrow, it would point to a course of development towards Pterodactyles or Birds."

The anti-evolutionary Owen hastened to add, "I mean to express no more than a degree of resemblance." Edward, Jr., then did further work on exposing the bones, noting that "close and careful work with the graver has uncovered the first and third phalanges of the fourth toe, seeming to show that the single phalanx on the right must have belonged to a fifth toe." For publication, he had life-size drawings of the bones prepared by his sister, Emily Hitchcock. They showed the large thumb, and he adopted Owen's suggested name *Megadactylus* ("big finger"), adding his own specific (trivial) name: "I propose the name POLYZELUS, 'much sought for', in allusion to the fact that for so many years other remains than simply tracks of the former inhabitants of the Connecticut valley, have been eagerly and anxiously sought for, and that now we have the much coveted bones."

This little dinosaur was later given a variety of names, each proving to have been assigned to a species already described, and eventually was classified as *Anchisaurus* along with the earlier bones. *Anchisaurus* was a primitive prosauropod, but had evolved coarsely serrated teeth similar to those of modern herbivorous lizards.

Supplement to the Ichnology of New England was produced in 1865, the year of the end of the Civil War and Lincoln's assassination. It was edited by Edward Hitchcock, Jr., with a supplement by another son, Charles Henry Hitchcock (1836–1919). By then the species recognized included 17 pachydactylous (thick-toed) birds; 17 leptodactylous (narrow-toed) birds; 21 ornithoid reptiles; 25 assorted reptiles and amphibians; 17 frogs or salamanders; 6 turtles; 2 fish; 1 marsupialoid; 45 insects, crustaceans, or larvae—a total of 151 species from 38 localities.

Charles Henry Hitchcock followed in his father's footsteps. He did pioneer geological mapping in New England and Hawaii, was State Geologist of Maine in 1861–62, and of New Hampshire in 1868–78, and concluded his career as a professor at Dartmouth College (1868–1908).

In 1866 he published "A Description of a New Reptilian Bird from the Trias of Massachusetts," followed by other papers on New England tracks. His description of the Dartmouth College ichnological collection was published in 1927 after his death. He also catalogued his father's great Amherst College collection, as well as one from Mount Holyoke.

In the same year that Charles Hitchcock described his "new reptilian bird," a new dinosaur collector—and a new dinosaur—appeared on the scene. Born the eldest child of a Quaker family of merchants in Philadelphia in 1840, Edward Drinker Cope (1840–97) was to become one of the most remarkable of all the people who studied dinosaurs. A child prodigy, he began drawing fossils in the Museum of the Academy of Natural Sciences at the age of eight. Although his father sent him to work on a farm at age fifteen, Cope studied science and published his first scientific paper at eighteen. He was able to persuade his father that Joseph Leidy's lectures on anatomy would help him in his work with farm animals, and he joined the Academy and recatalogued its reptile and amphibian collection in his spare time. In 1863, Cope's father sent him to Europe, probably to remove the fiery young Quaker from the dangers of involvement in the Civil War. There he met many of the leading scientists of the day. In 1864, at the age of twenty-four, he returned and became professor of zoology at Haverford College.

In 1866, Cope found fragmentary remains of a small carnivorous dinosaur in Late Cretaceous beds at Barsborough, on the New Jersey coast. A few teeth, a piece of jaw, some neck vertebrae, and limb bones were somewhat inadequate material, but Cope found enough to describe, and he named his find *Laelaps aquilunguis*. The generic name is a delightful literary joke, for in Greek mythology *Laelaps* is the name of a dog that was turned to stone in mid-leap.

After the Civil War, public attention could turn to science. Waterhouse Hawkins, who had built the dinosaur models for Owen at the Crystal Palace, visited the United States, and Phineas T. Barnum is rumored to have considered getting Hawkins to do figures for his American Museum, but was told there were no dinosaurs in North America. Hawkins received a letter from Andrew H. Green, comptroller of New York's newly created Central Park:

> Recognizing the interest that has long attended your restoration
> of the forms of extinct animals in Europe, the Commissioners of
> the Central Park have thought that a similar work in the direc-
> tion of reconstituting the phenomena of the ancient epochs of this

continent would be of equal scientific value, and of especial interest in an educational point of view. . . . It gives me great pleasure . . . to propose to you to undertake the resuscitation of a group of animals of the former periods of the American continent. . . . I think I may promise you the sympathy and support of the scientific men of this country, and that museums and collections of fossil treasures . . . will be freely opened for such examinations as you may wish to make in the prosecution of this interesting undertaking.

In accepting the offer in May 1868, Hawkins summed up the popular enthusiasm for dinosaurs over a century ago: "The interest in the remains of ancient animal life which Geology has revealed within the last century is world wide, and almost romantic in its influence upon the imagination." Patting himself on the back, he reminded Green that "the restorations which were committed to my charge in the Crystal Palace at Sydenham were the first efforts of the kind ever attempted, and their acknowledged success, both in commanding the cordial approval of scientific men, and also a large measure of public appreciation, encourages me to hope that a similar enterprise may meet with equal favor on this side of the Atlantic."

Hawkins stressed the educational value of his London models, despite their distance from town and the charge for admission, and grossly flattered his host by referring to the "higher condition of popular intelligence for which this country is pre-eminently distinguished."

By summer, Hawkins was visiting museums, including the Academy in Philadelphia, where he saw Leidy's *Hadrosaurus*, while the Park Commission planned a Crystal Palace–like building, to be called the Paleozoic Museum. ("Paleozoic" means literally "ancient life" and did not then have the connotation of the era before the Mesozoic, when the dinosaurs lived.) By the following year, the park reported on Hawkins's plans for "gigantic *Hadrosaurus* of the exact dimensions (one twenty-six feet, other thirty-one feet, long), . . . models of Laelap's Aquilunguis," and two plesiosaurs (marine reptiles).

Unfortunately, corrupt city politics in New York overthrew these ambitious plans before work could be completed. The Tweed Ring took control of the park programs, and (apparently not seeing any opportunities for illegal profit) insisted that the Paleozoic Museum be abandoned, the foundations demolished, and Hawkins's partly finished work broken up and buried in the park.

Hawkins's frustrated attempt to interpret the dinosaurs of the eastern states for the public may be said to end the first phase of discovery in the area. Significant remains, both of bones and footprints, had been discovered, they had been added to the scientific record by largely self-trained specialists, and an attempt at public interpretation had been made. Subsequent work would be founded on a more secure footing.

Over the years, more footprints and more bones were discovered. Later in the century, the bones went to Cope's rival, Othniel Charles Marsh, who was nine years older than Cope, and a much slower and more methodical worker. Marsh was the son of a New York State farmer, and his uncle was George Peabody, a wealthy financier. His mother died when he was three, and Marsh had a rather lonely childhood, enlivened by collecting fossils as the Erie Canal was widened. At twenty, he received a legacy, and went to study at Phillips Academy, in Andover, Massachusetts. Supported by his uncle, he then studied at Yale, and went to Europe to study during the Civil War. Then Marsh talked his uncle into a $150,000 endowment for a museum at Yale, which brought Marsh a professorship and a secure position to study fossils. It was Marsh who changed the name of Hitchcock's *Megadactylus* to *Anchisaurus* when the original name was found to have been used before.

A new prosauropod, *Ammosaurus*, was found in a quarry in Connecticut in 1884. Unfortunately, before its value was recognized, the block containing the front half of the skeleton had been built into the abutment of a bridge over Bigelow Brook, South Manchester. Despite all Marsh's efforts to locate the missing block, the rest remained in the bridge for over a century; recently some more bones have been recovered from the bridge. He estimated the whole dinosaur had been about 6 to 8 feet (2.0 to 2.5 m) long, and illustrated one of the hind legs, "as this was one of the animals that are supposed to have made the footprints." Another dinosaur from the same quarry, later named *Yaleosaurus*, was hailed by Marsh as "perhaps the most perfect Triassic Dinosaur yet discovered."

In 1906, the German scientist von Huene studied the dinosaurs of the area, and renamed some material. A new small dinosaur, *Podokesaurus holyokensis*, was discovered in 1911 by Mignon Talbot, when she was professor of geology at Mount Holyoke College. This tiny skeleton, only about 3 feet (90 cm) long, was the most northerly find in the area, and was in a boulder that had been carried from its original site by a glacier in the Ice Age. There was a gastrolith (stomach stone used to aid digestion) still in place near the backbone.

❖ ❖ ❖

Richard Swann Lull (1867–1957), an entomologist who had studied at Amherst College, worked on dinosaurs in the western United States, took his doctorate on a paleontological topic, and in 1903 returned to Amherst. There he made the first detailed overview of all the fossils of the Connecticut Valley since Hitchcock's, systematically surveying the footprints and bones found by earlier scientists. It was published as *Triassic Life of the Connecticut Valley* in 1915, and (after Lull become director of the Peabody Museum in 1922) appeared in a greatly extended version in 1953. At one quarry alone, that at Lily Pond, Lull recorded thirty-one genera and fifty-seven species of vertebrate tracks, and more of invertebrate tracks.

Lull had evidence of pairs of dinosaurs walking one behind the other, was able to relate some bones to particular tracks, and recorded breast and even bottom prints of dinosaurs among the tracks. Like Hitchcock, he supplemented his rigorous science with a romantic vision of the past:

> more than in any other act of paleontological history one is conscious of an obscuring drop scene in the middle distance, behind which may be seen with tantalizing clarity the passing and repassing feet of a host of players, some rapidly as though impelled by urgent impulse, others slow moving, ponderous, the like of which the paleontologist has never seen. Occasionally one passes before the curtain, and there while fully exposed to our scientific vision a tragedy is enacted, for bones are ever

symbolical of death; but the footprints are those of creatures in the full tide of life.

One of the best-known footprint sites is open to the public at Rocky Hill, Connecticut, where more than 2,000 dinosaur tracks can be seen with ripple marks, raindrops, and mud cracks. Further north, Donald Baird has found a number of bones of other small dinosaurs in Nova Scotia, many below tide line in the Bay of Fundy.

Recent advances in geology and paleontology have provided a couple of ingenious twists for those who had considered Hitchcock to be mistaken in his view that the tracks were made by birds. First, geologists who have studied the area for over a century have recently revised their opinion of the age of the beds, regarding them now as Upper Triassic and Lower Jurassic, and so somewhat more recent. Second, as birds are now regarded by many scientists as directly descended from dinosaurs, and by some as dinosaurs themselves, the difference between birds and dinosaurs becomes significantly lessened. Perhaps some of the tracks were made by creatures that were both birds and dinosaurs.

7

BONES BY THE TON

IN 1877—A SPECIAL YEAR FOR DINOSAUR DISCOVERIES—
no fewer than three major dinosaur sites were located in
the western United States. Although there had been earlier finds in the West—particularly in Montana, where
the Lewis and Clark expedition had made the first scientific expedition across what became the northern United States—such
finds were made by accident, as a secondary result of exploration.
Until the 1877 discoveries, no dinosaur site far from settled areas had
been the subject of sustained study. This year marks the beginning of
the serious pursuit of big dinosaurs in remote country by expeditions
of trained people.

What makes the coincidence even more remarkable is that there had
already been extensive geological study in the area, yet the bones had
been missed. One of the major discoverers, Samuel Wendell
Williston, remarked in 1878:

> For years the beds containing them had been studied by geolo-
> gists of experience . . . but with the possible exception of the
> half of a caudal vertebra . . . not a single fragment had been rec-
> ognized. This is all the more remarkable from the fact that in
> several of the localities I have observed acres literally strewn with
> fragments of bones, many of them extremely characteristic and
> so large as to tax the strength of a strong man to lift them. Three
> of the localities known to me are in the immediate vicinity, if

not upon the actual townsites of thriving villages, and for years numerous fragments have been collected by . . . tourists and exhibited as fossil wood. . . . I have no doubt that many hundreds of bones will eventually be exhumed.

The first discovery brought to a head the growing rivalry between Cope and Marsh. It was made by Arthur Lakes, an Englishman who was teaching school in Golden, west of Denver, Colorado. An Oxford graduate, Lakes had studied geology, and had perhaps gazed at the remains of *Megalosaurus* in the University Museum. Early in the spring he went looking for fossil leaves near the little town of Morrison, in company with H.C. Beckwith, a naval captain from Connecticut. When they found some huge bones on a hogback ridge fronting the Rocky Mountains, Lakes collected some samples. He knew he had something of importance, and had heard of the two great fossil specialists of the day, Marsh and Cope. Would either be interested? If so, which? In April 1877, Lakes sent some bones to Marsh, by then professor of paleontology at Yale College, who was known to be wealthy and willing to pay for specimens. He sent sketches, and perceptively suggested that they were "apparently a vertebra and a humerus bone of some gigantic saurian."

While waiting for a response, Lakes continued digging, until he had "no less than six different animals if not different species." He sent Marsh another ten boxes, and sent other specimens to Cope.

Marsh and Cope were, indeed, interested in the bones that had come their way. Marsh had secured a $150,000 endowment from his uncle for the foundation of the Peabody Museum of Natural History at Yale, and had secured a professorship there. Cope was by now an independent researcher who collaborated with surveys and governments when it suited him.

Marsh and Cope had at first been on friendly terms, and in the 1860s, when they courteously named fossils after each other, they might have cautiously collaborated in working on the finds. However, subtle antagonisms built up over the years, and after Marsh ridiculed Cope's erroneous restoration of the skeleton of a marine reptile, the two quarreled. Marsh later led a Yale College expedition into Wyoming and

Utah in 1870, the first expedition made into the American West specifically to collect fossils. Although it was not in an area that yielded many dinosaurs, some teeth were collected that resembled those of *Megalosaurus* (perhaps what later became known as *Allosaurus*). It was in that year that the surveyor Ferdinand Hayden (who was no fan of either of them) wrote that Marsh "is more ambitious than Cope ever was. He is raging ambitious."

Cope had also been in Wyoming and Utah in 1872, when he led a paleontological survey attached to the Hayden Geological Survey, while Marsh was with his own party in the area. Although few dinosaurs were found, Cope did describe what is now known to be a Cretaceous horned dinosaur, *Agathaumas* ("wonderful"), from an incomplete skeleton without a skull found in Sweetwater County, Wyoming.

Marsh felt that Cope was trespassing on his turf, so he convinced a member of Cope's party to act as a spy, ensuring that Marsh was always close when they made any important discoveries. Cope then tried to telegraph news of his discoveries for faster publication, but Marsh bribed the telegrapher to give him information. Leidy was already frustrated that Cope and Marsh were outbidding him for fossil specimens and was turning his attention to other fields of study; it is reported that when he heard of these antics he gave up vertebrate fossils in disgust. Cope and Marsh were left as the leading experts in the field—and the most bitter rivals. Both were fairly wealthy, and after their initial expeditions, they often found it more efficient to buy fossils or to pay other people to collect them than to keep going into the field themselves. Although Marsh enjoyed boasting of his western adventures, his assistants, who took most of the actual risks, painted a very different picture, and often resented the lack of credit that came their way. Samuel Williston once commented:

> In his publications, Professor Marsh has stated, or left it to be inferred, that his personal exploration in this as in other fields were extensive and that the larger part of the fossils described by him were the result of these explorations. The actual fact is that since 1875, when my personal relations with Professor Marsh began, he

himself did no field work, his knowledge of the formations being derived from a few transient and hasty visits to the different fields where his collectors were at work. His references to the personal dangers encountered by hostile Indians is amusing in the extreme . . .

When Lakes sent samples of his bones to Marsh in April 1877, he responded immediately with one hundred dollars, and asked Lakes to keep the discovery a secret. By July, Marsh had published an account of the large bones in the *American Journal of Science*, calling the animal *Titanosaurus montanus*, or "giant mountain reptile." (Later in the year he found that the name had already been used for a dinosaur from India, so he had to coin a new name, *Atlantosaurus* or "Atlas reptile.") By this time, Marsh knew that Cope also had some of the bones, and lost no time in trying to enlist Lakes for the Marsh team. He sent one of his henchmen, Benjamin Mudge (1817–79), who taught geology at the Kansas State Agricultural College, to convince Lakes.

Cope, meanwhile, had begun to describe for publication the new bones he had received, and was no doubt furious when Lakes wrote innocently and asked that the bones be sent on to Marsh. Marsh promptly named them *Apatosaurus ajax* "deceptive reptile." However, luck came to Cope from another direction.

O.W. Lucas, Superintendent of Schools in Canyon City, some miles south of Morrison, Colorado, found fossil bones in the Royal Gorge area and sent some to Cope. This time Cope's response was swift—he arranged for Lucas to hire a crew and collect for him. By August, Cope came to preliminary conclusions that the Canyon City dinosaurs were herbivores that measured up to 70 feet (21 m) long, and (he was no doubt delighted to record), exceeded "in proportions any other land animal hitherto described, including the one found near Golden City by Professor Lakes." Despite their size, the specimens represented young animals, but Cope revised his estimate of adult length to 60 feet (18 m). Cope called the monster *Camarasaurus*, or "chambered reptile," from the hollows that lightened the vertebrae.

Word of these finds got to Marsh, and he asked Benjamin Mudge to look over the area. Mudge confirmed that Lucas was indeed collecting large bones, and sending them to Cope. Despite offers of more than Cope was paying, and warnings that Cope could not be trusted, Mudge failed to persuade Lucas to change his loyalties.

Mudge then started up in competition, and requested help from a former student, Samuel Wendell Williston (1851–1918). Williston had been born in Boston but moved with his family to Kansas in 1857, and by the age of seven was collecting fossil clams. After a struggle to reconcile his Baptist upbringing with Darwinian ideas, Williston had become a dedicated fossil hunter, who worked first for Mudge and then directly for Marsh, who in 1876 hired him for three years at a salary of forty dollars a month. Williston wrote to Marsh, "I am very sorry to find that Cope is getting by far the best lot of fossils. . . . Prof Mudge thinks we had better work out these than use time in the risk of not finding better—but I am agoing to find better."

At a nearby site, Williston found "the hind leg, pelvis and much of the tail" of an 80-foot (24-m) skeleton. He was sent with "the innumerable pieces of bone" to Marsh. "I did observe that the caudal vertebrae had very peculiar chevrons," Williston later remembered, "and so I attempted to save some samples by pasting them up with thick layers of paper. Had we only known of plaster-of-Paris and burlap, the whole specimen might easily have been saved. When I reached New Haven, I took off the paper and called Professor Marsh's attention to the strange chevrons." Marsh recognized yet another new type of giant reptile, and in 1878 called it *Diplodocus* ("double beam") in allusion to the chevron structure. It was a relatively lightweight sauropod (about 10 tons [9 t]) but was one of the longest of the giants, up to 92 feet (28 m) long. Marsh also recognized the talents of his assistant, and a few weeks later instructed him by wire to work with Lakes at Morrison, which he did until they were interrupted by a rock fall. Later that same year, Williston was already "wrapping fossils with strips of paper dipped in flour paste," a technique developed by Cope and Sternberg the year before, but perhaps invented independently by Williston.

Marsh later sent another assistant, rancher M.P. Felch, to Garden City, where he discovered *Allosaurus* (the "different reptile," a large carnivore described by Marsh in 1877) and the nose-horned theropod *Ceratosaurus*, or "horned reptile" (1884).

The third great discovery of 1877 was made by William Harlow Reed, after he shot an antelope high on the slopes of Como Bluff, a long ridge in Wyoming. The weather was still cold in early March, but he was probably warm enough, carrying the antelope haunches down the ridge. It was not too cold for him to stop and look when he found large vertebrae and pelvic fragments sticking out of the ground.

Reed had been born in Hartford, Connecticut, in 1848, to a deeply religious Scottish family. As he grew up, the family moved slowly west, and he ran away to join the Union army in the Civil War. At the end of the war, he joined the Union Pacific Railroad, shoveling snow and hunting game for the construction crews. Later he married, farmed, and served the army as a scout, before his wife died in childbirth in 1874, when he rejoined the railway. There are suggestions that he had worked with Benjamin Mudge at some point in his career; at any rate, he knew about Professor Marsh and his interest in fossil bones. As Reed climbed down the slopes overlooking the Union Pacific rail line, he no doubt thought about what he should do. He consulted his colleague William Edwards Carlin, and they wrote to Marsh. By this time the paleontologist was used to receiving letters about bones from the West, but perhaps the detailed information gave him a hint of the exciting finds that were to come.

> I write to announce to you the discovery not far from this place, of a large number of fossils, supposed to be those of the Megatherium, although there is no one here sufficient of a geologist to state for a certainty. We have excavated one (1) partly, and know where there is several others that we have not, as yet, done any work upon. The formation in which they are found is that of the Tertiary Period.
>
> We are desirous of disposing of what fossils we have, and also, the secret of the others. We are working men and are not able to present them as a gift, and if we can sell the secret of the fossil bed and procure work in excavating others we would like to do so.
>
> We have said nothing to any-one as yet.

We measured one shoulder blade and found it to measure four feet eight inches 4 ft. 8 in. in length.

As a proof of our sincerity and truth, we will send you a few fossils, at what they cost us in time and money in unearthing.

We would be pleased to hear from you, as you are well-known as an enthusiastic geologist, and a man of means, both of which we are desirous of finding — more especially the latter.

Hoping to hear from you very soon, before the snows of winter set in . . .

His secretive correspondents called themselves Harlow and Edwards (using only their middle names). When the bones arrived in October (with a further letter telling of new finds), Marsh was enough of a geologist to tell that they were probably remains of dinosaurs from the Jurassic, and certainly not a *Megatherium* (ground sloth from the Ice Age). He sent a check for seventy-five dollars, and learned that Harlow and Edwards were willing to work for him, and that "there are plenty of men looking for such things." Marsh cabled Williston to investigate the fossils and their finders.

Williston found Como Station consisted of a couple of shacks, and at first all he could learn about Harlow and Edwards was that they apparently lived at a faraway ranch. A box of dinosaur fossils in the station suggested they might be closer at hand. "A freshly opened box of cigars, however, helped clear up things," recalled Williston in later years. Reed and Carlin acknowledged their subterfuge (which had prevented them from cashing the check), and Williston showed the telegram from Marsh. The two had collected an enormous quantity of bones during the summer, but Williston was even more impressed the next day when they took him up on the bluff.

He could hardly believe the richness of the deposit, and wrote Marsh with excitement, on November 14, that the bones "extend for seven miles & are by the ton. . . . The bones are very thick, well preserved and easy to get out." On November 16 he wrote "Cañon City & Morrison are simply nowhere in comparison to this locality—both as regards perfection, accessibility and quantity." He felt Carlin and Reed would be good workers, recommended pay of seventy-five dollars a month, and warned, "There will be great danger next summer of competition."

Ironically, Marsh had travelled the Union Pacific in 1868, nearly a decade before, and had actually been at Como Station, collecting living tiger salamanders. At another station he had found fossils, and had paid the stationmaster to collect more. Remembering the area, he immediately recognized the difficulty of keeping a rival collector away from a site that stretched for 7 miles (11 km) if word should leak out. He wrote a contract for Reed and Carlin, signing them exclusively for a year at ninety dollars a month each, and ordering them "to take all reasonable precautions to keep all other collectors not authorized by Prof Marsh out of the region and to use their best efforts in every way to promote Prof Marsh's interests." He also reserved the right to have someone supervise their work, and asked Williston (who had already spent eight months in the field and was being paid only forty dollars a month) to stay and take charge.

Carlin traveled east to meet Marsh while Reed and Williston opened Quarry 1. After a while, the huge bones started to move to the railway, and then on to Marsh. For a decade, the quarries supplied an average of a ton every week.

At first, the weather was a major obstacle. On November 30 Williston complained to Marsh, "The small saurian I have not yet sent and cannot for a few days till the snow blows off so that we can find it." In later years, Williston remembered that "inasmuch as mercury in the thermometer during the next two months seldom reached zero— upward I mean—the opening of this famous deposit was made under difficulties." Williston scratched his hand and it became badly infected; when Marsh sent him a hundred-dollar bill as a New Year's present to persuade him to stay through the winter, Williston used it to buy a train ticket east.

Although the bones were easy to extract, they were not easy to understand. Williston wrote that the quarries "are found containing remains of numerous individuals mingled together in the most inextricable confusion, and in every conceivable position, with connected limb bones standing nearly upright, connected vertebrae describing vertical curves, etc., precisely as though in some ancient mud holes these huge monsters had become mired and died, and succeeding generations had trodden their bones down and then left their own to mingle with them." Williston's explanation is probably correct; a number of other sites have now been found that preserve the bones in this way.

Marsh lost no time in naming his new material, rushing a paper into the December issue of *Silliman's Journal*. The first dinosaur named was *Apatosaurus grandis*. Other dinosaurs from the Como quarries named in the paper included the plated *Stegosaurus* ("roof reptile"); the giant sauropod *Atlantosaurus*; the fierce theropod *Allosaurus*; the small leaping *Hallopus* (now regarded as a crocodile); and a tiny *Nanosaurus* ("dwarf reptile"), an ornithopod only 2 to 4 feet (60 to 120 cm) long. Cope's *Camarasaurus* appeared in the quarry as well. The first quarry also produced a tiny mammal jaw—the first Jurassic mammal to be found in North America, and the first hint that, even in dinosaur country, small fossils could be as exciting as large ones. Marsh studied the smaller species of dinosaur after the big ones were out of the way, so that the ornithopod *Laosaurus* ("fossil reptile") was named in 1878, and the small theropod *Coelurus* ("hollow tail") in the following year.

Reed continued to explore with great enthusiasm, and wrote to Williston with more enthusiasm than accuracy in March 1878: "I had the worse time finding a good quary that a man ever had but now I wish you wer here to see the bones roll out and they are beauties to I think this quary eaqual no. 1 for good bones and quanity it outcrops for X80 feet length there is more than one animal it would astonish you to see the holes we have dug since we left no. 3."

By April, Williston was back at Como, and wrote to warn Marsh of potential rivals. A visitor named Haines had claimed to be selling groceries, but was asking a lot of questions about bones. Williston thought it might be Cope himself, but secured a specimen of his writing and found it did not resemble Cope's.

In the fall of 1878 Reed accused Carlin of laziness, and Carlin (the senior on the railway) forced Reed to leave Como Station. Reed wintered in a tent, which he called Camp Misery, near his quarry at Rock Creek. In March 1879, Reed told Marsh that Carlin had opened his own quarry, and was shipping fossils to Cope. When he had finished taking the best material out of a quarry, Reed smashed the rest so that no one else could profit from his work.

It was after this that Marsh brought Arthur Lakes over from Morrison, but Lakes and Reed did not get along either. Lakes found Reed rather uncouth, while Reed expected steady work with the pick and shovel and became frustrated when Lakes would stop to sketch the bones. Lakes did an entertaining series of watercolors of the excavations (which were used in this century to identify the quarries) and, in 1879–80, worked independently on another part of the bluff. Lakes was also a technical innovator, and in 1878 wrote to Marsh: "I have occasionally laid on a coat of plaster of Paris on the outside of the bone to preserve it while the rest of the rock was being jarred by the hammer." He, too, complained of winter work: "Collecting at this season is under many difficulties. At the bottom of a narrow pit 30 feet deep into which drift snow keeps blowing and fingers benumbed with cold from thermo between 20 and 30 below zero and snow often blowing blindingly down and covering up a bone as fast as it is unearthed."

In 1879, Reed discovered Quarry 9, which was found to be rich in fish, salamanders, frogs, lizards, turtles, crocodiles, pterodactyls, and mammals. But the new kinds of dinosaurs continued to be of prime interest. In the same year he discovered Quarry 13, which was the "source of the greatest accumulation of Stegosaurian remains ever discovered," and also produced four species of *Camptosaurus* ("bent reptile"), an ornithopod not named until 1885. Another sauropod, an almost complete skeleton except for the skull, was named *Brontosaurus* ("thunder lizard") in 1879, and in 1883 Marsh produced a reconstruction (the first of any sauropod) that erroneously had many features of the lighter *Camarasaurus* and used a skull from that somewhat different genus.

Marsh visited the sites in 1879, and it was in the same year that Cope first appeared on the scene in person. Although there are legends of fighting between the field parties, there is no real evidence that anything more serious happened than an unfriendly meeting or two. Reed was reporting regularly to Marsh, and would have had no reason to keep any altercations to himself: "The Cope party was up to [Quarry] 13 yesterday. They did not come to the quarey but was all around it the[y] went to those big Bones west of the quarey and I started out to see them and they left. . . . I find their tracks all round no. 9 but they have not done any work there."

Reed had a practical suggestion for Marsh, which seems to have been ignored: "there is one way in which to keep them away from our quaries and that is to preempt or take the land under the desert act by this act we can pay 25 cents per acre and hold the land three years and then by paying one dolar per acre more get a deed."

Lakes was favorably impressed by what he saw of Cope, and wrote of his visit: "The monstrum horridum [horrible monster] Cope has been and gone and I must say that what I saw of him I liked very much his manner is so affable and his conversation very agreeable. I only wish I could feel sure he had a sound reputation for honesty."

In November, Reed found a virtually complete skeleton of *Apatosaurus excelsus*, one of the best sauropods ever found. February 1880 saw Lakes working through snowdrifts to dig out a stegosaur skeleton from Robber's Roost on the western end of Como Bluff.

Despite Lakes's opinion of him, Reed was not uncultured. Finding reading material hard to obtain locally, he advertised for books in a Detroit newspaper, and his taste for Dickens, Twain, Thackeray, and Hebrew philosophy attracted the attention of a schoolteacher, Anne E. Clark, from Ohio. After some correspondence, they were married in 1880, and subsequently had two children.

Among a fluctuating army of helpers (including Frank Williston, Samuel's brother), Reed was a dedicated worker who was a constant figure in the quarries, although pay and money for supplies arrived irregularly. He made many of the most important discoveries despite the dangers and hardships of the work. On one occasion Reed almost drowned in an icy creek while rafting across it. Bones often had to be carried as far as 5 miles (8 km) to the station, and Reed once dragged a 400-pound (180-kg) partial leg bone for half a mile (0.8 km) down to the tracks. Perhaps he remembered how light the antelope had been in comparison, and wondered at his choice of a new career. At any rate, he complained in 1882 that he was disenchanted with the bone business, and in 1883 he resigned to take up sheep farming. Reed had worked for Marsh for six years in all. Although he was able to cope with the weather, he was frustrated by the lack of appreciation and the anarchic approach taken by Marsh's field crew; several people were often working independently and Reed sometimes found himself working for people he considered less well qualified than himself. He went on to try sheepherding and guiding hunting parties, but was soon back in the fossil business, first as an independent collector, and then as a scout for other institutions. Lakes eventually went back to teaching, and Frank Williston left to work for Cope.

E. Kennedy, who had worked with Marsh for some years, continued the excavations for Marsh. In 1884 he found Marsh had brought in Fred Brown (a previous assistant at Como who had spent a while at Canyon City) to take charge. Neither would work for the other, and for a year they worked independently in different quarries, disagreeing so violently when they met that, on one occasion, Brown brandished a couple of revolvers. Kennedy became so frustrated that he eventually left, leaving Brown to work alone until June 1889. Marsh did not hire anyone else to work on this site, which was abandoned for some years.

The remarkable series of dinosaurs produced at Como Bluff included twenty-six species new to science, and fine skeletons of others already known. The bones were in an excellent state of preservation, and for the first time numerous complete skeletons were found. These finds also mark the real beginning of the popular interest in dinosaurs, which has been growing steadily for over a century since then. Museum directors began to recognize the potential of spectacular dinosaur skeletons to attract the public, and eventually to help fund the less-dramatic work of other departments. Museum architects quickly grew to recognize the need for large exhibition halls in which giant skeletons could be displayed to advantage.

In the early 1890s, Cope lost much of his money in mining speculations, while Marsh was appointed to positions of great eminence, as president of the National Academy of Sciences and vertebrate paleontologist to the Geological Survey. The two continued their private war, which became a public scandal in 1890. The last straw came when Marsh tried to force Cope to transfer his personal fossil collection (for which he had paid out $75,000) to the National Museum (where Marsh would have access to it). Cope complained in the *New*

York Herald, and Marsh replied, each drawing on a private file of damaging information gathered about the other. Marsh suffered most from the publicity, as Cope was able to quote Williston's bitter—and credible—accusation that many of Marsh's dinosaur papers were "chiefly written by me." In reply, Marsh attempted to revive the old story about Cope's mistaken restoration of a marine reptile, and made unsupported accusations that Cope had stolen fossils destined for Marsh.

When funds for the Geological Survey were cut, Marsh was forced to resign. Cope sold his collection to the American Museum of Natural History for $32,000, and became a professor at the University of Pennsylvania, but died of kidney failure in 1897. Marsh's collections were in the Peabody Museum in New Haven, where in later years he found it necessary to ask for a salary. He died two years after Cope, in 1899.

The two men had remarkable careers, both working on many kinds of fossils and being responsible for the discovery and description of many kinds of dinosaurs. (Cope described nine genera of dinosaurs, Marsh nineteen.) They had also trained and supported a remarkable variety of people, some of whom were now ready to take up the hunt for dinosaurs, their scientific description, and the search for solutions to the complex problems their discovery presented. As new university departments and museums developed, it was to these people that they turned for expert assistance.

The American Museum of Natural History in New York was led by Henry Fairfield Osborn (1857-1935), who was brilliant as both a scientist and a communicator. He had another advantage, for he was not only rich, but well connected with people who were even richer. Osborn could mention casually in a discussion of great men that he had the privilege of calling the millionaire J. Pierpont Morgan "Uncle Pierpont." Born in 1857, he traveled west to collect fossils in 1877–78, and then studied in London, under Huxley, in 1879. That great scientist, by then at the peak of his career, was a pioneer of education as well as of science, and he inspired Osborn—"By his way of living and by the unlimited personal sacrifices he made he taught me that we men of science must do our part in public education," said Osborn in later life.

Through Huxley, he met Darwin, and many of the other great figures of Victorian science. He later trained with Cope, whom he regarded as "the most brilliant creative mind in comparative anatomy and evolution that America has produced," and in due course wrote the first biography of this great American scientist. In June 1897, Osborn started the Museum's Paleontology Department. He was interested in many aspects of vertebrate paleontology, publishing two mammoth monographs on fossil elephants, and took a strong interest in fossil man.

Osborn was a square, mustached, self-confident man. Many years later, Osborn's young assistant Edwin Colbert (now himself one of the most eminent vertebrate paleontologists of his generation) left vivid descriptions of Osborn in his prime: "Professor Osborn was quite aware of his eminence. I had seen him at a distance in the halls and corridors of the museum—a large and forceful looking person, generally clad in rather formal clothes. . . . He would often be seen striding along with two or three people in his wake, like a majestic ocean liner accompanied by several gulls."

Colbert remembers an instance of Osborn's self-importance when he ordered his chauffeur to go the wrong way down a one-way street in New York. When authority intervened, Osborn explained to the policeman who he was, behaving as if his importance gave him special privileges, even in traffic. However, the policeman was unimpressed, and insisted on a return journey.

The well-connected Osborn had no difficulty getting funding from the financial kings of the eastern establishment for his ambitious paleontological program. With these sources of funds, he was in a position to attract the best men and sustain them in the field for years at a time. He began to look for suitable staff, and put together a notable team of collectors and scientists. Osborn was determined to build a major dinosaur collection at his museum, anticipating both the scientific interest it would create and the public support such exciting exhibits would draw to his institution. Where better to start than Como Bluff, where Osborn felt there must be more fossils to be found. The day after Cope's funeral, Osborn dictated instructions for an expedition to Como Bluff.

Osborn set out to develop a team of specialists, and secured some remarkable men, including the young Barnum Brown (whose story is told in the next chapter). Another member of the team, Walter Granger (1872–1941) had hiked down from Vermont in 1890 at the age of seventeen and applied for a "job where I can learn taxidermy." Jacob Lawson Wortman (1856–1926) had worked for Cope, and came highly recommended. William Diller Matthew (1871–1930) was a Canadian who was studying under Osborn at Columbia University. Wilbur Clinton Knight (1858-1903) had done some fieldwork for the University of Wyoming in 1895, and was soon to become state geologist of Wyoming.

In 1897, the American Museum team was at Como Bluff, where they collected the rear halves of two sauropod skeletons from sites near quarries previously worked by Marsh's crews. Osborn and Brown worked on a *Diplodocus*, while Wortman and Knight excavated an *Apatosaurus*.

Technical methods had advanced by this time, but the modern plastering technique was still not in use. When struggling to excavate bones from crumbling clay, Wortman told his men to mix plaster and pour it onto burlap. "This mass was then drawn under the sacrum through a trench" to provide support, but when Wortman then asked his men to pull out the burlap, the setting plaster held it firm. Wortman soon realized he had stumbled on an improved method. He added more plaster and burlap and, after the bone was firmly wrapped, "the party declared a holiday."

While working for Marsh in 1881, Frank Williston had headed northwest of Como up to the Little Medicine River, and though Reed reported to Marsh that he had "found a very nice quarry in which the bones could be easily collected," nothing further was done in the area. It seems that when Frank went to work for Cope he explored this new quarry for a while, but greater riches were to be found in the area.

In 1898, the American Museum team was also working north of Como, looking for new sites. On June 11, Wortman sighted a cabin on a hilltop a couple of miles away, and decided the cabin would be the focus of the next day's search; "as I approached the hillock on which the ruin stands," wrote Granger later, "I observed, among the beautiful flowers, the blooming cacti, and the dwarf bushes of the desert, what were apparently numbers of dark-brown boulders. On closer examination it proved that there is really not a single rock, hardly even a pebble, on this hillock; all these apparent boulders are ponderous fossils which have slowly accumulated or washed out on the surface from the great dinosaur bed beneath."

When they reached the cabin the next day, they were astonished to find it was built of dinosaur bones, with the gaps filled in with adobe and sod. The local sheepherders had found a practical way of building a shelter in a treeless area. Thus was Bone Cabin Quarry—one of the most remarkable fossil quarries in the West—named. It was worked for the American Museum for seven years following 1898 by a small who's who of dinosaur men, including Peter Kaisen, Walter Granger, Richard Swann Lull, William Diller Matthew, and George Olsen. The quarry yielded 517 catalogued specimens, of which 98 percent were dinosaurs. Eighty-five percent of these came from three sauropod dinosaurs: *Apatosaurus, Camarasaurus* and *Diplodocus*. A small number of turtle and crocodile bones make up the rest. Most of the dinosaur material was strangely made up of complete legs and feet and sections of tail, perhaps implying a swamp in which dinosaurs had been mired, before flooding had carried away the rest of the bones. Only two skulls were found, both crushed. The small amount of non-sauropod material was important, including substantial parts of skeletons of *Stegosaurus, Camptosaurus,* and the rare *Ornitholestes*, a 6-foot, 6-inch (2-m) predator whose name means "bird robber."

In 1899 the Union Pacific Railroad collaborated with the University of Wyoming to conduct a tour of the fossil sites of the area, and scientists from universities and colleges around the country were invited, many of whom went home with a souvenir bone or two. In the same year, Sam Williston, of the University of Kansas, and his former student Elmer Samuel Riggs (1869–1963), of the Field Columbian Museum in Chicago, worked a number of quarries even farther northwest, in the Freeze Out Hills, finding fossils similar to those at Bone Cabin.

When one of the Bone Cabin dinosaurs was displayed in the American Museum, Samuel Clemens (Mark Twain) is reputed to have announced: "Professor Osborn has just reconstructed a 75-foot dinosaur. If the plaster had held out he would have made it 100." But in truth, the amazing animals needed no exaggeration to impress all who saw them, and thousands of people flocked to the exhibits.

8

TRICERATOPS
AND TYRANNOSAURUS

MILLIONS OF BUFFALO ONCE ROAMED THE GREAT PLAINS of the northwestern United States and Canada. They grazed on the short, dry grass and sheltered from summer storms and winter blizzards in the broad expanses of badlands that stretched along the major rivers. When they died, their bones sometimes mingled with those of much more ancient animals, weathering out on the surface of the rocky slopes. There the Peigan Indians found the "grandfather of the buffalo," and later cattlemen found fossil horned creatures that had preceded their long-horned herds. Across the Montana Territory of the United States and the parts of the Northwest Territories of Canada that later became the provinces of Saskatchewan and Alberta, people traveled west, looking for a route to the western sea. Some of them stayed to explore the badlands, and gradually unearthed a remarkable series of fossils, documenting the latest dinosaurs with names that would become household words.

The first United States expedition was sent out by Thomas Jefferson after he became president in 1800. He was himself a fossil collector; fascinated by the fossil mastodon remains that had turned up in the eastern United States, he dreamed that the great elephants might still live in the West. When the Louisiana Purchase of 1803 greatly extended the country, an exploring expedition became imperative.

The Lewis and Clark expedition in 1804–06 was a major triumph of American exploration. Jefferson appointed his own secretary, Captain

Meriwether Lewis, as co-leader, and naturally instructed him to search for "the remains or accounts of any [animals] which may be rare or extinct." He and Lieutenant William Clark were sent to Dr. Caspar Wistar (whose own dinosaur discovery was mentioned in Chapter 6) to be trained in geology before their departure.

Within two months of starting out, the expedition had reached what is now known to be rich dinosaur territory in what eventually became the state of Montana. About 100 miles (160 km) below the Great Falls of the Missouri, Clark named the Judith River after a young friend he was later to marry; long after her death her name is perpetuated for geologists in the dinosaur-rich Judith River Formation. The dinosaurs there are mainly in the topmost layers of gigantic bluffs 800 feet (240 m) above river level, and no bones were found by the expedition on the outward journey. Returning east, Clark discovered a bone in the cliff on July 25, 1806. It was large—"about 3 inches in Secumpherence about the middle it is 3 feet in length"— he noted in his journal. Although it was "semented within the face of the rock" and about 20 feet (6 m) above the water, Clark managed to extract several pieces. He thought it was the rib of a large fish, but it was almost certainly a dinosaur bone. Jefferson was perhaps disappointed that Clark had not brought back a living elephant, but after his return the president sent Clark — now a general—after the next-best thing: to dig for mastodon bones at Big Bone Lick in what is now Kentucky. Jefferson turned a room in the White House into a museum for them.

After Lewis and Clark's expedition, a number of others were undertaken, equipped to make a geological survey. One of these explorers, Ferdinand Vandiveer Hayden (1829–87), became well known to the Sioux, who often met him wandering the open country with his knapsack. One group of braves emptied his bag on the ground, and found it contained only stones. After that, they called him "Man-who-picks-up-stones-running," and regarded him as a harmless lunatic, so that he was left to carry on his collection in peace. The Blackfeet apparently had less reverence for the insane, as they drove Hayden out of the Montana Territory.

In 1855, Hayden brought back fossil teeth from the place where the

Judith and Missouri rivers join, near where Lewis and Clark had made their observation. He donated the teeth to the Academy of Natural Sciences in Philadelphia, where some of them were described by Joseph Leidy as being from fossil reptiles like the British *Iguanodon* and *Megalosaurus*, thus formally recognizing the first North American dinosaurs. The carnivore was named *Deinodon*, or "terror tooth," in 1856. In the same year, Leidy named other fossils (*Palaeoscincus* and *Troodon*), which he regarded as "lacertilian" (lizards) but which are both now known to be dinosaurs. The duck-billed dinosaur was named *Trachodon* ("rugged tooth") in 1865. Other teeth, which he left unnamed, later proved to have belonged to horned dinosaurs, unknown at that time.

These fragmentary dinosaur remains were not at first enough to arouse great interest, but as vertebrate fossils slowly accumulated over the next few decades, it became clear that the Northwest would yield worthwhile dinosaur deposits.

In what is now Canada, fur trader Alexander Mackenzie had crossed the continent through the Canadian West some twelve years before the Lewis and Clark expedition. He had portaged his frail canoes out of the Peace River canyon at what is now known as a major dinosaur footprint site, but failed to notice them. Dinosaurs were not recorded scientifically in the Canadian West until the arrival of the remarkable George Mercer Dawson. Dawson acquired his geological interests from his father, John William Dawson, an educator who in 1855 had become principal of and professor of geology and paleontology at McGill University in Montreal. As Dawson, Sr., was not only an expert paleobotanist, a pioneer of the study of fossil footprints, and a bestselling author on geology in its relation to religion, it is not surprising that his son grew up with a head start in the sciences. Unfortunately, he also had a severe illness (perhaps a tubercular spine) at about the age of eleven, which permanently stopped his growth at the height of about 4 feet, 6 inches (1.4 m), and left him with a severely deformed back.

After a few years of convalescence and private education, George went to London, England, to study geology at the Royal School of Mines, where he was a star student, and then headed back to Canada, determined against all odds to be a field geologist. In 1872, his father's connections and his own brilliance secured him a position as geologist and naturalist on the Boundary Survey across the western prairies. George geologized and photographed his way across the West with immense dedication, and his fellows nicknamed him the "Little Doctor."

In 1874, in what is now southern Saskatchewan and Alberta, Dawson found fragments of big bones, which he recognized as belonging to dinosaurs. In 1875, his fossils were referred to American paleontologist Edward Cope (by now one of the two leading authorities on dinosaurs) to be identified. Cope identified the large bones as those of duckbill dinosaurs, and also reported turtles and a fish. It was the first documented hint of the fossil wealth that was to be found in the Canadian West, and perhaps influenced Cope to explore the nearby Montana Territory for himself.

In the following year, Cope headed for Montana, bringing a couple of assistants, J.C. Isaac and Charles Hazelius Sternberg. Sternberg was a young but dedicated man who had started collecting fossil plants in Kansas while still a boy. Later, as a student at Kansas State Agricultural College, he had unsuccessfully tried to join a fossil-hunting party led by Benjamin Mudge, a professor at the college and a collector for Marsh. The young Sternberg wrote to Cope, earnestly offering to collect for him if he would fund a trip: "Although almost in despair, I turned for help to Professor E.D. Cope, of Philadelphia. . . . I put my soul into the letter I wrote him, for this was my last chance. I told him of my love for science, and of my earnest longing to enter the chalk of western Kansas and make a collection of its wonderful fossils, no matter what it might cost me in discomfort and danger."

Cope (who had never heard of Sternberg) trusted his judgment, and years later Sternberg remembered: "When I opened the envelope, a draft for three hundred dollars fell at my feet. . . . That letter bound me to Cope for four long years."

With Cope's financing, Sternberg began a professional career that would lead to his becoming one of the most remarkable fossil collectors of his time. He worked steadily in the early part of the summer, and was then asked to join Cope in Montana Territory in August.

Cope met Sternberg for the first time on the train heading for

Montana, and was surprised to find him lame from a childhood fall, as well as deaf in one ear. As they arrived at Helena, the news had just come in that the celebrated Colonel Custer and his men had been wiped out by the Sioux in the Battle of Little Bighorn. Cope reasoned that all the braves would stay together for fear of counterattack, so he proceeded with his plans, hired a scout and cook, and courageously set out on his expedition. When he strayed to within a day's journey of Sitting Bull's camp, his local men deserted, but the only Indians they met were Crows, who were sufficiently impressed by Cope's false teeth to leave him and his party strictly alone.

Sternberg has left vivid pictures of the Montana expedition, with himself riding close to his leader so that he could hear (with his good ear) Cope's flow of scientific talk: "He was not always in a talkative mood, but when he began to speak of the wonderful animals of this earth, those of long ago and those of to-day, so absorbed did he become in his subject that he talked on as if to himself . . . while I listened entranced."

Badlands on this scale were new to the party. They worked long hours, lost their way in the dark, and had to cover their faces with bacon grease to discourage the gnats. But Sternberg found the work rewarding: "We came upon localities literally filled with the scattered bones and teeth of dinosaurs, those terrible lizards whose tread once shook the earth."

Cope recognized the duckbill then known as *Trachodon*, but also found the first clearly identified horned dinosaurs, later describing three species of *Monoclonius*, which were estimated to have been around 25 feet (8 m) long. However, it was an exploratory trip. Sternberg noted: "We were in such haste that we secured few specimens, and the most important result of the expedition was our discovery of many new species of dinosaurs, represented chiefly by teeth."

Dinosaur bones were difficult to collect, as they often broke up when they were carried over rough ground. To prevent this, the team made an important technical breakthrough.

> When we uncovered these bones we found them very brittle, . . .
> and we were obliged to devise some means of holding them in
> place. The only thing we had in camp that could be made into a
> paste was rice, which we had brought along for food. We boiled

quantities of it until it became thick, then, dipping it into flour bags and pieces of cotton cloth and burlap, we used them to strengthen the bones and hold them together. This was the beginning of a long line of experiments, which culminated in the recently adopted method of taking up large fossils by bandaging them with strips of cloth dipped in plaster of Paris, like the bandages with which a modern surgeon encases a broken limb.

Sternberg, Isaac, and Cope stayed in the badlands until the first November snowstorm, and then shipped back by paddle steamer.

The year before Cope's Montana trip, the diminutive George Dawson (still only in his mid-twenties) had joined the Geological Survey of Canada as its chief geologist. In 1881, he was back on the prairies with his assistant Richard McConnell, hunting for Cretaceous coal deposits that could be used by the railway then being built across Canada. McConnell discovered a small area of badlands named Scabby Butte, near present-day Lethbridge, Alberta, where he found numerous dinosaur bones, including the thighbone of a duck-billed dinosaur. McConnell was unaware of the techniques being developed in the United States, so he collected the bone in many pieces, and it was eventually repaired at the Survey's base in Ottawa.

In 1883, Dawson became assistant director of the Survey, and returned to the field with two new assistants, Thomas Chesmer Weston and Joseph Burr Tyrrell. Weston (1832-1910) had been born in England, the son of a mineral dealer, and had been invited to bring his skills to the Geological Survey in Canada. As a technician he had repaired some of the bones Dawson had collected in previous years; now he was out in the West as a collector, and made further finds at Scabby Butte and other localities. These bones, including parts of a carnivore attributed to Cope's genus *Laelaps*, were lost when the ship *Glenfinlas* sank in Lake Superior. Weston returned the following year with botanist John Macoun, and found a new locality in the Cypress Hills, at Irvine Coulee.

The most important geological specimen found . . . was the scapula of an extinct animal, probably a Dinosaurian. It was a bone three feet long, eight or ten inches wide and half an inch to one or two inches thick. I spent six or eight hours uncovering this bone, and Mr. Macoun walked sixteen miles—to Medicine Hat and back—to get glue or some other material with a view to preserving this specimen. It was like most of these fossil bones, cracked in all directions. Well after all our trouble, while lifting it from its sandy bed, it fell into a thousand fragments, and now lies at the bottom of one of the great excavations in these soft sandstones. Still I mourn the loss of this bone.

Tyrrell was a Canadian, the son of a wealthy stonemason in the Toronto area. Scarlet fever in childhood had left young Tyrrell somewhat deaf, which hampered his relations with his fellows and was perhaps partly responsible for his character, which one of his biographers has called "heavy-handed, imperious, and ambitious." After taking a law degree, Tyrrell found science more to his taste, and (with the help of Prime Minister Macdonald, an acquaintance of his father) obtained a job with the Geological Survey, unpacking thousands of fossils which had been moved from Montreal to Ottawa.

Before long he found himself in the field, but did not like working for Dawson, who worked all hours and expected his men to do the same, and became anxious for autonomy. This he obtained in 1884, when he was sent to survey an area of 45,000 square miles (116,500 km²) north of the border region where Dawson and McConnell had worked. The area was crossed by the Red Deer River, then a little-known waterway, and Tyrrell decided the deep canyon was a good place to sample the geology. As well as coal deposits, Tyrrell found a few dinosaur bones, and soon located something more spectacular. Tyrrell wrote: "As I stuck my head around a point, there was this skull leering at me, sticking right out of the rock. It gave me a fright."

Tyrrell recognized the importance of his find, which was the first dinosaur skull to be found in Canada, and eventually became the type specimen of the carnivore *Albertosaurus*.

We spent the afternoon excavating these bones from the rock, but unfortunately we had no appliances but axes and small geological hammers . . . but in spite of all we could do some of the bones, teeth etc. were broken . . . we had no proper means of packing them, and no boxes but the wagon box to put them in. However, we got together the skull and some of the best of the leg and other bones. . . . Our journey to Calgary took us a week, for we were obliged to drive slowly and carefully . . . because we were anxious not to jar the brittle dinosaurian bones any more than necessary, . . . since our course for the most of the way was over the rough unbroken prairie.

This was Tyrrell's only contribution to dinosaur study, but the site of his discovery chanced to be close to where the Alberta government opened a major fossil museum in 1985, and the Royal Tyrrell Museum of Paleontology now bears his name. After undertaking major explorations in arctic Canada, Tyrrell left the Survey, became a wealthy mining engineer in the Klondike and Ontario, and died in 1957 at the age of ninety-nine.

Weston was sent to explore the Red Deer River dinosaur beds in more detail, and did paleontological work that was much more significant. In 1888, the timid Englishman started a voyage down the Red Deer River on a crude raft, but was deterred by the rough water and the inexperience of his men. The following year, with better equipment and assistance, he made a major voyage down the Red Deer River in search of bones, the first of many trips by successive generations of paleontologists. For much of its route the river flows in a deep canyon between high walls of tumbled badlands, representing the higher (Edmonton) beds in the Drumheller area. Further southeast, an area of lower cliffs represents the marine Bearpaw Formation, which does not contain dinosaur remains. Southeast again, the river runs into the area of spectacular badlands near the former town of Steveville, representing the Oldman (now Judith River) Formation. Weston was enthralled by the scenery, and described it later in his autobiography: "The river cuts through a fertile valley from 400 to 600 feet deep. Here nature has used her scooping shovel to an enormous extent, for between the prairie level and the river sandy buttes interstratified with bands of sandstone form pyramid-like structures."

In this location, dinosaur bones were abundant, but, alas, Weston was not equipped to collect them. Three hours were spent digging out a single carnivore leg bone: "three pairs of hands carefully lifted our precious specimen to put it into the rude box we had made from part of the upper floor of our boat, when to our surprise the thing crumbled into a thousand fragments."

Weston recognized the significance of the region, and described it as "the most important field in Canada, so far as bones of extinct animals is concerned." It was not until many years later that the area became Dinosaur Provincial Park in Alberta, and the first World Heritage Site ever to be established because of a paleontological resource.

❖ ❖ ❖

Cope had beaten Marsh to the horned dinosaurs, with the skull-less *Agathaumas* and then *Monoclonius* from his 1876 expedition. Ten years later Marsh was responsible for bringing what became the best-known horned dinosaur to scientific attention — but mistakenly described it as a fossil buffalo.

Marsh's first specimens were a pair of large bisonlike horn cores found by George L. Cannon in 1887 at Green Mountain Creek, in the area of Denver, Colorado. They came into the hands of Whitman Cross, a government geologist who was studying the age of the Denver beds (now known as the Lance Formation), and Cross sent them on to Marsh. Although Cross said they came from Cretaceous beds, and Marsh's assistants supported this view, Marsh decided the horn cores must belong to a very recent bison, which he named *Bison alticornis* in December 1888.

If Marsh had been a little slower off the mark, he would have been saved some embarrassment, for, in the same year, the key to the situation was already in the hands of one of his assistants, John Bell Hatcher. His cooperation helped Marsh to redress his error, and Hatcher was led to discoveries that eventually made him a world authority on horned dinosaurs.

Hatcher had been born in Illinois, but his family moved to Iowa when he was young. They were not well off, and to pay for college, Hatcher took work in a coal mine. There he developed an interest in fossils. When he graduated from Yale in 1884, the twenty-three-year-old Hatcher went to Marsh and offered to collect fossils, with place, time, and salary being no object. Hatcher was sent to Kansas to learn fossil-hunting methods. His tutor was to be Charles H. Sternberg, whose hero and sponsor Cope had lost much of his money in unfortunate investments, so he had ended up collecting fossil rhinoceros bones for Marsh.

Sternberg tried to be positive about his unsought assistant, and later wrote that he "gave promise of a future even then by his perfect understanding of the work in hand and the thoughtful care which he devoted to it." The less-charitable Hatcher was critical of what he considered Sternberg's careless and unscientific work, and insisted on working independently on the other side of the ravine.

Hatcher soon became an independent collector for Marsh, working the West for a couple of years for fossil mammals. He married in 1887 and made his home in Nebraska. The following year he went to Montana, collecting from some of the rocks that Cope had explored. Even though he found only fragments, he was able to send a ton of bones to Marsh. On his way back, he met Charles Gurney, a rancher in Converse County of eastern Wyoming. Gurney's cowboys had told him of a skull "with horns as long as a hoe handle and eye holes as big as your hat." The cattlemen had found it sticking out of the side of a bank, and tried to lassoo the maverick skull. When they put a lariat around the horn to loosen it, the skull rolled down the bank and broke into pieces. Hatcher sent the horn to Marsh, who realized it was the same as that of his "bison." Hatcher was sent after the rest of the fossil, and in May he wrote "The big skull is ours." It weighed more than a ton, but Hatcher got it back, and it became the type specimen of Marsh's *Triceratops horridus*, the "terrifying three-horned face."

This success inspired Hatcher, who spent the next four years (1889–92) rounding up more of the huge, awkward horned dinosaur skulls in greater number than anyone else had done. He obtained more than fifty individual ceratopsian skulls from the Lance Formation near Lusk, Wyoming, and thirty-three of those were nearly perfect.

He was not just a fine collector, but carefully observed the situations in which the bones were found, interpreting fine details to understand the precise situation in which the bone was buried: "on one side of a bone the matrix will be made up entirely of sand, while on the opposite side the stem and leaves of plants have been dropped. . . . This . . . shows the direction of the current to have been from that side containing only sand, and toward the side containing the plants. So shallow were the waters, the bone itself became an obstacle sufficient to produce an eddy on the lower side, in which the leaves and other vegetable materials accumulated, and sank to the bottom."

Such careful observations helped him not only to interpret the situation in which the animal had died and the fossil had been preserved, but also to find other bones.

Although Marsh valued his assistant's capabilities, he paid him infrequently and would not let him publish any of his finds. Hatcher was increasingly frustrated, but also did not take kindly to efforts by others to help him. Cope's disciple Osborn approached Hatcher in 1890 to collect for the American Museum of Natural History, but when Hatcher found Osborn did not yet have a position at the museum he accused him of dishonesty. Osborn was very angry, and at first found it difficult to forgive Hatcher.

Marsh became notorious for treating his assistants poorly. He had actively prevented one from pursuing academic training, and Williston claimed that Marsh's published papers were "either the work or the actual language of his assistants." Despite such frustrations, Hatcher continued to provide fine specimens to Marsh, such as the skull of the horned dinosaur named *Torosaurus* in 1891, the animal with the longest skull of any terrestrial animal. During that year Marsh had agreed to give Hatcher a raise, along with the title of Assistant in Geology, and the opportunity to write up some of his work. Hatcher was still in the field in 1893, and he finally left Marsh to become curator of Vertebrate Palaeontology at Princeton, where the forgiving Osborn was able to get him an honorary degree. Although Hatcher was increasingly rheumatic and needed help just to climb onto his horse, he conceived the idea of an expedition to Patagonia in South America, which he not only successfully carried out but is reputed to have financed largely by his skill as a poker player.

On his return, Hatcher moved to the Carnegie Museum in Pittsburgh. When Marsh died in 1899, the Geological Survey asked Osborn to arrange for completion of his work. Osborn chose Hatcher to finish the descriptions of the Ceratopsia (horned dinosaurs), so many of which Hatcher had himself collected. Normally, a paleontologist tries to borrow specimens so that direct comparisons can be made, but the horned dinosaurs were so huge, this could not be done. Hatcher had to travel from museum to museum, measuring huge skulls. He was paid for the work for two years, but spent most of his funds on fees to the preparators, draftsmen, and clerks who helped him. Although Hatcher died of typhoid in 1904, leaving much of his important work unfinished, he was remembered as a man who tolerated disrespect from none, and readily criticized powerful figures. His great monograph was finally finished by Lull and published three years after Hatcher's death. Osborn noted in the introduction that Hatcher had produced 204 plates and no text. He wrote in conclusion: "I trust that this volume may prove to be a lasting monument to the rare and noble spirit of John Bell Hatcher."

❖ ❖ ❖

Although the dinosaur beds of Canada were not receiving so much attention, Weston was followed down the Red Deer River in 1897 and 1898 by another Canadian paleontologist, Lawrence Lambe (1863–1919). He found remains of carnivorous, duck-billed, armored, and horned dinosaurs, but could only compare them with the best-known dinosaurs of the day, which were mainly from the much older American Jurassic beds.

In 1900, Lambe was able to visit New York to study with Osborn at Columbia University and the American Museum. Osborn was an admirer of Cope, and when in due course he wrote his biography, Osborn called him a "master naturalist." Despite his strong interest in fossil elephants and a major administrative load, Osborn found time to do much important work on dinosaurs. He also succeeded Cope as the paleontological adviser to the Canadian Survey. Osborn was able to teach Lambe much that would help him, but Lambe was able to make only one more expedition to the Red Deer, spending three months in the field and making important collections.

In 1902, Lambe and Osborn published a study of the dinosaurs found to date in Alberta, clearly distinguishing two faunas of different ages. From this time onward, Lambe described new genera or species of dinosaurs from Alberta almost every year. New genera included the duck-bill *Stephanosaurus*, or "Stephan's reptile" (1902); the armored *Stereocephalus* (1902), renamed *Euoplocephalus* or "well-armored head," in 1910 when it was found the original name had been used for an insect; the horned *Centrosaurus*, or "horned reptile" (1904); and the first bone-headed dinosaur, *Stegoceras* or "horny roof" (1902). There were new species belonging to known genera, such as an armored dinosaur *Palaeoscincus*, or "ancient skink" (a skink is a kind of lizard); a new duckbill assigned to *Trachodon*, or "rough tooth"; a "one-horned" *Monoclonius*; and a little "bird mimic" *Ornithomimus*. Osborn also published descriptions of the carnivore found twenty years earlier by Tyrrell. After having been referred earlier to Marsh's Jurassic genus *Dryptosaurus*, it was named *Albertosaurus* ("Alberta reptile") by Osborn in 1905. This large carnivore would have become well known for its size and presumed ferocity had Osborn's staff not already found an even larger and more spectacular relative.

Osborn's favorite dinosaur hunter, Barnum Brown, was born near Carbondale, Kansas, on February 12, 1873, a few days before the great showman Phineas T. Barnum's "Great Traveling World's Fair" arrived in town. The baby was left unnamed for a few days, and while the family discussed the matter, his older brother Frank, obsessed by the incoming show, suggested "Let's call him Barnum." The name was chosen, and proved to be rather appropriate, for Barnum Brown seemed to spend much of his adult life in a sort of perpetual traveling circus, though with fossil instead of living animals.

His father, William Brown, was born in Virginia in 1833, and joined the great trek west. He met his wife, Clara, in Wisconsin, where a daughter was born before they left for Kansas in an ox-drawn covered wagon in 1859. At Carbon Hill, Kansas, he both farmed and ran a coal mine, and developed a thriving freighting business during the Civil War. While William was away with his bull team, his wife fed troops from both sides, as well as renegades and Indian refugees, successfully steering the difficult course of neutrality and emerging unscathed.

Barnum was the youngest child, and grew up helping his mother in the kitchen, where he developed a life-long interest in the preparation and enjoyment of food. (His second wife later noted appreciatively that he could cook, make jam, and loved housekeeping. Years later, in a snowbound camp, he was known to use an old sourdough trick, putting the pancake batter in a bottle and taking it to bed with him to make sure of having pancakes for breakfast.)

Outside his mother's kitchen, young Barnum was left to amuse himself, and he observed the geology of his father's coal mine and collected the fossil shells turned up by the plow. His collection of fossils, plants, and shells overflowed the house until his mother made him move it into the laundry building on the family farm. In 1889, when he was sixteen, his father took him as cook on a four-month, 3,000-mile (4800-km) wagon trip to Montana in search of a ranch site. Although the family did not, in the end, move from Kansas, Brown got a remarkable overview of the West, and perhaps made plans to return to Montana.

Though the little town of Carbondale had developed near the family farm, it still had no high school, so Barnum was sent to Lawrence, Kansas, to study. Barnum finished high school and went on to the University of Kansas. One of Marsh's former assistants, vertebrate paleontologist Samuel Wendell Williston, was teaching a course that was not open to freshmen, but Brown arranged to take an exam in the prerequisites so that he could register. Barnum started serious fossil collecting as a student, going on a university field trip to Nebraska and South Dakota in the summer of 1894 with his fellow students. (One of his friends was Elmer Riggs, who later joined the Field Museum in Chicago and became another important fossil collector.) The following year, 1895, the party went to Wyoming and Brown found his first dinosaur fossil, a skull of the three-horned ceratopsian *Triceratops*.

In 1896, he was again in the field, and met a party from the American Museum of Natural History led by Dr. Jacob Wortman (1856–1926). Brown must have impressed him, for he was asked to join the museum staff in 1897, when he was still a few courses short of graduation. Brown became so busy that he did not finish his degree until 1907, when he took graduate courses at Columbia University.

At the American Museum, Brown found his niche in life. Osborn thought very highly of him, and was later quoted as saying: "Brown is the most amazing collector I have ever known. He must be able to *smell* fossils. If he runs a test-trench through an exposure it will be right in the middle of the richest deposit. He never misses."

Brown had started work on dinosaurs at Como Bluff, Wyoming, and was then sent (literally at a day's notice) to Patagonia with Hatcher, returning to New York in 1901. In the following year, Brown started a collecting campaign for the American Museum of Natural History in Montana.

Brown first went by train to Miles City, and then began to search the badlands south of the Missouri River. In June he wrote to Osborn, "this country promises well and has never been examined." Later, he hired a wagon and team and went five days north to a small settlement, Jordan, and then into the badlands at the head of Hell Creek, where cowboys and sheepherders had reported bones. On his first day, July 12, he picked up some *Triceratops* bones, which showed that he was on the right track.

A few days later, in a hard yellow sandstone bluff, Brown found bones of a carnivore even larger than Tyrrell's Alberta find. He spent the rest of the summer and most of the following one excavating the specimen, which proved to be an almost complete skeleton. He had to use dynamite to remove some of the hard sandstone, but as he got closer to the bones, a pickax and then a chisel were used. In turn, a partial skull, shoulder blade and vertebrae, and hind legs were uncovered. The fragile bones were hardened with shellac and then the bones were wrapped in sacking soaked in plaster of Paris. The pelvis presented a problem, as it weighed 2 tons (1.8 t) when wrapped in its plaster block. Brown had to build a stoneboat (a wooden sledge) and drag it with four horses, and even then it took all day to get the pelvis out to the nearest road. Then there was a journey of 124 miles (200 km) to the railroad in Miles City.

Brown married in 1904, but this did not stop him going into the field. Osborn described Brown's great carnivore in 1905 and chose the name *Tyrannosaurus rex* ("king of the tyrant lizards").

In 1908, Brown made a second *Tyrannosaurus* find north of the previous locality, in an area which is now submerged by the Fort Peck Reservoir. He reported by letter that he had made a "ten strike," as he found "15 caudals connected, running into soft sand." Brown dug a trench that followed the tail bones into hard sandstone, and gradually unearthed a fine skeleton, of which he told Osborn "I have seen nothing like it before."

Osborn wrote back, "Your letter . . . makes me feel like a prophet and the son of a prophet, as I felt instinctively you would surely find a *Tyrannosaurus* this season." The more Brown dug, the more excited he became, telling Osborn later that it was a "magnificent specimen. This skull alone is worth the summer's work, for it is perfect." The skeleton proved to be nearly complete, and the two together gave a remarkable representation of this spectacular animal. The heads were more than 3 feet (90 cm) in length, and the largest teeth were 6 inches (15 cm) long and 1 inch (2.5 cm) wide. Fortunately, by now the American Museum laboratories were equal to such demanding material. The pneumatic hammer had been adapted to paleontology by former American Museum staffer Elmer Riggs about 1903, and in the following year Osborn's labs had not only adopted it but were experimenting with sandblasting equipment.

When the Second World War later raised fears that New York would be bombed, the first *Tyrannosaurus* was transferred to the Carnegie Museum in Pittsburgh. Brown delighted in showing off the other, which he introduced to visitors as "my favorite child."

While Brown was busy in Montana, Charles H. Sternberg had continued his work in the West. After the deaths of Cope and Marsh, Sternberg had become the leading freelance collector of his day, searching out fossils across the continent, and selling them to a variety of museum clients in North America and Europe. By the early years of the century, Sternberg was in his fifties, but his enthusiasm for the tough life of the field was unabated. From their teenage years his three sons—George Fryer (1883–1969), Charles ("Charlie") Mortram (1885–1981), and Levi (1894–1976) — had joined him the field. Working closely as a team, they developed skills as fossil hunters and collectors, and were often responsible for important finds.

In 1908, the Sternbergs were following in Hatcher's footsteps in Converse County, southern Wyoming, looking for remains of the great horned dinosaur *Triceratops*. The badland countryside was used largely as unfenced cattle and sheep range, and there was no source of groceries for many miles. Charles and Levi located a somewhat damaged skull, and excavated it while George surveyed a neighboring area and found a few bones sticking out of a high sandstone escarpment.

Charles left Levi to help George follow the bones into the rock, and took the skull off on a five day trip to the town of Lusk, 65 miles (105 km) away, to ship it off to the British Museum in London and get supplies. "While we were taking in our skull," remembered C.H. Sternberg, "George and Levi ran nearly out of provisions, and the last day of our absence lived on boiled potatoes. But in spite of this they had removed a mass of sandstone 12 feet wide, 15 feet deep, and 10 feet high."

George and Levi soon recognized that their find was a duck-billed dinosaur. On the third day, there was a moment that George recalled many years later, as their chisels removed the overlying sandstone from the breastbone.

> There was nothing unusual about that, but when I removed a rather large piece of sandstone rock from over the breast I found, much to my surprise, a perfect cast of the skin impression beautifully preserved. Imagine the feeling that crept over me when I realized that here for the first time a skeleton of a dinosaur had been discovered wrapped in its skin. That was a sleepless night for me. . . . It was about dusk on the evening of the fifth day when we saw the wagon loaded with provisions roll into camp. "What luck?" was my father's first question. And before he could leave his seat I had given him a vivid sketch of my find. . . ."Let's go and see it," he shouted, as he jumped from his seat on the wagon. I grabbed some food from the boxes on the wagon, and away the two of us went, leaving the others to prepare the meal for us. Darkness was nearly upon us when we reached the quarry and there laid out before us was the specimen. One glance was enough for my father to realize what I had found and what it meant to science.

Charles also recollected the great moment: "Shall I ever experience such joy as when I stood in the quarry for the first time, and beheld lying in state the most complete skeleton of an extinct animal I have ever seen, after forty years experience as a collector. The crowning specimen of my life work!"

George vividly remembered his father's exact words: "Will I ever forget his first remark as we stood there in the fast approaching twilight? It thrills me now as I repeat it. 'George, this is a finer fossil than I have ever found. And the only thing which would have given me greater pleasure would have been to have discovered it myself.' "

The famous fossil, an *Edmontosaurus*, went to the American Museum where it was labeled "the mummy dinosaur." The skeleton was not complete—the tail was missing—but the impression of the flesh and surviving skin make it remarkably lifelike.

The skeleton "lay on its back with front limbs stretched out as if imploring aid, while the hind limbs in a convulsive effort were drawn up and folded against the walls of the abdomen. The head lay under the right shoulder. . . . It lay there with expanded ribs as in life, wrapped in the impressions of the skin whose beautiful patterns of octagonal plates marked the fine sandstone above the bones."

It was at first thought to have been preserved away from predators in arid conditions, which had delayed decomposition and allowed the flesh to mummify. The flesh had then decayed and been replaced with sand after it had already been buried, leaving the skin impressions in the shape of the body. Technically it was a fossil of what had once been a dried or mummified body. Richard Lull described it as "the most marvellously preserved dinosaur known to science." More recent interpretations suggest it may have been rapidly buried in a stream.

This mummy was the first of two such finds by the Sternbergs, the second going to the Senckenberg Museum in Frankfurt-am-Main, Germany, despite efforts of the Canadian Geological Survey to obtain it. Although it was shown to have webs between the toes, when, in 1922, its stomach contents were studied, the mummy's last meal had not included any water plants, but instead a mass of needles from a coniferous tree, and twigs, seeds, and roots from other land plants.

❖ ❖ ❖

By 1909, Barnum Brown was beginning to feel he had skimmed the cream from the Montana beds and was wondering where to go next.

That spring, before he had left for the field, a letter to the American Museum at New York from rancher John C. Wegener had told Brown that his ranch in Alberta, Canada, had similar bones. At the end of his Montana season, Brown went up for an exploratory visit. The ranch was on Michichi Creek, near the present-day city of Drumheller, and Brown was sufficiently impressed to plan his next season further north.

Before he left, tragedy struck. In April, his wife, Marion, and their young daughter both caught scarlet fever, and Marion died within a few days. Brown left the baby with his parents-in-law and headed for the field, nursing his grief. The party left the train in Calgary, and Brown visited important contacts to develop support for his expedition. He probably knew of Weston's boat expeditions, and headed for Red Deer, where he ordered a 12-foot–by–30-foot (3.6-m–by–9-m) raft, which he equipped with 22-foot (7-m) sweeps for steering, and a tent and a stove for the crew. Loaded with equipment and supplies, the party drifted down the gentle Red Deer River, through a beautiful and wild landscape. Tall cottonwoods grew on flats by the river, and farther back the high walls of the badlands beckoned the fossil hunter, while overhead eagles and hawks soared. They would tie up along the bank at promising places, dine on fish caught in the river, and fall asleep to the lullaby of coyotes and horned owls.

The dinosaur hunting was not so easy, as the valley can be hot and windless, and the mosquitoes swarmed so badly the men often had to wear gloves and hats with nets to cover their faces. The discoveries soon came, however, and Brown began to excavate promising finds. When there was overburden, dynamite was used, or a local farmer was hired to bring a horse-drawn scraper. The fine work was first with pick and shovel, then with hammer and chisel, and finally scraper and brush. It took only three days to uncover a skeleton, but it could be another three weeks before it was boxed and ready for carrying or dragging down to the raft.

Major finds included a new horned dinosaur, later called *Leptoceratops*, or "slender horned face," which was found in the middle of a cow trail, its limb bones shattered by the passage of successive generations of cattle. By September, the raft was full of boxes, and ice was forming on the river, but Brown had seen great potential. He shifted his load to wagons and beached the raft at Tolman ferry crossing, ready to start again next season.

In 1911 a find was made on the hillside within sight of Tolman ferry. They excavated bones of a duckbill that was thought to be the familiar *Trachodon,* until the skull was exposed. A long crest extending behind the head made it clear that a new kind of duckbill had been found. A box was built around the skeleton, and the 700-pound (315 kg) load was lowered to the valley with a block and tackle. Since Professor Osborn visited the field camp, the new duckbill was eventually given in 1912 the name *Saurolophus osborni,* or "Osborn's crested saurian."

Osborn was also shown an ankylosaur (armored dinosaur) quarry, opened by blasting a cut 30 feet (9 m) long, 40 feet (12 m) high, and 20 feet (6 m) back into the hill. (Brown had described the armored *Ankylosaurus* from Montana in 1908.) Brown and Osborn then took an exploratory trip by canoe down the river, leaving the rest of the staff to continue the dig. The two paddled downstream as far as the Judith River Formation exposures. That season's finds made up a complete carload of fossils on the train.

As more and more tons of bones were sent to New York, local people began to realize how rich the deposits actually were, and to fear they would be mined out. Local interests (including the University of Alberta) put pressure on the Canadian government to limit the export of fossil bones. Protective legislation was being planned in 1913—against the opposition of Lawrence Lambe of the Survey— but it was never enacted. During the discussion, important questions were raised. Should not some of the dinosaurs be retained in Canada? Why had Canada not built a complete national collection before allowing the export of its fossil heritage?

The Canadian government (through the Geological Survey) had started planning a national museum to be built in Ottawa early in the century. Although some of the specimens collected by Dawson, Tyrrell, and Weston were to be on display, there were no complete dinosaur skeletons such as those Brown was collecting. The major stumbling block was that the Survey had no trained dinosaur collectors other than Lambe, who was busy developing the fossil galleries in the new museum and acquiring fossils in the United States as well as Canada. Since it was not politically possible to ban Brown from Alberta, their only choice was to start up a competing collection.

In 1911, Lambe had ordered a *Triceratops* from the Sternberg family, and the museum also bought from them a large fish, a marine reptile, and a Tertiary mammal, *Titanotherium*. Arrangements had been made for the Sternbergs to come to Ottawa to mount the mammal specimen, and as they were the most qualified collectors available, Lambe no doubt planned to hire them to work in Alberta. As the elder Sternberg was now in his sixties, it seems probable that Lambe intended to ask George, the oldest son; unfortunately, George visited the American Museum in New York on his way to Ottawa and had been invited to join Barnum Brown's team. The second son, Charles, was next asked, but he felt too inexperienced to work without his father, so Charles Sternberg, Sr., found himself in charge of the Canadian field party.

The Sternbergs arrived in the Drumheller area at the end of July 1912. Initially, they worked with a rowboat, and had fair success in finding skeletons. On August 13: "Charlie found . . . the wonderfully complete skeleton of a duck-billed dinosaur. . . . It measured thirty-two feet in length. . . . Lying on its right side, the hind limbs were doubled on themselves . . . and the head bent towards the front limbs. The animal lay like a dead dog. I thought I had never seen anything so pitiful and forlorn."

They had a difficult time collecting it, and it ended up sliding out of control downhill into the wagon, forcing the fossil hunters to leap for safety. The fossil hunters may have been bruised, but the specimen arrived intact. Despite technical difficulties, the Sternbergs successfully prepared it the following winter, producing the first dinosaur mount to be placed in a Canadian museum. This was one of many Canadian dinosaurs described by Lambe during the next few years; he called it *Trachodon marginatus,* and eventually it became the type specimen of *Edmontosaurus*, or "Edmonton [Formation] reptile." Lambe died in 1919, having named many of the Sternberg finds as well his own. Eventually, he was commemorated in the name of a duckbilled dinosaur, *Lambeosaurus.*

Brown's response to the rival team was to move rapidly down-stream to Steveville, where he was already aware that the great valley of Deadlodge Canyon offered rich pickings from a different period. In 1913, the Sternbergs started again in Drumheller, where they acquired a 5-horsepower motorboat, and adopted Brown's techniques by building a flatboat. George Sternberg rejoined the family firm, and the rival teams kept up friendly competition, meeting sometimes on Sundays for social gatherings. Wonderful fossils were found. Brown's prizes included the crested duckbill *Corythosaurus* ("helmet reptile"), and a *Monoclonius* so complete that the skeleton even included the tongue bones. His first four seasons had netted three-and-a-half carloads of fossils, including twenty skulls and fourteen complete skeletons of large dinosaurs. The Sternbergs' chief prize was a complete skeleton of a carnivore named *Gorgosaurus* ("terrible reptile"), but more recently considered to be identical to *Albertosaurus*.

Brown continued work in 1914 and 1915, and then returned to New York with another carload of fossils. Canada and the United States were now embroiled in the First World War, and money was tight. C.H. Sternberg resigned when he was told there was no money for a 1916 field season. He and Levi continued independently for a while, selling their material to the British Museum, but after the ship carrying two fine duckbills in transit across the Atlantic was sunk by a German sub-marine, Sternberg gave up in disgust and eventually returned to the United States. All three of his sons remained in Canada, working for different institutions.

When Brown arrived in the Deadlodge Canyon area near Steveville, he was approached by a local homesteader, William Cutler. Born in London, England, about 1878, Cutler had some scientific training and since 1912 had been trying to make a living on a farm in the vicinity of the badlands. He had already located a number of fossils, and he offered Brown a skeleton in exchange for instruction in col-lecting techniques, and a promise to name the animal after its finder if it should be new to science. Brown recognized the skeleton of a horned dinosaur with skin impressions that was well worth collecting, and so had little choice but to accept the offer. However, the collaboration was apparently not a happy one, and although *Monoclonius cutleri* was added to the list of Alberta dinosaurs, Cutler was not added to the list of American Museum workers.

In June 1913, a group of members of the Calgary Natural History Society formed the Calgary Syndicate for Prehistoric Research, an agency to raise money to support Cutler in independent fieldwork for an embryonic Calgary Museum. Cutler collected a small duck-billed dinosaur for Calgary, and fended off an attempt by Brown to obtain it in exchange for a "larger common specimen."

In 1914, Cutler made a more important find, of a nearly complete skeleton of an armored dinosaur with all its armor intact. This he sold to the British Museum in 1915, where it was eventually described in 1928 as *Scolosaurus cutleri* by the eccentric Franz Nopcsa (1877–1933), a Hungarian baron who did important work on dinosaur classification in the intervals of a political and personal career of great diversity. At the end of the season, Cutler joined the Canadian Forces and served in France during the First World War. Subsequently he returned to western Canada and collected for the University of Manitoba and the British Museum, before in 1924 being selected by the British to lead an expedition to the African dinosaur locality of Tendaguru (see Chapter 16). The First World War marked the end of a major period of discovery, and the western rivers were left to the eagles and coyotes for a while. But three Sternbergs remained in Canada, ready to start a new series of discoveries.

9

THE MOST COLOSSAL ANIMAL FOUND OUT WEST

THE *NEW YORK HERALD* HAD DONE WELL WITH DINOSAURS in 1890, when it featured the unseemly squabble between Cope and Marsh in its columns. Less than a decade later, in 1898, it had another dinosaur story, which it published under the headline "Most Colossal Animal Ever On Earth Just Found Out West." The story described in purple prose the discovery of a huge monster: "When it walked the earth trembled under its weight of 120,000 pounds, when it ate it filled a stomach enough to hold three elephants, when it was angry its terrible roar could be heard ten miles, and when it stood up its height was equal to eleven stories of a sky-scraper."

The animal in question was described in the article as *Brontosaurus giganteus*, which was claimed to have been 130 feet (40 m) long (nearly twice the size of any known *Brontosaurus*). The story was accompanied by photographs showing the skeleton, some footprints, and the finder, "Bill Reeder," standing next to an 8-foot (2.4-m) long thighbone. The finder was actually William Reed, whose discoveries at Como Bluff were described in Chapter 7. He was now working in Utah, where he was destined to make more remarkable discoveries.

❖ ❖ ❖

Dinosaur bones had been found in Utah as far back as 1859, when J.N. Macomb led a military expedition through the area. A member of the expedition, John Strong Newberry (1822–92), found bones in

Cañon Pintado (now called Painted Canyon). He recognized that the greater part of a skeleton was present, but as he had few tools, he was able to work only for two days, during which time he excavated a few bones. There was a complete femur (which was apparently too large to collect), but Newberry did pick up most of a humerus and several phalanges (toe bones) and bits of ribs. All the bones were handed over to Joseph Leidy at the University of Pennsylvania, but he did not publish a report on them.

In 1877, Cope studied the bones and named a new sauropod, which he called *Dystrophaeus viaemalae*, or "wasted one." Cope thought they might be of Triassic age, but they are now regarded as Morrison (Jurassic), the same age as the Como Bluff localities. Cope claimed this as the first dinosaur discovery in western North America, but he should have been aware of Hayden's discoveries, described by Leidy. (The Lewis and Clark find was not recorded as a dinosaur and was still unpublished at the time.) The German paleontologist von Huene (perhaps attracted by Cope's attribution of the bones to his favorite period, the Triassic) described and illustrated the material in 1904. It is probably the sauropod now known as *Camarasaurus*.

Meanwhile, the explorer of the Grand Canyon, one-armed Major John Wesley Powell (1834–1902) had recorded "reptile remains" during his second trip down the Green River in 1871. Hayden had reported vertebrate fossils from Wyoming in his 1872 geological expedition, and in 1893 Olof August Peterson (1865–1933), a Swedish vertebrate paleontologist from the American Museum, had recorded dinosaur bones of Morrison age during a trip to the Uinta basin of Utah.

After Reed's sheepherding venture failed, he became a night watchman for the Union Pacific Railroad, combining it with guiding hunting parties and some freelance dinosaur collecting. In 1894 he began to collect regularly for Wilbur Clinton Knight (1858–1903) at the University of Wyoming, Laramie, and stayed a collector for the rest of his life. In later years, Reed wrote down the requirements of his chosen profession: "The necessary outfit for a fossil hunter is first, an interest in the work; secondly, if he be a good fossil hunter, he will necessarily take a great interest in all branches of natural history; and third, he must be endowed with a large portion of patience and an immense amount of perseverance and energy. He will find sooner or later that he must learn comparative anatomy to a certain extent, the more the better."

In the following year, Reed was given the job of guiding a hundred people round the major fossil sites in Wyoming. At first he was still selling bones independently, both to Knight and to other museums and collections. In 1896, Knight was able to hire Reed to collect exclusively for the University of Wyoming. Knight was mainly interested in marine reptiles, and Reed wrote to Marsh about his frustration that no work was being done on his dinosaur collections: "if I could support myself would leave and sell fossils . . . have found 36 quarries 1 mile from camp . . . have 320 acres in my name claimed . . . many new things at University of Wyoming but not much hope of them being worked on soon."

In 1897 Reed was appointed assistant geologist and curator at the University of Wyoming geological museum (which had been founded in 1887) at a salary of $900 a year, but from that income he had to supply his own horse and wagon. His main work was done in localities that Knight had found south of Laramie. There Reed collected *Stegosaurus, Camarasaurus, Barosaurus* ("heavy reptile"), and *Allosaurus*— a total of 10,000 specimens—between 1896 and 1899. By the end of the decade, the University of Wyoming was close to overtaking the remarkable Marsh collection. The university's accumulation of North American Jurassic vertebrates weighed more than 80 tons (72 t), and to house them a hall of science was planned, of which the lower floor was to be devoted to museum purposes. Until 1896 Reed was still selling some material to Marsh, causing friction with Knight. However, his main interest was the university collection, for he wrote to Marsh: "Hope to see this museum one of the finest in the land before I get too old to work in the field."

The exaggerated press report of Reed's find was read by Andrew Carnegie, the Pittsburgh millionaire industrialist. Carnegie was born in near poverty in 1835, and had emigrated from Scotland as a youth. At age thirty-three, he found his income exceeded $50,000 a year, and he determined to use his wealth for public benefit. Although he became best known for his work in support of music and libraries, Carnegie was also actively interested in museums. He had spent $24 million on the Carnegie Institute in Pittsburgh, which had a concert hall, an art gallery and a natural science museum. He felt that something "big as a barn" should be acquired for the museum. In 1898 he hired as director of the museum William Jacob Holland (1848–1932), a clergyman, entomologist, and paleontologist, who had been born in Jamaica and (like Carnegie) had traveled to Japan. Carnegie sent a clipping of the dinosaur story from the paper to Holland with a terse note saying, "Buy this for Pittsburgh."

Holland was able to identify "Reeder" as Reed, and later met him in Wyoming, where he offered him a position at the Carnegie Museum to work on the skeleton. Reed explained that his expertise was in finding and collecting fossils, and not in preparation, and suggested that others should be hired for this part of the work. When Holland agreed, Reed handed over part of the bone, gave six months' notice to the University of Wyoming, and signed a one-year contract to start in May 1899. Holland hired Jacob Lawson Wortman (1856–1926) and Arthur Coggeshall (formerly at the American Museum of Natural History) to help Reed.

The three met at Medicine Bow, Wyoming, and loaded supplies, including a ton of plaster and a bale of burlap, onto a farm wagon. After wading through streams swollen with spring rain, they went northwest to the foot of the Freezeout Mountains, but found only a few fragments of bone at the site. Reed confessed that the newspaper story had been exaggerated, but that he expected to find more bones. They worked through the neighboring country until, 30 miles (48 km) east, they located a dinosaur toe bone near Sheep Creek (north of Como Bluff). Both Reed and his companions have been credited with the discovery.

On July 4, 1899, they discovered that the toe bone was associated with a nearly intact skeleton of the sauropod *Diplodocus*. When this was reported to Holland, he came out to see the site, and it was included in the Fossil Fields expedition organized by the University of Wyoming and the Union Pacific Railroad. Reed worked for the winter on the material and, the following year, traveled back with Coggeshall and Peterson to collect the rest. Another partial *Diplodocus* skeleton was found as the quarry was enlarged. Holland now put Peterson, formerly an assistant, in charge of the excavation, and, after protest, Reed resigned. (Reed later worked for the American Museum and then returned to the University of Wyoming after Knight's death created a new opportunity.)

To replace him, Holland hired Charles Whitney Gilmore, who had been born in the area of Rochester, New York, in 1874. At the age of six, an aunt had taken him to visit Ward's Natural Science Establishment in Rochester. The natural-history supply house, which provided specimens to museums and colleges for educational purposes, left a deep impression on the little boy: "Upon my return home, the 'museum bug' had been firmly implanted, for immediately collections of fossil shells, rocks, birds' eggs, and insects were started. . . . This was the time when the idea of following museum work as a life profession was implanted, an idea that never deserted me."

When he was eight the family moved to Michigan, and after graduation Gilmore went farther west: "Upon entering the University of Wyoming, the idea of preparing myself for some line of museum endeavor . . . was still fixed in my mind . . . the collection of dinosaur specimens in the university soon attracted my attention, and from then until graduation all my spare time was devoted to the study and collection of fossil specimens."

While at the University of Wyoming, Gilmore had collected with Reed. After graduation, Gilmore joined the Carnegie Museum, where he started his progress toward becoming a great authority on dinosaurs.

The new species was named *Diplodocus carnegii* after its patron, though the staff nicknamed it "Dippy." Its 84-foot - (26-m-) long skeleton (made up from parts of four individuals) was not only the first sauropod skeleton to be mounted, but also one of the longest.

The world was fascinated, and there was a strong demand for life-sized copies. Carnegie hired a team of Italian plasterers to make them. Holland went on a grand tour as the millionaire's representative, and gave casts to a number of museums in different countries, often stopping to supervise the mounting. He was feted and given honors. The lucky museums were in France, England, Germany, Austria, Italy, Russia,

Spain, Argentina, and Mexico. Arthur Coggeshall noted that "to *Diplodocus carnegii* goes the credit for making 'dinosaur,' a household word . . . presidents, kings, emperors, and czars besieged Andrew Carnegie for replicas to be installed in their national museums." Many years later, Gerhard Ernest Untermann (1898–1975), director of the Utah Field House in Vernal, acquired the original molds and made a cast from a new material, fiberglass, which is now visible outdoors to the traveler on Highway 40.

In 1908, Holland was involved in another major dinosaur find. He was visiting Earl Douglass, one of his collectors. Douglass had been born in Minnesota in 1862, and educated at both the University of South Dakota and the Agricultural College. He later taught school in Montana, where he found some fossils. His interest in the natural sciences was sharpened by an expedition with a botanist on a collecting trip to Mexico and a year at the Missouri Botanical Gardens. Douglass had studied under paleontologist William Berryman Scott (1858–1947) at Princeton, and then was hired by the Carnegie Museum in Pittsburgh to work on early mammals.

Holland was with Douglass in his field camp in Utah, when Holland looked at mountains of the Uinta Range, visible from the camp, and recalled that Hayden's survey had reported Jurassic beds there.

> We decided that we would set forth early the next day with our teams of mules and visit the foot-hills, where Hayden had indicated the presence of Jurassic exposures. We started shortly after dawn and spent a long day on the cactus-covered ridge of Dead Man's Bench, in making our way through the gullies and ravines to the north. . . . The next day we went forward through the broken foot-hills which lie east and south of the great gorge through which the Green River emerges from the Uinta Mountains on its course towards the Grand Canyon of Arizona. As we slowly made our way through the stunted groves of pine we realized that we were upon Jurassic beds. We tethered our mules in the forest. Douglass went to the right and I to the left, scrambling up and down through the gullies in search of Jurassic fossils, with the understanding, that, if he found anything he was to dis-

charge the shotgun which he carried, and, if I found anything, I would fire the rifle, which I carried. His shotgun was presently heard and after a somewhat toilsome walk in the direction of the sound I heard him shout. I came up to him standing beside the weathered-out femur of a Diplodocus lying in the bottom of a very narrow ravine in which it was difficult to descend. Whence this perfectly preserved bone had fallen, from what stratum of the many above us it had been washed, we failed to ascertain. But there it was, as clean and perfect as if it had been worked out from the matrix in the laboratory. It was too heavy for us to shoulder and carry away, and possibly even too heavy for the light-wheeled vehicle in which we were traveling. So we left it there, proof positive that in that general region search for dinosaurian remains would probably be successful.

Did Douglass feel a prickle of anticipation when he saw this "perfectly preserved bone"? Although he could not have known it at the time, it was a turning point in his life, which came to revolve almost obsessively around the dinosaurs at this site.

In the following year, Douglass was back in the area, looking for more bones, assisted by a local farmer, George "Dad" Goodrich, who was a Mormon elder with a long white beard. During the spring and early summer they had little success, but on August 17, 1909, they again saw the ridge near where the femur had been found. Douglass walked up the ridge of Morrison sandstone. He wrote: "At last, in the top of the ledge where the softer overlying beds form a divide—a kind of a saddle—I saw eight of the tail bones of a *Brontosaurus* in exact position. It was a beautiful sight."

Douglass fired his gun twice to summon Goodrich, and the two decided there was a chance that there might be a complete skeleton buried in the rocks. Douglass gathered more local help and began an excavation. On August 23 he wrote to Holland: "I have discovered a huge dinosaur Brontosaurus and if the skeleton is as perfect as the portions we have exposed, the task of excavating will be enormous and will cost a lot of money, but the rock is that kind to get perfect bones from."

Holland came to visit, and secured ongoing support from Carnegie. Douglass continued his exploratory excavation, and was able to excavate his initial discovery.

Douglass directed what became known as the Carnegie Quarry from 1909–1922. The nearest town, Vernal, was some 20 miles (32 km) to the west, so Douglass preferred to live on the spot. During the first summer, as it became clear that he would be there for a long time, he asked his wife, Pearl, if she would leave Pittsburgh and bring their one-year-old baby son out and live with him. At this time, most dinosaur hunters' wives stayed home when their husbands were afield, but Pearl was ready for adventure and the family arrived in September. Through the cold winter, a frame of two-by-fours covered with canvas, kept warm with an iron stove, served the family as living and dining room. They slept in a tent, and kept their equipment in another one, while three local workmen slept in a sheepherder's wagon. No doubt Pearl Douglass found herself expected to be the unpaid cook for the entire camp.

As the years went by, the camp turned into a settlement. Douglass took out a homestead, built a log cabin, and bought a cow and chickens. He cultivated a vegetable garden, though there was not enough water for the farm he had planned. Eventually, his sister and father also came out to live at the quarry.

Douglass and his men worked every day except during the worst weather. During the day he supervised the excavations, and every evening he wrote down his copious observations. He was a naturalist of the old school, interested in everything, but his observations now stayed in his field notebook, with the careful maps he made of the bones. Although he had published important papers on early mammals, his publications ceased as the quarry absorbed more and more of his attention.

The four men gradually exposed the skeleton, but for some time the shoulders appeared to be the foremost part present. Eventually, they found the neck twisted back into the rock—but there was no skull. When excavated, the whole animal was about 98 feet (30 m) long, and its tail alone was 30 feet (9 m) long. When it was cleaned and mounted, it became the type specimen of a new species of brontosaur, *Apatosaurus louisae*, which was named by Holland in honor of Carnegie's wife, Louise. As it was being prepared for exhibition at the Carnegie Museum, Holland was left with the problem of deciding what to do about a skull.

Many otherwise fairly complete dinosaur fossils are found without skulls, and have become known to collectors as "headless wonders." This happens when a large animal's carcass has floated for a time before burial—as the decaying neck breaks, the skull separates and falls apart or is buried elsewhere.

Though the explanation is logical, such a discovery is highly frustrating for the fossil hunter. The skull gives important information about the animal's lifestyle (for instance, the size of the mouth and type of teeth are the best evidence to show what it may have fed on). As many dinosaurs have similar bodies but different heads, the skull is also of vital importance for identification, and many dinosaur skeletons cannot be named with certainty if a skull is not present. Although there was no skull on the *Apatosaurus* skeleton, a possible candidate was available, for unassociated among the bones of later skeletons found unearthed in the quarry was a long and narrow sauropod skull resembling that of a *Diplodocus*. Could this skull belong to the great skeleton? No one could be sure, for no one knew what the skull of *Apatosaurus* was really like.

The original finds of *Brontosaurus* had been headless. Marsh's men had found two relatively broad and blunt skulls—4 miles (6 km) and 400 miles (640 km) away—and although these were apparently associated with bones of *Camarasaurus*, Marsh had complacently described them as *Brontosaurus* skulls so that his skeletons would be complete.

Holland's first intention was to mount the new head on the *Apatosaurus* skeleton in the museum. This would have amounted to a public declaration of disagreement with Marsh, whose reputation was so great that even after his death reputable scientists hesitated to disagree with him. Osborn of the American Museum (who in this instance supported Marsh and felt the *Camarasaurus*-like skull was probably the correct one) challenged Holland to put his new skull on the skeleton, with the obvious intention of blasting him in the scientific press if he did. Holland found it more comfortable to leave the skeleton without a skull.

A later director in 1932 crowned *Apatosaurus* with a "Marsh" skull of unknown origin. It was not until 1979 that two paleontologists, John

S. McIntosh and David S. Berman, carefully studied Douglass's field records and decided that Douglass and Holland had been right. The correct *Apatosaurus* skull was finally mounted on the skeleton in October 1979.

Besides this original great find, there were three other sauropod skeletons close by, including one of a very small juvenile. The rocks of the Carnegie Quarry have been tilted by earth movements, so that the surface on which the fossils were deposited now slopes at about seventy degrees. Douglass and his men dug a trench along the front of the fossiliferous beds, using explosives to blast the overburden and then digging with hand tools until the bones were exposed. Horses and mules helped to shift the blocks of debris and plastered bones. As the years went by, the trench was deepened and lengthened until it was 600 feet (180 m) long and 80 feet (24 m) deep. The debris was removed along a narrow-gauge rail track, which was relaid as the quarry extended. Between 1909 and 1922, Douglass and his crew removed a sandstone layer 300 feet (90 m) long and 75 feet (23 m) high, and 700,000 pounds (315 t) of fossils were taken by buckboard 50 miles (80 km) or so to Dragon, Utah, and sent back to Pennsylvania by train.

During that period, 20 or more skeletons were found, with articulated segments representing perhaps 300 other individuals. Careful analysis showed that the fossils had been deposited in a shallow place in an ancient river. Carcasses had drifted down and stuck in the river bottom. Often the undersides of skeletons had all the bones in place, while the bones of the upper parts were scattered, as the stream's flow had removed them. Tails and necks of the skeletons were strung out, positioned by the flow of the river.

Over the years, Douglass excavated to the west and east of the original quarry, finding many more skeletons. Most remarkable was a juvenile *Camarasaurus* which proved to be the most complete sauropod ever found, and the first sauropod skeleton ever to be mounted that could be completely based on the bones of a single individual. It was 17 feet (5 m) long, and in comparison with the adult, the skull was relatively larger and the neck relatively shorter.

During 1922, Arthur Coggeshall spent several weeks filming in the quarry. Although the Dominion Motion Picture Bureau (ancestor of the National Film Board of Canada) had made one in 1921 in

Canada, the resulting movie, *Monsters of the Past*, is still one of the earliest films ever made of fossil-vertebrate collecting. It was shown to the Washington Academy of Sciences in 1924, and the only surviving copy has recently been rediscovered.

When Andrew Carnegie died in 1919, the funding for the Carnegie Museum project dried up. By this time the museum storage space and the staff were exhausted by the deluge of 300 tons (270 t) of fossils, which had been received in not much over a decade. Director Holland retired in 1922, and it was decided to close off the quarry, though work would continue in 1923 to crate and remove the remaining fossils. Over the years the quarry had been worked, the Carnegie Museum had become filled with splendid skeletons, which had been laboriously prepared and the best mounted for display.

❖   ❖   ❖

Since the rivalries of Cope and Marsh, paleontologists had become cautious about trespassing on each other's terrain. Although a richly fossiliferous area might attract more than one expedition from competing institutions, courtesy demands that the working of a single quarry should be left to those who had found and opened it, as long as they were interested in doing so. As soon as the Carnegie Museum was unable to continue work in the Carnegie Quarry, others lined up for a chance at the big dinosaurs.

First in line was the U.S. National Museum, part of the group of museums run by the Smithsonian Institution. In charge of the work was Charles Whitney Gilmore (1874–1945), who had now been with the Smithsonian for twenty years. After his early work with the Carnegie Museum, he had joined the U.S. National Museum in 1903, but retained a continuing interest in the Carnegie dinosaurs. Gilmore became a full curator in 1923. In the same year, the museum moved into the Carnegie Quarry as soon as the Carnegie Museum had cleaned up its work. Gilmore and his men collected thirty-three crates of bones, including a *Diplodocus*. Gilmore continued extensive studies of Morrison dinosaurs, and studied at the Carnegie Museum at length during his later career until his retirement in 1945.

With the completion of the Carnegie Museum's involvement in the quarry, Earl Douglass had left the museum and moved to Salt Lake City.

However, he was soon back at his beloved quarry with a team, collecting for the University of Utah. He collected another thirty-three crates of specimens, including an incomplete skeleton of a very large *Allosaurus* with a good skull. Unfortunately, he was denied any credit and did not get a position he had hoped for at the university. Douglass died in 1931 in comparative poverty, but he has left a noble monument: less than a quarter-century after his death, his visionary ideas for the Carnegie Quarry began to come to fruition.

When Douglass started work on the quarry, it was in a wild place, far from populated places, and over the years he watched the advancing tide of settlers. A few years after the quarry was started the U.S. government opened the area for settlement. Concerned that homesteading might interfere with his scientific work, Douglass filed for the mineral rights. After some delays, the government decided that dinosaur bones could not be considered minerals, and the claim was denied. Holland, the director of the Carnegie Museum, had an old friend in high places— Charles Doolittle Walcott (another paleontologist and discoverer of the now famous Burgess Shale) was secretary of the Smithsonian, and influential in government circles. As a result of Walcott's intervention, President Woodrow Wilson protected the area as Dinosaur National Monument in 1915. An area of 80 acres (32 ha) was set aside to protect what was somewhat startlingly described as "an extraordinary deposit of Dinosaurian and other gigantic reptilian remains of the Juratrias [*sic*] period which are of great scientific interest and value." The U.S. Department of the Interior became responsible for the site, and permits were issued for continued excavation.

Douglass had wanted to develop an exhibit in place as early as 1915. At the end of the Carnegie Museum's work in the quarry in 1923, he spelled out his proposal in a letter to Walcott at the Smithsonian: "I hope that the Government, for the benefit of science and the people, will uncover a large area, leave the bones and skeletons in relief and house them in. It would make one of the most astounding and instructive sights imaginable."

There was at the time no precedent for such an idea, and the crowds that now tour western parks were not on the road in the days when Henry Ford had only just started to produce popular and inexpensive motor vehicles. Nevertheless, within a decade the government took the idea seriously, and from 1933 to 1938, during the Depression, crews of unemployed men from the WPA (Works Progress Administration) deepened and enlarged the quarry. Although a few bones were exposed, they were not removed. The National Park Service brought in Barnum Brown from the American Museum of Natural History to advise them. Detailed plans were made for a building, and Brown wrote a popular article to promote the idea in 1937. However, no exhibit had been prepared by the outbreak of the Second World War.

When the idea was revived again in the 1950s, the National Park Service feared that all the bones might have been removed. Theodore White, a paleontologist who had worked for the Smithsonian, did some exploration to see if bones were still to be found. He located several significant specimens, including two of *Camarasaurus*. One was a neck and skull, and the other an 80 percent complete skeleton. By the mid-1950s, part of the quarry was covered with a large tin shed, and in 1957 work began on the present visitor center. By mid-1958 this unique building was open to the public. Part of the original quarry, the north wall consists of a sandstone bed 190 feet (58 m) long and 30 feet (9 m) high, with a 70-degree dip. A glass-walled building against the cliff allows visitors to watch the work in progress from two levels.

White was the first one of a succession of paleontologists (supported by preparators) who have worked at the site. Over the years they have exposed the bones in a 15-foot (4.5-m) thick layer of 70 percent of the cliff face, leaving them in high relief, just as they were laid down 145 million years ago. About 2,000 bones are currently exposed, including new or better finds than have been previously made. Not surprisingly, the site receives more than 400,000 visitors annually. A large library and research facilities are available to specialists, and other research continues elsewhere in the monument, which has been enlarged many times since 1915. In the 1980s, the University of Utah collections were transferred back to Dinosaur National Monument. This innovative design has been imitated a number of times, in other parts of the United States and in China.

Dinosaur National Monument has become one of the most remarkable dinosaur sites known anywhere in the world. During his years at the quarry, Douglass assigned specimen numbers up to 410, representing more individuals than have been found in any other Jurassic quarry. These include ten genera of dinosaurs, as well as turtles and crocodiles. The site has produced thirteen skulls, and more juvenile dinosaurs than any other Morrison quarry. The 350 tons (315 t) of bones shipped out from site include 20 mountable skeletons, belonging to 10 species of dinosaurs.

While he was planning the development of Dinosaur National Monument in 1931, Barnum Brown ran into a local fossil enthusiast, Mrs. Austin. She told him about a report of large bones on the ranch of Barker Howe, near Shell, at the foot of the Bighorn Mountains in Wyoming, east of Yellowstone. In 1933 Brown and his assistant Roland Thaxter Bird (1899–1978) went to visit the ranch. Like Brown, Bird was an eccentric figure. Born in Rye, New York, he was the son of an amateur entomologist, and spent his youth on farms. After losing his investments in the 1929 crash, Bird built a motorcycle camper and went on the road. In Arizona in 1932, he found part of a fossil skull, and sent it to his father, who showed a drawing of it to Barnum Brown. When the two met, Bird became Brown's faithful disciple. He collected with Brown and for Brown all over North America, doing particularly important work with dinosaur footprints.

At the ranch in Wyoming, Howe, a crusty eighty-two-year-old rancher, showed them the bones, weathering out from a horizontal rock layer quite near the ranch buildings. Brown, Bird, and their colleagues began careful excavation, watched with increasing impatience by the rancher. After a week of painstaking work, Howe showed up with a pickax, and was with difficulty restrained from doing a quick and dirty excavation of his own. It soon became clear that they had located another fine concentration of sauropod bones, like that in the Carnegie Quarry. Brown sought financial help from the Sinclair Oil Company, which had often provided support as the company advertising featured dinosaurs.

In 1934, Brown returned with a full team. As the bones were laboriously excavated, Bird made a map of the entire site on a 3-foot

(1 m) grid, working from a barrel slung 30 feet (9 m) up in the air. The entire deposit, about 60 feet (18 m) by 54 feet (16 m) at its widest dimensions, was in the form of a lens, thickest in the middle and thinner at the edge. Though there were many bones, there were no complete skeletons. Brown recalled his problems: "It soon became apparent that . . . there was a veritable herd of dinosaurs, their skeletal remains crossed, crisscrossed and interlocked in a confused and almost inextricable manner. . . . Through the warping of the strata incident to the nearby mountain uplift, the bones had been checked and fractured to a high degree, so all had to be thoroughly shellacked as soon as uncovered. Never have I seen such a thirsty lot of dinosaurs."

More than 4,000 bones, representing at least 20 individual dinosaurs, had been collected. They included *Barosaurus*, *Camarasaurus*, and *Camptosaurus*, and teeth of the carnivore *Allosaurus*. There were partial skeletons—long sections of vertebrae and large limb bones—piled up like logs. They were not water-worn, and had not been chewed by predators. Single bones of smaller species were scattered around the edge. In the center, several limbs of larger dinosaurs stood upright in what had once been soft gray mud. Brown's joke about thirsty dinosaurs has a second, and sinister, meaning. He interpreted the site as a drinking pool in an area that was gradually drying up, and visualized them coming to a sticky end: "The dinosaurs became more and more concentrated in the remaining pools as they were pushed together in huge herds. As the water receded, weaker dinosaurs were trampled and their bones scattered on the borders of the pool, the larger ones huddled closer and closer together as they made their last futile stand against fate."

This dramatic scene inspired part of Disney's *Fantasia*, in which dinosaurs trudge across a desert and die of thirst.

The bones of the Howe Quarry, packed in 144 cases, and weighing 35 tons (32 t), filled an entire boxcar. They have still not been described.

❖ ❖ ❖

As westerners became more aware of dinosaur bones, new sites and discoveries continued to appear. One of the earliest large monsters to be discovered, *Brontosaurus*, was so called because Marsh imagined that its steps must have sounded like thunder. In more recent years, it seems that as fast as one huge monster is named, another, even bigger, is discovered. The namers are beginning to run out of superlatives, and nowhere is this so much of a problem as in Utah.

James Jensen grew up on a farm in the state and, at the age of ten, he found some fossils: "I began collecting them and became curious as to what they were. My father bought a used geology textbook, and in the back of it were pictures of dinosaurs. While some boys dreamed of a new bicycle, I dreamed of finding dinosaurs. I would always wake up just before I could dig them up. I never did have a bicycle, but I've never stopped dreaming of dinosaurs."

Although "Dinosaur Jim" Jensen did not have much college education, he became curator of the Vertebrate Paleontology Research Laboratory at Brigham Young University, in Provo, Utah. There he developed a great reputation as a finder of fossils, and on the strength of this was chosen to be part of Edwin Colbert's team in a fossil-hunting trip to the Antarctic in 1968 (see Chapter 17).

Back in Utah and neighboring Colorado, he developed a network of informants—people who spent their time in the country, such as farmers, herdsmen, and rockhounds—who kept their eyes on the lookout for fossils. Jim Smith of Henrieville, Utah, told Jensen of a skeleton he had found back in the 1940s. When Jensen located it, he found a message in a bottle beside the skeleton, which explained, "This critter belongs to Jim Smith. This is as far as I could lead him."

Jensen found a new carnosaur (flesh-eating dinosaur) with a heavy body and short arms with slashing claws which he named (with Peter Galton) *Torvosaurus*, or "savage lizard," in 1979. But Jensen has had most luck with sauropods. One, found in 1967, he called *Cathetosaurus*, or "upright lizard," in 1988. Another, named in 1985, is *Dystylosaurus* or "two beam lizard," named from a single vertebra more than 3 feet (1 m) high.

Another informant, a sawmill operator in Delta, called Eddie Jones, directed Jensen to Dry Mesa, Colorado, where late Jurassic rocks were exposed. There, in 1972, Jensen had a bulldozer make a cut across 300 feet (92 m) of the site. An assistant commented, "All along that cut, there was bone everywhere we looked." Jensen's son Ron located an enormous shoulderblade, uncovered the whole thing, and concealed it with burlap bags before calling his father. When he removed the bags, there was an 8-foot (2-m) bone. It had belonged to a sauropod, which as far as its available bones went seemed to resemble the giant African sauropod *Brachiosaurus*. If its proportions, extrapolated from the bones found, were the same as *Brachiosaurus*, the new dinosaur would have weighed 55 tons (50 t), and been 80 to 100 feet (24 to 30 m) long. Jensen informally called it "Supersaurus," or the "super reptile." It took over ten years (until 1985) to collect all the available pieces, then prepare and describe them, and until that point *Supersaurus* was not the animal's official name. Because of its spectacular size, the dinosaur was widely discussed, even though it had not been formally described, and the name "Supersaurus" appears in many dinosaur books from that period in quotes, representing its informal status.

At the same site in 1979, Jensen was being filmed by a Japanese television crew when he found a shoulder blade and vertebrae of an even larger dinosaur. The shoulder blade alone is more than 9 feet (3 m) long, and he informally named it "Ultrasaurus," or "ultra lizard." Estimates of its total size are staggering: 90 feet (27 m) long and 52 feet (16 m) tall; its weight has been estimated as high as 144 tons (130 t). It would have stood 25 feet (8 m) at the shoulder, and its 60-foot (18-m) neck would have allowed it to peek in fifth- or sixth-story windows (if any had been available). National Museum of Canada paleontologist Dale Russell has speculated that the dinosaur might have lived as long as 114 years, which is rather longer than its name did.

Jim Jensen retired in 1983, but continued his research. By the time he officially named *Ultrasaurus* in 1985, there had been an unexpected development. Another new sauropod dinosaur found in Korea, smaller than *Brachiosaurus*, was named by paleontologist Haang Mook Kim in 1983 — under the name of *Ultrasaurus*. By the rules of scientific nomenclature, the first published use of a name accompanied by a description has priority, so *Ultrasaurus* is now properly the Korean dinosaur, and the animal already well known informally as "Ultrasaurus" needed a new name. Jensen has published more on his "Ultrasaurus," but in an unorthodox manner which has confused other paleontologists, and has abandoned further work.

New Brigham Young University staff are continuing work in the quarry. In August 1988, two collectors—Cliff Miles and Brian Versey—both hit bone, several feet apart. As they exposed it, they found they were working on the same bone; a pelvis 6 feet (2 m) long and weighing 1,500 pounds (675 kg).

Even before its name could be finalized, the Utah "Ultrasaurus" lost its status as the biggest dinosaur. In New Mexico, yet another large sauropod has been found, and Utah state paleontologist David Gillette began excavations in 1985 which are still continuing. Some large bones (surrounded by Indian petroglyphs) had been found by a group of backpackers on land belonging to the Bureau of Land Management. Gillette started the excavation, removing several vertebrae, but found they pointed under a hillside. He enlisted unexpected assistance in locating the rest of the skeleton when he lectured about it to the scientists at Los Alamos National Laboratory. They tried to find more bones with sound waves, ground-penetrating radar, and sensitive tests for uranium and magnetite, and even undertook a night search using ultraviolet light, but none has yet been really successful. More conventional blasting removed enough of the hill to expose the rear half of the dinosaur. Only then did it become clear that it was probably the longest dinosaur recorded.

Although Gillette is cautious in his estimates, he feels 140 feet (43 m)—half as long as an American football field—is a fair estimate, making it the longest known by about 25 percent. Much of the skeleton is articulated, and includes the front half of the tail, the pelvis, and the vertebrae of the back. Apart from its size, another rare feature is the presence of 230 stomach stones (gastroliths) with the skeleton. It is hoped that the front legs, neck, and skull can be recovered, but Gillette estimates the total pricetag as a million dollars—far in excess of his available resources. It was unofficially known for some years as "Seismosaurus" ("earthquake lizard"), and this name was formally published in 1991. It seems to be even bigger than the grossly exaggerated estimate for the 1898 sauropod. The last two decades have shown clearly that "the most colossal animal ever found" is out west somewhere—but when will we find the last and biggest?

10

LARGE DUCKBILLS
AND SMALL CARNIVORES

IN NOVEMBER 1916 TWO FINE DUCK-BILLED DINOSAURS from Alberta were loaded on a ship, the S.S. *Mount Temple*, before it set off on its dangerous journey across the Atlantic to war-besieged Britain. During its perilous journey, the *Mount Temple* was torpedoed, and the dinosaurs sank to the bottom of the ocean. They had been collected by Charles H. Sternberg, by then in his middle sixties, and their loss was a serious blow to him.

Sternberg and his three sons had been kept busy collecting for the Geological Survey of Canada as long as Brown was in Alberta working for the American Museum of Natural History in New York. But, when Brown left Alberta in 1915, the pressure was off. Worse, on February 16, 1916, the central block of the Houses of Parliament in Ottawa burned down, and the new museum was requisitioned as a temporary space for the business of government. The Senate was placed in the cleared fossil gallery, which amused the museum staff but was small consolation for the handicaps to their work. C.H. Sternberg was told that there was no more money to support fieldwork on the former scale. Characteristically, he resigned from the Survey in May 1916 and returned to Alberta as a freelancer. He wrote to his other clients, and before long it was agreed that his new material would go to the British Museum in London. It may seem strange that there was money in Britain for fossil collecting in the middle of the First World War, but the British Museum had access to a bequest, the Sladen

Memorial Fund. Cutler's finds were no doubt used as evidence to convince the trustees that Alberta could produce good material.

C.H. Sternberg was in the field with his son Levi as early as the beginning of June, even though the money had not yet been approved. They worked for four months, assisted by local help, and although Charles was injured falling from his wagon, the two Sternbergs collected three fine skeletons of the helmeted duckbill *Corythosaurus*. The first one was complete except for the end of the tail and a part of the skull, but collecting it was not an easy job.

> It lay up a narrow gorge, too narrow to get a horse up. We were obliged to cut steps up and down the rough way from the nearest point we could reach it from camp, and Levi had to carry nearly all the water, plaster, burlap and paper, etc., necessary to wrap a skeleton nearly thirty feet long. The distance from the wagon was nearly an eighth of a mile.
>
> [Levi] . . . would have to strap his burlap strips beneath the specimen in such a way that the rock did not fall out. It would often take him many minutes before he could get a strip to stick. He lay on his back and patted the plaster-soaked burlap with the ends of his fingers until the blood came. Often the plaster would harden before he could get it to stick. Then he had to take a new strip and again go through the same hard and patience-trying labor, filling his eyes with burning lime. . . . After the specimen was ready for hauling out of the brakes, we had to build a sled road to it from the prairie, and haul it to camp around the badlands, a distance of about six miles, while in a bee-line it was only about a mile to camp.

The second specimen was even better: "It was in a splendid matrix— a strong sandstone—and the bones were beautifully preserved — a specimen that could have been easily prepared. One hind foot was all that was exposed. I could not believe that this meant anything but a few loose bones. It pointed heavenward, from the side of the cliff. We followed the foot down to the body and found the entire skeleton except for a few inches of the tail and THE HEAD."

Sternberg was ready to deal with another "headless wonder": "With a restored head (and we found one that could have been used), as far as the public was concerned, the British Museum could have mounted these two lords of the ancient bayous in that great storehouse of treasures, more rare than gold or silver, to be the heritage of the ages to come."

Alas for his dreams, the duckbills were destined for that even greater storehouse of treasures, the bottom of the Atlantic. Sternberg suffered greatly from the loss, not only because his hard work had been wasted, but because the insurance claims were not settled until May. For by now he had sold his house in Ottawa and moved back to Kansas.

Although Sternberg was eager to go to Alberta again for the British Museum, no more funding was available, and he worked for a while in Texas. Sternberg did work with Levi in Alberta again in 1917. They found another carnivore (*Gorgosaurus sternbergi*), a hooded duckbill, and a skeleton of a small ankylosaur, which Sternberg referred to the poorly known genus *Palaeoscincus*. The British Museum refused to buy the new material, and Sternberg sold the carnivore and the armored dinosaur to the American Museum (on the recommendation of his old rival, Barnum Brown) and the duckbill to the San Diego Museum of Natural History in California. C.H. and Levi Sternberg in due course mounted the duckbill in its new home, leaving the other two brothers in Canada. This move finally broke up the remarkable family team of dinosaur collectors, but all the four individuals continued separate careers in the fossil field. C.H. Sternberg continued fossil collecting until his eighties. When his wife died in 1938, he joined Levi in Toronto, where he died in 1943 at the age of ninety-three.

George Sternberg, C.H. Sternberg's eldest son, once spent part of a summer helping a farmer with the harvest. The farmer asked about George's regular work, and he explained that he went out West to collect dinosaurs. The farmer was impressed. "You must be a very brave man," he said, "to capture such big, ferocious creatures."

Though the dangers he faced were not quite what the farmer imagined, George Sternberg too earned his reputation as an intrepid fossil hunter. His father's right-hand man since he was a boy, George had been the first to break away from the strong parental influence, working with Barnum Brown in Alberta before returning to the family team, and then doing more independent fieldwork in 1915. When his father left the Survey, George initially stayed on, and spent a short time in the field in 1916, completing the previous season's effort and finding a large flat-headed duckbill (*Edmontosaurus regalis*) and the type specimen of a new bird mimic, *Ornithomimus edmontonicus*. In 1917 there was no fieldwork, and he remained in Ottawa, preparing material that had been collected. When there was still no prospect of fieldwork by the middle of 1918, George also resigned from the Survey, and worked for a while with his father. But money was tight, so George went off on his own.

He was offered a job with the Field Museum in Chicago by Elmer Riggs, but did not take it. He came back into the field in Alberta in 1920, collecting near Little Sandhill Creek, and sold some of his material (including skulls of the duckbill *Corythosaurus excavatus* and the horned dinosaur *Chasmosaurus kaiseni*) to John Andrew Allan at the geology department of the University of Alberta. This was the first Alberta-funded fossil collecting since Cutler's short-lived attempts to develop a collection in Calgary. Allan had started the department in 1912, and headed it for twenty-nine years. Although he necessarily concentrated on economic geology, he attempted to develop a dinosaur collection too, and lobbied for funds behind the scenes. In November 1920, George applied for a position with the University of Alberta, presumably with some assurance that funds might be available.

Riggs tried again to lure George to Chicago in January 1921, but the University of Alberta must have found funds, for George stayed in Edmonton for the 1920–21 winter, and returned to Little Sandhill Creek in 1921. This time he found a nearly complete *Corythosaurus* skeleton, and the skull and incomplete skeleton of the carnivore *Gorgosaurus* (later regarded as *Albertosaurus libratus*, but other identifications are recently being considered). He also solved a mystery by finding the first reasonably complete skeleton of the bonehead *Stegoceras validus*. This small dinosaur had a thick, solid crown to its skull, now thought to have been used in battering-ram contests with rival males, as bighorn sheep use their horns. The heavy skull caps had previously been described by Lambe, but the rest of the skeleton is much more fragile, and had not previously been found.

In a mildly comic incident, the Dominion Motion Picture Bureau came in the field to film the work of George's brother Charles M. Sternberg, who was still with the Geological Survey. Presumably the filmmakers asked at the nearest town for Mr. Sternberg's camp, and were directed to George by mistake. The finished film shows George in the field and Charles in the laboratory.

In 1923 George finally accepted a position with the Field Museum in Chicago under Elmer Riggs, and his collection of that year went to Chicago. Riggs had been born in Indiana in 1869, had taken degrees at the University of Kansas, and had worked in the field with his friend Barnum Brown. Riggs was in Alberta with George Sternberg when the museum's director wired for them to head off immediately for an expedition to South America.

Some of George's material at the University of Alberta was described by Charles Gilmore of the U.S. National Museum (part of the Smithsonian Institution), and George returned briefly to Alberta in 1935 to complete preparation of his collection at the university. Otherwise, his career remained based in the United States, and eventually he became curator of what is now the Sternberg Memorial Museum at Fort Hays State University in Hays, Kansas. George died in 1969.

C.H. Sternberg's second son, Charles Mortram (known in the family as Charlie), also remained with the Geological Survey of Canada— for more than forty years. Charlie, too, had worked independently in Little Sandhill Creek in 1917, where he found a horned dinosaur, *Centrosaurus longirostris,* and the skull of a new *Lambeosaurus* (which was later named *lambei* in double honor of Lawrence Lambe). There was also an incomplete armored dinosaur, *Panoplosaurus mirus,* the "wonderful fully armored reptile." After the war, there was money again for fieldwork. In 1919, he was back in Alberta, where he found several new duckbills. During that year Lambe died, and Charlie began to take responsibility for the scientific work of paleontology as well as collection, first finishing one of Lambe's papers and then publishing his first independent paper in 1921. Nevertheless, these were not good times for dinosaurs at the National Museum, for there was pressure to close down the dinosaur gallery yet again, this time to make room for a national art gallery.

In 1921, Charlie was collecting at Morgan Creek in Saskatchewan, where Dawson had made the original western Canadian dinosaur find. Here he found a three-horned *Triceratops*, and the skull of a new duckbill, which he called *Anatosaurus saskatchewanensis*. Later in the season he moved on to Little Sandhill Creek in Alberta and found a skull and a partial skeleton of *Gorgosaurus libratus*, and skulls of *Corythosaurus* and *Centrosaurus*. In this year Charlie used an automobile as well as a team and wagon—one of the first instances in which an engine was used to help the dinosaur collector.

Charlie was in western Canada again in 1924, 1925, 1926, and 1928. In 1926, he found a skeleton of *Thescelosaurus*, one of the latest dinosaurs. In 1928, he began a long collaboration with the amateur collector H.S. "Corky" Jones, an Englishman who had come from the Isle of Wight (and perhaps knew of dinosaurs there) to the little town of Eastend, Saskatchewan. In 1930, Charlie visited the Peace River canyon of British Columbia, where he documented a number of striking dinosaur footprints along the rock ledges beside the wildly flowing river. In the 1930s, the Depression slowed virtually all fieldwork to a halt.

In the years 1935 and 1936, Charlie Sternberg mapped all the quarry sites in the Steveville area (many of which he had worked on or at least visited during the dinosaur rush of the First World War period), and helped to produce a remarkable geological map of the area, which surely shows the highest concentration of dinosaur quarries in the world. Even now new finds could be made, and Sternberg located a duckbill that was named in 1949 *Brachylophosaurus canadensis,* "Canadian short-crested reptile."

In 1937 he visited the Manyberries area in southeastern Alberta, where he found an almost complete *Lambeosaurus*. Although its field photograph soon became familiar through reproductions, the specimen lay unprepared in three packing crates in Ottawa for thirty years.

Fieldwork was again suspended during the Second World War, but in 1946 Charlie returned to the Big Valley area of the Red Deer River. Here he found the first Alberta skull of the large three-horned dinosaur *Triceratops*, which was placed in a new species named *albertensis*, for the province. Another dinosaur was *Pachyrhinosaurus*, or "thick nose," a most spectacular relative of the horned dinosaurs, which relied for offense and defense on a massive thickening of the skull bones instead of horns.

In 1948 the vertebrate paleontology program was transferred from the Geological Survey to the National Museum of Canada, followed by an administrative separation of the two programs in 1950. Charlie, who had by now spent almost fifty years collecting and studying dinosaurs for the Canadian government, and had become well known as Canada's "Mr. Dinosaur," decided to retire. This was by no means the end of his professional career, for he continued to work on his beloved dinosaurs in retirement. Over his professional life he had described seventeen new species of dinosaurs in forty-seven scientific papers, and supplemented his high-school education with a number of honorary degrees. Late in life, the National Film Board (whose predecessor had failed to film him in the field) made him the subject of an entire movie, affectionately named *Charlie*, using some of the earlier footage. Charlie himself remained modest about his accomplishments. "I enjoyed every minute of my work," he said. "If I could do it all over again I would be a dinosaur *expert*."

Charlie's own scientific work was not his only contribution to the study of Canadian dinosaurs. One of his sons (and a grandson of C.H. Sternberg) was Raymond Sternberg (who later changed his surname to Martin). He had worked with his father in the field in 1936, and in 1940 described a strange fossil that he had found. The main part of the fossil was a pair of toothless, birdlike jaws, and there was also a breastbone (wishbone) which was then thought to be absent in dinosaurs. Raymond accordingly described his fossil as a bird, *Caenagnathus* ("recent jaw"), and it was not until long after, when more complete material of similar fossils was found in Mongolia, that it was recognized as a dinosaur of the *Oviraptor* group.

The youngest Sternberg son, Levi, continued to collect with his father for some time after his brothers were working independently, but eventually he decided to settle down in Canada. In the 1920s, the one player besides the National Museum was the Palaeontology Museum in Toronto. What is now called the Royal Ontario Museum was established in 1912 as an adjunct to the University of Toronto. Initially, it was made up of five separate and independent museums, and both Benjamin Bensley of the Zoology Museum and William Arthur Parks of the Palaeontology Museum took an active interest in Canadian dinosaurs.

Parks (1868–1936) had been born in Hamilton, and graduated from the University of Toronto in 1892 in Modern Languages and Natural Sciences, going on to work as a chemist for a mining company. In his youth he did geological fieldwork in the Ontario back country, and soon learnt to carry enormous loads, for the native porters did not recognize the significance of his rock samples, and to save labor would surreptitiously dump one set of rocks and pick up others near the next camp rather than carry the specimens he had so carefully collected. Parks joined the staff of the University of Toronto as a Fellow in Geology in 1893, and earned his doctorate in 1900 (the first geologist in Canada to receive that degree). He became professor of paleontology when he added the subject to the curriculum in 1915, and was head of the Geology Department in 1922. He managed to secure space for a geology museum in 1904, and began to build an important collection of fossils, including a mosasaur from Kansas that he purchased from C.H. Sternberg.

Parks was known for work on the obscure fossils called stromatoporoids, but was interested in dinosaurs as well. Even before he began teaching paleontology, he had sent out one of his staff, Alexander McLean, to Alberta as early as 1912. McLean had no experience and achieved poor results. Parks led an expedition in 1918 at the age of about fifty. He found a specimen of the duckbill *Kritosaurus*, "noble reptile," and used it to learn the techniques of collection. After leading another expedition, Parks hired the experienced Levi Sternberg in 1919, who mounted the *Kritosaurus*, which was exhibited in 1920. Once a dinosaur could be seen in the museum gallery, funds were easier to obtain. Levi was able to go into the field year after year, and brought his brother-in-law Gustav Lindblad onto the staff. In 1923, Levi took a year's leave of absence to help his father (aged seventy-one) collect in New Mexico, leaving Lindblad to lead the expeditions.

From this time onwards, Parks visited the field parties only occasionally, concentrating his efforts on the scientific description of the stream of material that Levi collected. A striking find was *Parasaurolophus walkeri* (found in 1920 and described in 1922). It had an even longer crest than *Saurolophus*, so its generic name means "beside *Saurolophus*." It was named *walkeri* after Sir Edmund Walker, who had facilitated the gathering of financial support for the expedition. Parks followed Brown's opinion (about the related *Saurolophus*) that the crest supported a flap of skin, but did not speculate further. It was only in later years it was shown that the hollow crest contained a long air tube. At first this was regarded as an adaptation to underwater feeding, but it was later suggested that it could have been used to make a call like a French horn. Before he died in 1936, Parks had published twenty-two articles and papers on dinosaurs, and described a number of new ones. Levi continued at the museum until his retirement in 1962, as associate curator; he died in 1976.

❖ ❖ ❖

For a whole generation of vertebrate paleontologists in Canada, dinosaurs had been a major preoccupation. Lawrence Lambe, all of the Sternbergs, and even William Parks had given them a major share of attention, though none had had the luxury of concentrating exclusively on dinosaurs and all had done significant work on other groups. Gradually, a feeling developed in both the United States and Canada, that the dinosaurs were becoming fairly well understood. This impression was supported by the prominence of dinosaur exhibits in museums. Other significant vertebrate fossils existed, and many paleontologists felt that they had been unduly neglected, yet deserved attention for the scientific puzzles they presented. Consequently, a whole generation of vertebrate paleontologists grew up for whom dinosaurs were interesting, but not a principal preoccupation. In Canada, which supported very few vertebrate paleontologists at all, this would have resulted in a significant neglect of dinosaurs, but for one remarkable man.

Loris Russell was born in New York in 1904, but his parents moved to Alberta when he was small. He was raised in Calgary, became a student at the University of Alberta in the 1920s, and graduated in 1927. While still a student, he had the opportunity to work with Charlie

Sternberg in 1923, excavating an *Edmontosaurus* at Bleriot Ferry near Drumheller. Loris pursued his interest in vertebrates in the new area of focus, fossil mammals, and went to Princeton to study with William Berryman Scott, completing his master's degree in 1929 and his doctorate in 1930. The Depression was not a good time to earn a living in paleontology, but Loris found a position with the Geological Survey of Canada and spent seven years in the field. Although formally a field geologist, he published a steady stream of paleontological work, including a number of publications on dinosaurs. These moved away from the descriptions of new species that had been done by his older colleagues, and often addressed important theoretical questions. In 1930, for instance, Russell produced a summary of the Upper Cretaceous dinosaur faunas in North America. In 1932, he published papers on an obscure little dinosaur known as *Troödon*; one of the first to be named from the western States, but whose great importance was not to be fully recognized for another half-century. He published another paper on the Cretaceous–Tertiary transition, the time when the dinosaurs became extinct.

On Parks's death in 1936, his protégée Madeleine Fritz became acting director of both the vertebrate collections and the invertebrates, where her training lay. In 1937 Russell moved to the Royal Ontario Museum of Palaeontology, where he was assistant director from 1937 to 1940. In 1938 he was married to Grace LeFeuvre, who challenged orthodoxy by regularly accompanying Loris in the field. Although not a paleontologist she has become almost as well known in the paleontological world as her husband.

Loris Russell built an amateur interest in ham radio into a distinguished career in the Canadian Corps of Signals during the Second World War, and then returned to the Royal Ontario Museum of Palaeontology as director in 1946. In this position he was able to play an active part in bringing the five museums closer together into what eventually became the single Royal Ontario Museum.

In 1950, Loris Russell moved to the National Museum of Canada as chief of the zoology section until 1957, when he became director of the museum. In 1956, he was the first since Huxley to seriously suggest that dinosaurs might have been warm-blooded. "The silence was deafening," said Russell, for the idea was virtually ignored. However, he did not forget the idea, and continued to believe that the success of the dinosaurs might be explained by this unorthodox view.

> It is quite proper, [he said later] to speculate that the circulatory system of dinosaurs had already passed from the crocodile to the bird stage of organization, and this might have been the secret of success during more than one hundred million years of dominance. A complete separation of venous and arterial blood would have permitted . . . a stepped-up metabolism in general. . . . I have long held that the great success of the dinosaurs over other reptiles implies a fundamental difference, and that this difference was the possession by the dinosaurs of a better circulatory system and an independent body temperature.

In 1963 Russell moved back to the Royal Ontario Museum as chief biologist, and was also a professor of geology at the University of Toronto. Now retired, he continued to do fieldwork until he was eighty-three, and in his late eighties is still an active researcher in the laboratory, continuing to publish papers on dinosaurs and on the historical development of dinosaur collecting in Canada.

❖ ❖ ❖

From 1935 to 1943, Alberta was governed by a Social Credit government led by fundamentalist preacher William "Bible Bill" Aberhart. It is reported that in one of his broadcasts, Aberhart claimed that paleontologists went out into the badlands and made dinosaur bones out of plaster of Paris to confuse true believers. When he heard this, Charlie Sternberg's wry response was "how clever we were."

With the Alberta government so unsympathetic to dinosaurs, it is not surprising that for many years there was little provincial support to develop the dinosaur resource. Although the richness of the dinosaur deposits in Alberta was widely recognized, and many individuals were interested, the province was relatively slow to support scientific research, protective parks, and interpretive exhibits.

Calgary, the city nearest the dinosaur beds, had tried to develop a museum with Cutler's collections (see Chapter 8), but it failed in the

1920s. A new initiative came from the Calgary Zoo, after curator Lars Willumsen visited the zoo at Stellingen, near Hamburg, in 1931. There the famous animal collector Carl Hagenbeck had developed a prehistoric zoo of life-sized models of various extinct animals. Willumsen was so impressed that he came home determined to develop a similar attraction in Calgary. Several model makers, principally John Kanerva, labored over the years to make life-sized models of various dinosaurs. Although some Alberta dinosaurs were featured, most effort went into the huge Brontosaurus, which was popularly known as "Dinny" and became the zoo's emblem. It was formally unveiled in 1938 by Prime Minister R.B. Bennett.

The little coal town of Drumheller, with a population of only a few thousand, had grown up in the badlands, not far from the location where Tyrrell had found his only dinosaur on the Red Deer River. A number of local people began to take an interest in the dinosaur fossils of the area, and as a result of lobbying, a nearby area between Munson and Morrin had been set aside in 1939 as a park reserve, but only given nominal protection. During the 1940s and 1950s, a collection of fossils was displayed in a room next to the Rotary swimming pool. In 1955, at the instigation of W.R. Reade and Irene McVeigh, the Drumheller and District Museum Society was formed, and a small museum was developed. The society "borrowed" a 29-foot (9-m) *Edmontosaurus* from the National Museum, and it was installed by Charlie Sternberg. Gradually, Drumheller began to develop its tourist image as the "Dinosaur Capital of Alberta." In the 1950s a circular route of country roads was developed and advertised as the Dinosaur Trail, and in 1959, a local man, Tig Seland, constructed a life-sized *Tyrannosaurus* model out of chicken wire and concrete, the first of a number of models that decorate the area. Seland ended up president of the Museum Society, and the museum succeeded in attracting around 100,000 visitors a year. A local guidebook, the *Badlands of the Red Deer Valley,* was published annually, presenting more or less accurate information about dinosaurs, geology, and other tourist features. By 1960, the museum was home for a number of important specimens, including a skull of the "thick-nosed lizard" *Pachyrhinosaurus* found near Munson. By the early 1970s the tourist trade was growing to sufficient size to encourage dinosaur-related commercial developments such as the model collection called Prehistoric Parks.

South and east of Drumheller, the less-populated Steveville area had by this time produced about 45 percent of the world's known Upper Cretaceous dinosaurs. With depopulation in the "dirty thirties," the town of Steveville had disappeared, and the new center of population was Brooks, some distance away from the dinosaur exposures. A lobby for a park was headed by doctor and homesteader Winfred George Anderson. In 1937, the federal government took an interest in the area becoming a national park, but as Alberta already had a bigger area of national parkland than any other province, negotiations were unsuccessful. Finally, in 1955, the Alberta government decided to protect part of the Red Deer River. Despite a lobby from the Drumheller area, the government asked the advice of recently retired Charlie Sternberg, and chose the Steveville area for what was at first known as Steveville Dinosaur Provincial Park. An Alberta naturalist, Roy Fowler, was appointed park warden, and in 1958 he started to preserve some skeletons in place, as they were found, covering them with little "fossil houses." Charlie Sternberg continued to provide assistance until 1965, when Fowler retired. With various changes in boundary, the park grew to be around 35 square miles (90 km^2), but for many years remained underdeveloped, without a paved road to connect it to the nearby Trans-Canada Highway.

After Charlie Sternberg's retirement, there was relatively little dinosaur work from the National Museum for some years. In 1954, the museum hired a new vertebrate paleontologist, Wann Langston, Jr., who had been trained at the universities of Oklahoma and California. Although he was interested in dinosaurs, other fossil areas in Canada had been neglected and he devoted much of his attention elsewhere.

Apart from a little work by Charlie Sternberg, the southern Alberta locality of Scabby Butte had been almost totally forgotten. In August 1955, Loris Russell and Wann Langston rediscovered the site, and found two skulls of the little-known dinosaur *Pachyrhinosaurus*. Langston excavated these in 1957 with assistance from the Geological Survey and Chevron Oil Company. As well as the skulls, Langston obtained another 200 bones from a bone bed. Bone beds—layers of rock containing concentrations of single bones—have been the only available evidence for dinosaurs in many parts of the world, but in Alberta so many fairly complete skeletons had been found that bone beds had largely been ignored. Langston made Alberta's first careful analysis of the fauna from a single bed, recording remains of thirty-two different animals, including fish, amphibians, several kinds of water reptiles (turtles, champsosaurs, mosasaurs, and crocodiles), as well as seven kinds of dinosaurs and some mammals. Another innovation involved securing pollen samples from inside one of the *Pachyrhinosaurus* skulls, which when analyzed showed evidence of twenty-eight species of plants, including relatives of the swamp cypress, other conifers, and the gingko.

An oil strike in 1947 led to Alberta gradually moving from being a "have not" province to its new status as one of the richest areas of Canada. Recognizing that nothing much had been done about developing the dinosaur resources, the University of Alberta managed to fund a 1963 conference on vertebrate paleontology in association with the International Congress of Zoology in Washington, D.C. In August and September, a select party gathered in Edmonton for discussions, which were followed by a three-day field trip. The thirty-four attendees included a number of eminent dinosaur specialists and other leading vertebrate paleontologists, such as Edwin Colbert, Bjorn Kurten, and Alfred Romer. Canadian vertebrate paleontology was represented by Loris Russell, Charlie Sternberg, Wann Langston (in transition from the National Museum to a new position in Texas), and William Swinton, a British dinosaur specialist who had moved to the Royal Ontario Museum. Local representatives included University of Alberta paleontologist Charles Stelck, geologists Potter Chamney and Don Taylor, and amateur collectors and museum specialists.

Loris Russell hoped to see Alberta establish "a first-class program of research in vertebrate paleontology and a public museum where the fruits of this work can be displayed, in such a manner as to make the information available to the public." Russell speculated on the sort of budget that might be needed, and envisaged some $800,000 dollars to operate a paleontology program. Saskatchewan Museum of Natural History's Bruce McCorquodale pointed out that "the more you show the public, the more interest you arouse."

The general consensus was, inevitably, that more needed to be done, and by the time the conference proceedings were published in 1964 the preface announced new developments: "a vertebrate paleontologist will be appointed to the staff of the University. These developments coincide with the foundation of a Provincial Museum which we hope will eventually be able to display specimens and add greatly to the public interest in Vertebrate Palaeontology."

In due course the University of Alberta hired Richard Fox, a paleontologist from the United States who was particularly interested in a new and important area of paleontology, the tiny mammals that were contemporaries of the dinosaurs. By using new techniques, Fox found a wealth of important and unknown mammal material in the beds which until then had been famous for their dinosaurs. While collecting new dinosaur material, he developed new techniques, collaborating with the Canadian Armed Forces to use helicopters to lift heavy fossils out of the badlands. He also trained a new generation of vertebrate paleontologists on Alberta material.

The Provincial Museum and Archives of Alberta got under way with a fossil-collecting program in 1966, when curator of earth sciences Don Taylor began to acquire many single bones and partial skeletons from localities around the province. I myself joined the staff in 1967 as head curator of natural history. The *Lambeosaurus* collected by Charlie Sternberg in 1937 had been lent to the new museum, and was at last prepared for exhibition by technician John Poikans. The first curator of palaeontology at the museum was John Storer, a former student of Loris Russell's, who combined a strong interest in Tertiary mammals with an ability to collect what dinosaur material could be located. The museum was able to gradually evolve a dinosaur exhibit, using life-sized models and miniature dioramas as well as partial skeletons to supplement the *Lambeosaurus*.

❖ ❖ ❖

Since Barnum Brown's work, Montana's dinosaur resources had been generally even more neglected than those of Alberta, and there were only occasional expeditions until the 1960s. As in Alberta, new dinosaurs were found in what was considered well-trodden ground, particularly as it was realized that the smaller dinosaurs had been relatively ignored

in the search for large and spectacular display specimens. Small carnivores, in particular, were little known; the first dromaeosaur had been
discovered by Barnum Brown in 1914, but apart from the skull there
were only a few other bones. Half a century later, a small carnivorous
dinosaur became one of the most important dinosaurs known.

In August 1964, John Ostrom (a professor at Yale and curator of vertebrate paleontology at the Peabody Museum) and his assistant Grant
Meyer found a new locality in the Early Cretaceous Cloverly Formation
of Southern Montana. Ostrom and Meyer were leading the third Yale
University field expedition to the northwestern United States in a
conscious effort to fill the gaps in the early Cretaceous, which is relatively less well-exposed than the Jurassic and later Cretaceous. Over 930
miles (1500 km) of outcrops in Wyoming and Montana had been
checked, revealing a number of new reptiles. At the end of the summer the leaders were reviewing possible sites for the following year,
when something caught their attention: "We both nearly rolled down
the slope in our rush to the spot," said Ostrom later. "In front of us,
clearly recognizable, was a good portion of a large clawed hand protruding from the surface. My crew had missed it. I saw their footprints just a few feet away."

The bones were weathered, so had clearly been on the surface for
some time, but Ostrom was excited. "I knew . . . that this was the
most important thing we'd found so far." Because they were
prospecting they were without tools, but immediately began digging
with knives and uncovered the whole hand and some carnivore teeth.
The next day they unearthed a foot, which was even more substantial, with an inner toe bearing a long, thin sickle-shaped claw.

Over the next two years, the team unearthed several hundred
bones (representing three nearly complete skeletons) of the new carnivore. When it was described in great detail in 1969 under the name
Deinonychus ("terrible claw"), it became the best-known example of
the group.

The animal was relatively small—8 feet (2.4 m) long and perhaps
5 feet (1.5 m) tall. It was lightly built, weighing around 175 pounds
(80 kg). The skull had backward-pointing teeth, to hold struggling prey.
Its long arms were clearly not used for walking, but were handlike, with

three flexible digits. The femur was shorter than the lower-leg bones, an adaptation for fast running. The most striking feature was the second toe of the hind foot, which had a huge claw, pointed and curved, which gives *Deinonychus* its name. The toe joint permitted the claws to be raised during walking, so they were probably carried in a position where they did not touch the ground. Thin rods of bone were arranged beside the tail vertebrae, apparently supporting the tail in a horizontal position as a balancing pole but permitting some flexibility. The picture that emerged was somewhat like the modern cassowary, a huge bird that can disembowel a man with a single kick. However, *Deinonychus* was clearly carnivorous. Bones of the primitive hypsilophodont *Tenontosaurus* were found in the excavations, and loose teeth of *Deinonychus* at *Tenontosaurus* sites, suggesting it was a possible prey. *Deinonychus* probably grabbed its prey with jaws and hands, disabling it by vicious kicks with the claw on the hind foot. If such behavior was not expected from cold-blooded dinosaurs, one could almost picture it hunting in packs.

Similar dinosaurs (*Velociraptor*) had been found in Mongolia. Previously, only two major groups of carnosaurs had been recognized, but Ostrom showed that *Deinonychus* was intermediate between the big and small carnivores already known, having characteristics of both groups, as well as similarities to birds.

As a graduate student in the 1950s, Ostrom had discussed the possibility that dinosaur physiology had been mammal-like, but had failed to convince his supervisor, Edwin Colbert. But, in 1964, the fossil evidence of *Deinonychus* demanded revision in the conventional views. "It does not surprise to see an eagle or a hawk slash with its talons, or stand on one foot and lash out with the other," explained Ostrom. "But to imagine a lizard or a crocodile—or any modern reptile—standing on its hind legs and attacking is ridiculous. Reptiles are just not capable of such intricate maneuvers, such delicate balance, poise and agility."

Somewhat cautiously, Ostrom presented the implications of these interpretations in the same year at the North American Paleontological Convention in Chicago. Dinosaurs had previously been assumed to be sluggish and therefore seen as indicators of warm climates, but Ostrom suggested that this view was wrong. "There is considerable evidence," he pointed out, "which is impressive, if not compelling, that many different kinds of ancient reptiles were characterized by mammalian or avian levels of metabolism."

One of Ostrom's students, Robert Bakker, had been present on the dig in 1964, and was commissioned to draw the reconstruction of *Deinonychus*. His graphic vision of a dynamic, running animal became one of the key icons of the next two decades, when new and still-controversial views of dinosaurs were vigorously debated, with Bakker as one of the most vociferous proponents.

11

LITTLE DINOSAURS
AND BIG TREES

THE SOUTHWESTERN DESERTS OF THE UNITED STATES ARE not the most inviting places to search for fossils. Unbearably hot in summer, they are unpleasantly cold in the middle of winter, yet winter was the favorite time for collector David Baldwin. In the summer's droughts there was no water available, but in winter he could at least find water for himself and his burro by melting snow. Baldwin had been hired by Marsh in 1876, and sent to collect from Cope's sites. He was so successful that Cope bid even more for his services. Baldwin felt that he and his finds were not appreciated by Marsh, and he readily shifted his allegiance to Cope. In 1881 Baldwin's headquarters were in the little New Mexico town of Abiquiu, northwest of Santa Fe, which provided easy access to a range of Permian and Triassic rocks to the northwest. In early 1881, Baldwin found a number of small fossil bones which he bundled up and sent to Cope. His original label was reexamined many years later: "Label Sack 2 Box 1 Prof E.D. Cope Contains Triassic or Jurassic bones all small and tender. All in this sack found in same place about four hundred feet below gypsum strata 'Arroyo Seco' Rio Arriba Co New Mexico February 1881. no feet—no head—only one tooth. D Baldwin—Abiquiu." Later in the year he sent in another collection: "Box 2. Contains sack 3. Part of fossil dug out Gallina Canyon. April 12 - May 1. Three reptile teeth. Triassic or Jurassic. 400 feet below gypsum horizon. 180 feet above grey sandstone."

Cope identified leg bones, vertebrae, pelvic bones, and rib fragments of a small dinosaur in Baldwin's boxes. In 1887, he published the opinion that the specimens belonged to the same genus as Marsh's small Jurassic (Morrison) dinosaur *Coelurus*, but considered that he had two new species. Instead of honoring the finder, he named a new species after Marsh's assistant, George Baur, thus subtly fomenting discontent in the ranks of Marsh's team and perhaps hoping to flatter more of them into his service. A larger species, the size of a greyhound, he called *longicollis*, "long-necked." He did not give away the localities, illustrate the specimens, or indicate the specimen numbers that had been assigned to them.

Later in the same year, Cope published a survey of North American Triassic vertebrates and gave more detailed descriptions. He now decided his new finds were distinct from *Coelurus* because of the hollow ends of the cervical vertebrae, and he assigned the bones to *Tanystropheus*, a fossil reptile described by the German von Meyer. (*Tanystropheus* has a skeleton so bizarre that, when found in incomplete sections, the front half was first regarded as a flying reptile, while the rest was thought to be a primitive dinosaur—it is now known to be a giraffe-necked marine reptile, and not a dinosaur at all.) Another new form was described, an even smaller kind which he named after another of Marsh's assistants, Samuel Wendell Williston.

In 1889, Cope changed the name to *Coelophysis* and included all the previously described material. For sixty years almost no new information appeared about the little *Coelophysis*, though a few new finds were referred to it. On Cope's death, his fossils came to the American Museum of Natural History in New York, and the German paleontologist von Huene asked for casts from Osborn, and redescribed the material in 1915. For the first time, illustrations were made available, but von Huene confused the picture somewhat by not taking full account of Cope's original information. Although in 1912 Samuel Williston and Ermine Cowles Case (1871–1953) rediscovered Baldwin's locality, they found little new material. It seemed that *Coelophysis* was destined to remain one of many small dinosaurs inadequately known from fragmentary material.

❖ ❖ ❖

In 1947, paleontologist Edwin (Ned) Colbert of the American Museum was traveling through Arizona with a party, including colleague George Whitaker and Colbert's friend and amateur fossil hunter Thomas Ierardi, a professor at City College, New York. The small expedition was on its way to the Petrified Forest National Monument, a site that was zealously protected by the federal government, even against paleontologists. Colbert had gone to a lot of trouble to get a permit to collect in the Petrified Forest, pursuing it all the way through the bureaucracy up to the secretary of the interior. On the way to the Petrified Forest, Colbert wanted to check another site. He had previously studied some crocodilelike fossil reptiles called phytosaurs, which had come from Ghost Ranch, and he was naturally curious to see if he could find any more.

On June 19, 1947, they arrived at Ghost Ranch, and were intrigued to see that its gate was decorated with a silhouette of a cow skull, the logo for the ranch. They later learned it had been designed by neighboring artist Georgia O'Keeffe, long before she became famous. Colbert was unprepared for the splendid view of richly colored rocks, as the bright red sandstones of the Triassic Chinle Formation formed hills of eroded badlands up to 150 feet (46 m) in height, some of which were topped by chocolate-colored beds of the Morrison Formation and even brownish Cretaceous beds. The ranch owner, Arthur Pack, met the party and invited them all for lunch, and afterwards they set up camp in a shady place at the edge of Arroyo del Yeso. The same day, Whitaker found fragments of a phytosaur skull on a talus slope behind the ranch buildings, and the party spent two days excavating it.

On June 22, Whitaker again found a small claw and some bone fragments on a talus slope about half a mile (1 km) east of the ranch. Colbert realized that these belonged to Cope's little-known dinosaur *Coelophysis*, and everyone moved to the new site. It soon became clear that they had found an unusually rich source of bones. As they dug down into the hillside, they uncovered a number of articulated skeletons. Colbert remembered that "within a few moments of scratching around on that talus slope we had found more materials of the little dinosaur than had previously existed."

The party broke off and went for lunch, and no doubt discussed how these little skeletons would fit into their plans. If the Petrified Forest permit was not used, the museum's credibility might suffer; yet here was a find of special importance. Perhaps a fossil in the hand was worth two in the Petrified Forest. After lunch, they followed the bone fragments up the hill, locating the outcrop, and for two days they dug into the side of the hill. "The more we dug the more we found," said Colbert later. "It was a paleontological treasure beyond one's wildest dreams. We therefore abandoned all of our original plans and settled down for a summer of digging at Ghost Ranch."

As they dug deeper into the mountain, there was a lot of overburden to be removed. The small skeletons were lying in a tangled mass of overlapping bones. Colbert noted that "it was a problem of how to excavate the skeletons without damaging them because to cut around one specimen it frequently was necessary to cut through another."

The individual skeletons were among the most complete dinosaurs ever discovered anywhere. Overnight, the little-known *Coelophysis* became the Triassic dinosaur that could be best understood— once its bones had been collected and described.

The party was not well equipped for working at this site. They were camping and cooking over a gasoline stove, and the Coleman lamp Colbert used to write up his notes in the evening attracted all the local insects. Fortunately, the warm hospitality of the ranch was proof against the unexpectedly extended stay. The paleontologists were delighted when Arthur Pack invited them to move into the empty Johnson house—the unused summer residence of Mr. Johnson of Johnson & Johnson, the pharmaceutical company. "The most posh living in all my experience of fossil collecting," wrote Colbert later. The house even had a swimming pool.

Feeling the need for extra help, Colbert wrote back to the museum and asked them to send out Danish-born senior lab technician Carl Sorensen. A week later, they were able to meet him at Lamy, the nearest railway station.

As they realized the extent of the deposit, the work became systematic. Using pick and shovel, the party exposed the quarry floor, which was eventually 30 to 40 feet (9 to 12 m) wide and ran 15 feet (5 m) back into the hillside. The rough work stopped a foot (30 cm) above the bones, which were then carefully uncovered. They were very delicate, and had to be immediately treated with shellac and Japanese rice paper so that they did not fragment when exposed to the air.

A wooden roof was built over the quarry to protect the bones and their diggers from the hot sun and sudden showers. The skeletons were divided into blocks about 5 by 5 by 2 feet (1.5 by 1.5 by 0.6 m) for removal, and sometimes the fossils were so close together that they had to remove actual bones to make the narrow trenches, "all of which involved much time, much profanity, and many scraped knuckles."

As the work developed, it attracted visitors. Georgia O'Keeffe lived only half a mile (1 km) away from the ranch, and her interest in bones led her to make regular visits. A visiting paleontologist felt that the 1,500 pounds (675 kg) of plaster Colbert had brought from the town of Espanola was far too much, but Colbert had to get another 1,000 pounds (454 kg) before the season finished. As each block was plastered, it was turned over with a chain hoist, with everyone watching anxiously in case the plaster was not strong enough to hold it together. Ranch foreman Herman Hall made a road to the quarry with his bulldozer, and then dragged the blocks back on sleds to the ranch headquarters. The trucker who eventually took them across country said it was one of the heaviest loads he had ever transported.

❖ ❖ ❖

In the summer of 1948, Whitaker and Sorensen continued work at the site, though Colbert had to be elsewhere. More and more skeletons emerged. A most intriguing discovery was a *Coelophysis* skeleton with another tiny skeleton inside it, the first of two such finds from the site. On close examination the small bones proved to be of the same species. Could *Coelophysis* have given birth to live baby dinosaurs, or did they eat their own young? Analogy with modern reptiles suggests that both theories were legitimate possibilities. Some modern snakes retain their eggs inside the body until they hatch, so that baby snakes are born directly from the mother. However, the size of the pelvic opening of *Coelophysis* suggests that it laid eggs, as other dinosaurs are known to have done. As for the second theory, many modern reptiles, such as the Oro (or Komodo dragon), and many species of crocodile, are quite ready to munch on young of the same species that are unwise enough to stray within reach.

The whole team was together again in 1949, and assistance was obtained from geologists of the U.S. Geological Survey. The intention was to relate the little dinosaurs as closely as possible to their environment by obtaining information on the conditions of deposition and their geologic age.

Meanwhile, preparation of the blocks of bones was slowly progressing at the American Museum. The small bones were so delicate, and mixed up in such a complex way, that it was decided to share out the work. Several of the plastered blocks were sent to other institutions for preparation and display, and in due course over the years Edwin Colbert followed them to make careful measurements and observations, for he was committed to the analysis and publication of this unexpected find.

Part of the work involved checking through the literature to see if other dinosaurs similar to *Coelophysis* were already known. Colbert was naturally aware of the many dinosaur footprints from New England (Chapter 6), and soon learned of the little dinosaur that had been described in 1911 as *Podokesaurus*. Although the type specimen had by then been lost in a fire, he was able to study a surviving cast and in 1958 assigned it to *Coelophysis*. It is now known that the New England fossils are later in time, and so the apparent relationship between *Podokesaurus* and *Coelophysis* is rather tenuous.

❖ ❖ ❖

John Muir, the celebrated wilderness explorer, was the first to write seriously about the Petrified Forest in northern Arizona. In 1906, Muir had just lost his wife, and sought solace as always in wild places. He was fascinated by the "stone forests," the abundant remains of tree trunks from the Triassic, and wrote: "I sit silent and alone from morn til eve in the deeper silence of the enchanted old old forests . . . the hours go on neither long or short, glorious for imagination . . . but tough for the old paleontological body nearing 70."

Although he never wrote the magazine articles he had planned, Muir did find fragments of fossil reptiles, and in the same year was able to influence President Theodore Roosevelt to set aside the site as a national monument.

Gradually the fossil life of the area became known. It received national-park status in 1958, and was formally named Petrified Forest National Park in 1962. Over 200 species of fossil plants, and at least 60 kinds of fossil animals have been found there. Although the rocks of the Petrified Forest are of the same Chinle Formation as those at Ghost Ranch, bones of dinosaurs were so rarely found that they were ignored in early reconstructions of the life of the area. As the fossils became better known, more effort was put into interpretation, and Edwin Colbert's wife, Margaret (herself the daughter and granddaughter of paleontologists), painted a mural in 1978 for the interpretive center.

A new bone locality was finally discovered in 1982 by Ann Preston, who with her husband, Robert Preston, was exploring the park for caves and prehistoric carvings that might suggest that astronomical observations had been made by natives in the area. Working in the southwest area of the square-shaped northern part of the park, near Lacey Point, they found three low hills that were almost entirely covered with bits of reptile bone. In the same area was a field party from the University of California Museum of Paleontology. By coincidence, they had come to begin a paleontological survey of the Chinle Formation outcrops in the park. As they began to collect at the Prestons' site, it seemed that most of the bones were a random mix of odd bones from a number of different kinds of fossils. Such a "float" can show what animals are present, but rarely adds much to the information about any one kind. As the search persisted, however, three fairly complete skeletons were located. Along with a fossil amphibian and a crocodilelike reptile, there was a small theropod dinosaur.

Later, a second dinosaur locality in Petrified Forest National Park was found, at a place called "Lot's Wife." The park has older dinosaur sites than any other localities in the area, and they were at the time the oldest in North America, and perhaps in the world. Along with a great range of other kinds of reptiles, these rocks contain fragments of little fabrosaurs, and primitive anchisaurs, 15 feet (4.5 m) or more long. In the younger beds *Coelophysis* appears, along with the first North American staurikosaur found in 1984. Scientifically it is as yet unnamed, but it has been nicknamed "Gertie" after the first cartoon dinosaur. Although it at first appeared to be a candidate for the oldest known dinosaur, it was later found to be more recent than at first thought.

Although the American Museum excavations were completed in a few years, the dinosaurs became an ongoing part of the history of Ghost Ranch. Mr. Pack eventually donated the ranch to the Presbyterian church, which developed a conference center there. When the Reverend James W. Hall became director of the center in 1961, he took a great interest in the quarry, and expressed the feeling that the church had an obligation to protect and develop the site. To gain a better understanding, he brought Colbert to the center to teach seminars about the paleontology of the area. Hall's wife, Ruth, became fascinated with the dinosaurs, and spent a lot of time searching for fossils and talking about them to children in the area.

It was no doubt in part this receptive atmosphere that encouraged David Berman of the Carnegie Museum in Pittsburgh, to request permission to reopen the quarry in 1980. Colbert (who was still studying the fossils) was kept in touch with the new developments. In 1981 the quarry was reopened by a team representing the Carnegie Museum, the New Mexico Museum of Natural History, the Museum of Northern Arizona (to which Colbert had by this time "retired"), and the Peabody Museum of Yale University. James Shibley of the ranch used his bulldozer to reduce the overburden and provided a heavy crane to lift out the heavy blocks when the field season ended. A number of blocks were removed and shipped to the various museums for preparation and display. Half of one block was purchased by the [Royal] Tyrrell Museum in Alberta. One block was left at the site, and exhibited in the Ruth Hall Museum of Paleontology, part of the Florence Ellis Hawley Museum. As the doors would not be big enough to accommodate the block, it was placed in the building during construction. Preparation of the block was undertaken by Lynnet Gillette, curator of the Ghost Ranch museum and wife of David Gillette of the New Mexico Museum.

In 1977, the Department of the Interior made the Ghost Ranch site a national landmark. *Coelophysis* has also become the state fossil of New Mexico and the logo of the New Mexico Museum of Natural History.

❖ ❖ ❖

In 1989, forty-two years after the discovery of the Ghost Ranch site,

Colbert finally published his monograph on *Coelophysis*. He had (as he quite reasonably explained) been distracted by his discoveries in the southern continents (some of these "distractions" are chronicled in Chapter 17). With Colbert's analysis, it was now possible to fully assess the importance of the site. Colbert felt that all the skeletons belonged to the same species, *Coelophysis bauri*. As more and more specimens could be measured, it became clear that the different species Cope had described were all within the range of variation of a single population.

Geological examination showed that the skeletons were buried in a shallow stream channel, and that they had been transported by moderately strong currents (powerful enough to carry their bodies). However, the skeletons were fairly complete, showing that they had been transported only a short distance. There was no evidence of predation, as the bones were generally unbroken, and the tightly closed jaws showed that decay had not relaxed the muscles before burial. Of eighteen skulls, fifteen had the jaws closed—an extremely frustrating obstacle to the study of the dinosaurs, as the teeth are a most important source of information. The heads were often bent over the backs, possibly a result of drying of the body contracting the neck ligaments. All the fragile skulls were somewhat distorted or broken, but most had survived in some form with the skeletons. The tails were often broken off and some separate tails were found in the rock.

It seems most likely that the living *Coelophysis* were probably trapped unexpectedly by floodwaters or quicksand. Colbert had a persuasive early theory suggesting a Mount St. Helens–type of hot ash flow or volcanic eruption. Unfortunately, when the rocks were analyzed, these ideas had to be rejected as no evidence was found to support them. The mineral bentonite, indicating a volcanic source, occurs in many exposures of the Chinle Formation, but is not present at Ghost Ranch.

Almost all the bones found were of the little dinosaur *Coelophysis*, though there were a few bones of other animals (phytosaur skulls and other thecodont reptiles). In Upper Triassic times dinosaurs were a small minority among the great diversity of other reptiles, and the *Coelophysis* deposit was a remarkable concentration, which suggested that the dinosaurs must have been together in some sort of herd when they were overtaken by disaster. This evidence of a gregarious lifestyle is supported by the evidence of footprints in other areas, and it is possible to make comparisons with such modern herd animals as caribou and buffalo. Could *Coelophysis* have been migratory, like those species? Certainly, mass drownings today are usually of migratory species. The *Coelophysis* deposit has juveniles, but they do not dominate, and the sex of the adults cannot be determined. (In many mammals, females have larger pelvises to accommodate live births, but in egg-laying reptiles this is not apparent.)

From the richer environment of the Petrified Forest, we can visualize the world in which the herds of little dinosaurs roamed. Three natural communities have been identified, of which the lowest is a flood plain with cycads and ferns, phytosaurs and fish. A lowland forest is dominated by ferns and the huge tree known as *Araucarioxylon* (related to the spiny-leaved monkey puzzle or Chile pine). An upland forest has gymnosperms (primitive trees that include the modern conifers) and dinosaurs. The climate may have been warm arid or semiarid, or (depending on the interpretation of the plant evidence) a humid one. Colbert prefers the latter explanation, and points to the large amounts of wood and the association of lateritic soils with forest. At the time, its location on the surface of the earth would have been about eighteen degrees north, or about the latitude of Mexico City today.

In addition to *Coelophysis*, the fauna included other dinosaurs (*Fabrosaurus*, trilophosaurs); other reptiles, including several phytosaurs and a crocodile; an amphibian (*Metoposaurus*); and a number of fishes (including freshwater sharks and a lungfish similar to the modern Australian one).

The little dinosaur was relatively lightly built, as it was up to 7 feet (2 m) long, yet must have weighed only about 40 to 50 pounds (18 to 23 kg). In size they ranged from juveniles at 3.3 feet (1 m) to adults at 10 feet (3 m). The smallest skull was only 3 inches (8 cm) in diameter, but the hatchlings were probably even smaller. The biggest adult skull was three times as large as the smallest.

Coelophysis seems to have been a very active animal. Its long hind legs show that it ran actively on two legs. Its tail was used as a counterweight—a modern running lizard that has lost two-thirds of its tail is unable to rise on its hind legs. The hands must have been used for grasping prey, and the long neck allowed it to dart the head in many directions when trying to catch a prey animal. The front teeth were spikelike for grabbing, while the back ones were flat and bladelike, and serrated like a steak knife.

There can be little doubt that *Coelophysis* ate a wide variety of animal prey, which might have included smaller reptiles and even slow-moving lungfish. The little skeletons within the ribs show that it could be cannibalistic. The number of skeletons suggest that it traveled in groups, so that it perhaps attacked larger reptiles, such as phytosaurs or thecodonts, in ferocious packs. Scientists distinguish between "feeding aggregations," such as a gathering of crocodiles on a riverbank without much social interaction, and true herds that feed and travel together, showing a strongly social behavior. The first perhaps is a more appropriate model for *Coelophysis*.

An early dinosaur, *Coelophysis* was thought to be ancestral to its Jurassic relative *Compsognathus,* whose similarity to the early bird *Archaeopteryx* has been considered to suggest a common ancestor a few million years before. Yet, in the 1990s, another group of "small and tender" bones from the Triassic of nearby Texas has aroused a storm of controversy about the origin of the birds.

This find was made by Sankar Chatterjee, a professor at Texas Technical University in Lubbock. Born in 1943 in Calcutta, Chatterjee was the son of a chemist, and his brothers were engineers. He studied geology at the prestigious Indian Statistical Institute, and had found primitive sauropods in India (see Chapter 17) and done other research in China before coming to Texas Tech as a geology professor in 1979. Despite limited funding, he secured support from the National Science Foundation for three expeditions to the Antarctic, as well as National Geographic Society support for his research in Texas.

In the early 1980s, Chatterjee was collecting in the bluffs outside the town of Post, about 50 miles (80 km) southeast of Lubbock. The rocks belonged to the Late Triassic Dockum Group, which overlaps the Chinle Formation in age; his finds from the area date from about 225 million years ago. The badlands had already yielded crocodilelike reptiles and pterosaurs; some poor material had been tentatively assigned to *Coelophysis*, and Chatterjee had found a small new dinosaur which he named *Technosaurus* in 1984 after the university. It was no surprise therefore when he found in 1983 a group of delicate white bones which reminded him of a little dinosaur he had previously found in India. The bones represented two individuals of an animal smaller than a crow, yet the fused bones showed that they were adults. He only made sketches of the finds, and the pressure of other work created a gap of two years before he began to try and interpret them.

As he cleaned and pieced together the bones, he became more and more excited. A shoulder bone was longer than expected, and the neck vertebrae showed a saddle—both features more typical of birds than dinosaurs. The skull fragments seemed to show only one hole in the skull—unlike the two characteristic of dinosaurs. As he reexamined other bones, Chatterjee identified small bumps on the bones which suggested feather insertions. Could he have a bird, dating some 80 million years before *Archaeopteryx*? When the National Geographic Society heard the news they considered a press conference, but decided to be cautious and fly John Ostrom to Lubbock to provide an independent view. After a hasty visit, Ostrom responded that the bones did look birdlike, but he didn't recognize feather nodes and was concerned about the fragmentary nature of many of the bones. In 1986, the National Geographic Society (who made it a condition of their grant that they have the right to publicize discoveries) issued a press release, indicating that Chatterjee intended to name the fossil *Protoavis*, or "ancestral bird." Coming from such a source, the story soon hit the international headlines.

Publicity about new finds is likely to encourage public support for funding agencies, and many scientists (or their institutions) make sure their discoveries are publicized. However, other scientists are more likely to be frustrated by newspaper reports of important discoveries. In this instance, virtually every scientist whose work involved dinosaurs or birds was potentially affected by the new find, yet until a formal description had been published by the discoverer it would not be possible to weigh the evidence.

Chatterjee worked on a paper describing the bones, while a number of paleontologists came to Lubbock to see the fossils. Many of them went away unconvinced that Chatterjee had a bird, putting increasing pressure on the finder to study the possible bird connections as carefully as possible before publishing. In 1991 a paper, "Cranial Anatomy and Relationships of a New Triassic Bird from Texas," was published in the prestigious *Philosophical Transactions* of the Royal Society of London. Chatterjee analyzed the skull fragments in detail, and illustrated the rest of the bones, but left a detailed description of the remainder of the skeleton for a later paper.

Although far from complete, the skeleton has numerous fragments of a skull, much of the backbone, and substantial parts of both fore and hind limbs. A single bony knob is interpreted by Chatterjee as part of a wishbone—a vital bit of equipment for a flying bird. The quadrate—one of the jaw bones—is considered particularly birdlike. Chatterjee considers that the skull is, in fact, more birdlike than that of *Archaeopteryx*.

With *Protoavis* now officially described, the critics responded more formally. Some argued that Chatterjee has not satisfactorily demonstrated that the bones all belong to the same animal—and feel that some of them belong to other creatures. Others felt the wishbone was not convincing, and raised concerns about the fragmentary nature of the bones, making interpretation difficult. The arguments inevitably involved alternative theories about the origin of birds. A convincing *Protoavis* from such an early date would make a dinosaur origin for the birds more difficult to sustain, while those who still felt that a predinosaur ancestor was most likely were more comfortable with the idea. Even supporters of *Protoavis* do not necessarily agree that it had feathers, seeing it as a tree-dwelling reptile which was not yet a bird, and *Archaeopteryx* as a much later evolutionary dead end. Chatterjee plans a more detailed publication of the rest of bones, partly based on new finds which bring the skeleton to 80 percent completeness, and include a better wishbone.

Since the discovery of Baldwin's "bones all small and tender" the American southwest has yielded with abundant *Coelophysis* fossils a remarkably complete story of a remote age when dinosaurs were just beginning their long career of world domination. Meanwhile, *Protoavis*—whatever meaning science will eventually give to it—reminds us that the remote Triassic may yield other surprises, which will perhaps take the dinosaur story in unexpected directions.

12

THE GOOD MOTHER
AND THE DINOSAUROID

DURING THE MID-1870S, THERE WERE A NUMBER OF important discoveries that changed our view of dinosaurs. Those in the localities of Como Bluff and Garden City in the western United States, and Bernissart in Belgium, were all made within a couple of years of each other. The massive fieldwork that followed produced the first major collections of complete dinosaur skeletons, and in turn led to new theoretical evaluations of the anatomy and lifestyle of dinosaurs, which were current until well into this century.

Coincidentally there was a similar conjunction of events almost exactly a century later. By the 1970s most major dinosaur localities in the world seemed to have been identified, and most new discoveries came from ongoing systematic exploitation of well-known fossiliferous regions. Some of the most significant developments took place during studies of the Upper Cretaceous rocks of northwestern North America, in the U.S. state of Montana and adjacent provinces of Alberta and British Columbia in Canada.

In 1970, attention was drawn to Bug Creek in Montana, where controversial evidence suggested that dinosaurs may have lived beyond the end of the Cretaceous. In the same year, Peter Dodson, then a student at the University of Alberta, completed a detailed thesis reinterpreting the circumstances of burial of the dinosaurs of Dinosaur Provincial Park. In 1976, new work started on footprint localities in the

Peace River Canyon of British Columbia. In the much-trodden area of Dinosaur Provincial Park, a new bone bed was located in 1977, which was systematically excavated from 1979 on. Meanwhile, a rich dinosaur egg site was located in Montana in 1978.

Important as many of these finds were, their significance was increased by the background against which they took place. For dinosaur discoveries no longer depended only on new fossil finds, but also came from the reexamination of collections that had been made in earlier years. Both the process of reexamination and the new investigations were often inspired by the asking of new questions. After focusing for almost a century on bones, many scientists were now asking about the importance of footprints. Others were investigating the circumstances in which animals had died and been preserved, not only as skeletons, but in bone beds. Although penetrating observations of these circumstances had been made since the beginning of scientific paleontology, the study of the environmental conditions that could be inferred from the way an animal had been preserved was only named by the Russian paleontologist Ivan Antonovich Efremov in 1940. He called it taphonomy—a term meaning the "laws of burial." Increasingly, scientists were addressing from fresh perspectives the old questions about the evolution of the dinosaurs and their relationship to birds, the extinction of the dinosaurs, and above all their physiology and behavior.

By the mid-1970s, a combination of recent discoveries and new theoretical approaches started what has become known as the "dinosaur renaissance." The power of the media ensured that this time the preoccupation of a few scientists would be shared with a wide public, and the excitement that was generated led to many conferences and publications, the protection and interpretation of sites, and even the development of new museums. These, in turn, provided opportunities for a new generation of scholars to carry on their studies, in sometimes innovative ways, advancing the research and pace of discovery even further.

Although others had raised the possibilities, new theoretical explorations were dramatized by two people. Robert Bakker had been present on John Ostrom's *Deinonychus* dig in 1964, and had moved to Johns Hopkins University. Although he had already expressed similar ideas in more specialized journals, in 1975 Bakker published an article in *Scientific American* entitled "Dinosaur Renaissance," which argued that dinosaurs were warm-blooded and had directly given rise to the birds. Unlike the deafening silence that greeted Russell's similar but milder views a couple of decades earlier, Bakker's opinions were greeted with a roar of mingled enthusiasm and disapproval, pitchforking him into the center of a controversy that is still unresolved.

Two years later in 1977, Dale Russell of the National Museum of Canada convened what became known as the first K-TEC conference, bringing a diversity of specialists together to discuss the Cretaceous–Tertiary boundary and the extinction of the dinosaurs. ("K" is the geologist's abbreviation for the Cretaceous, "T" for the Tertiary, "K-TEC" stands for "Cretaceous–Tertiary Environmental Change.") In the same year, boundary rock samples were found in Italy that showed startlingly high iridium content. Similar samples have since been found around the world, and have been interpreted as evidence that an extraterrestrial event, such as a meteor collision with earth, coincided with the boundary. The controversies that followed have led to the reevaluation of much existing evidence from around the world, as well as the search for new information.

It was less these events than the slow achievement of critical mass that led at last to major public recognition of the dinosaurs of Alberta. By the late 1970s, the new scientific and popular interest in dinosaurs made it possible for Dinosaur Park to be selected as the first World Heritage Site anywhere in the world to be chosen largely for its fossil resources. Shortly afterwards, the provincial government of Alberta announced the construction of what became one of the world's largest fossil museums, building on a foundation of new paleontological work that had started more than a decade before.

❖ ❖ ❖

The Provincial Museum of Alberta had planned to include dinosaurs as an important part of its paleontology program from the beginning, but was not able to hire its first dinosaur specialist until 1976, when

Philip Currie became curator of paleontology. Currie's fascination with dinosaurs began when he found a plastic triceratops in a cereal box at the age of six. Unlike many boys, Currie retained his interest with dogged persistence, haunting the dinosaur galleries at the Royal Ontario Museum in Toronto, where he grew up. At the age of eleven he had discovered Roy Chapman Andrews's books on dinosaur collecting in Asia, which with Knight's paintings inspired an ongoing interest in dinosaurs. He later persuaded his parents to take him west to Alberta to visit dinosaur sites and museums, but there was so little to see that he was disappointed. Currie completed a bachelor's degree at the University of Toronto, taking all Loris Russell's courses and becoming a volunteer at the Royal Ontario Museum. He then took an M.Sc with Robert Carroll at McGill, and had embarked on a Ph.D program when the Alberta position was advertised. Knowing how few positions there were that would allow him to study dinosaurs in Canada, Currie put his doctorate on temporary hold, applied, and was appointed.

One important project was already in hand. Dinosaur footprints had been reported from the Peace River Canyon across the provincial border in British Columbia by C.M. Sternberg in 1930. A Calgary oilman on a fishing trip brought them to the museum's attention, along with the news that B.C. Hydro, the electric company, was planning to dam the river. The red tape involved in working in an adjacent province was sorted out, and as Currie had never worked on footprints, trace fossil specialist William Sarjeant at the University of Saskatchewan was asked to lend a hand. Working in the canyon was not easy—the walls were mainly rocky cliffs (though a rough trail gave access to the shore at one point) and the raging river had 4-foot (1.2-m) standing waves, which could be traversed only by powerful jet boat. The results of a reconnaissance of the canyon were astonishing—there were far more footprints there than anyone had realized. Most would disappear as the reservoir filled, and the dam was already under construction. The initial concept of a small rescue expedition expanded, and Currie led three more annual expeditions to the canyon until 1979, collecting about 100 footprints and documenting a total of about 1,700 footprints, of which many were in trackways,

and the oldest bird footprints known. The expedition was documented in a film that shows (among other aspects of the work) some of the
most spectacular trackways from the air. One of these shows a small
group of duckbills moving in parallel, and changing direction simul-
taneously on meeting a carnivorous dinosaur—a moment of ancient
life frozen in time, showing clearly that the duckbills were behaving
as a herd. Currie followed up his footprint work on the canyon site
by identifying a number of previously unstudied footprint sites at a number of locations in the foothills and Front Ranges of the Rockies in both
British Columbia and Alberta.

Where previous curators of palaeontology at the Provincial Museum
of Alberta had kept pace with the amount of new dinosaur material
that turned up, Currie soon had more located than could be collected. A gradual increase of staff support made collection easier, but
also brought increasing amounts of new material to light, and the paleontology program began a period of growth that startled older paleontologists. Despite the shortness of the Alberta field season, Currie
managed to run around five major excavations each summer, in a number of different sites around the province. Specimens up to 4 tons
(3.6 t) were being removed from some quarries, but most were split
into blocks under a ton in weight so that they could be removed by
helicopter—a technique that now became a regular part of the field
season. In 1978, fragments of dinosaur eggs were found in Alberta
for the first time.

❖ ❖ ❖

Dale Russell (who is not related to Loris Russell) is an American-born
paleontologist who studied with Edwin Colbert at Columbia University
in New York. He joined the staff of Canada's National Museum of
Natural Sciences in 1965 as curator of fossil vertebrates. During his
years at the National Museum, he has devoted much time to in-
depth research on many aspects of dinosaurian life, emphasizing the
Canadian fauna, but always in a world—indeed, a cosmic—context.

Russell early recognized that extended study and reinterpretation of
the fossils of Dinosaur Provincial Park was an important direction to
pursue. In 1967, he brought together a census of the dinosaur speci-

mens known from the park, and published a joint paper with an Alberta geologist, T. Potter Chamney, relating the dinosaurs and microfossils of the Edmonton Formation. In 1974, he was able to establish a palynology laboratory in Ottawa with palynologist David Jarzen. Along with other microfossils, fossil pollen had been studied for many years and had produced much information useful in dating rocks. Russell and Jarzen were interested in the evidence that pollen could produce about the environment in which the dinosaurs had lived. The laboratory gathered a large collection of recent pollen samples from around the world, and of fossil pollen from a great variety of sources in the Cretaceous and Tertiary. Alberta was shown to have the longest clear sequence of Cretaceous terrestrial rocks in Canada. Pollen evidence suggested an environment that was subtropical, with affinities to the Indomalaysian region of today.

In 1977, Russell published *A Vanished World: The Dinosaurs of Western Canada*, a book summarizing in popular terms a picture of the rich life of the Canadian terrestrial Mesozoic. In the following years, he published with Pierre Béland, several papers on the park. The first discussed the paleoecology—the ecology of the past—represented by the rocks and fossils of the park. The second reviewed the evidence for hot-blooded dinosaurs provided by the evidence in the park; and the third explored the same topic from a different angle, looking at predator-prey ratios.

The authors noted that there have been certain biases built into the collection of display specimens; for instance, carnivores are relatively rare, so that any found are likely to be collected. Charlie Sternberg's map of the fossil sites showed a ratio of one carnivore to nine noncarnivores. The exact proportion is potentially important for testing the truth of hot-blooded dinosaur theories, as it has been suggested that cold-blooded predators (needing to eat less often) would be found in a higher ratio to prey than hot-blooded predators. The authors calculated that 6 percent of the dinosaur biomass was carnivorous, which is in the range expected for hot-blooded predators.

Fragments of small carnivorous dinosaurs had been found in Alberta from time to time, but they had been neglected because their fragile bones were relatively hard to find, and they did not make such spectacular display specimens as their larger relatives. Matthew and Brown had described *Dromaeosaurus* from the Red Deer in 1922, and, in 1932, Charles M. Sternberg gave the name *Stenonychosaurus inequalis* to fragments of a small carnivore from Alberta.

In 1967, Dale Russell saw in the American Museum of Natural History a small dinosaur skull collected by the Sternbergs in Alberta in 1917. It was exhibited as an ostrich dinosaur, but Russell was struck by the large size of the brain for such a small dinosaur and thought other interpretations were possible: "I knew the flaming thing was not an ostrich dinosaur, and I also knew that the thing had a very big brain. It amazed me because I'd never seen a dinosaur with a brain that large for such a small animal."

In 1968, Russell's National Museum team spent six weeks looking for small theropods in Dinosaur Provincial Park. Little was found, and Russell complained to park employee and amateur paleontologist Hope Johnson that he would have to go back to Ottawa more or less empty-handed. Johnson connected him with Irene Vanderloh, a local amateur fossil hunter who had found a small carnivore fossil outside the park six years earlier. Vanderloh was uncertain that she could recall the site of her discovery, but when the team went searching, National Museum technician Gilles Danis found a skull of the small carnivore. Dale Russell initially ascribed it to the genus *Saurornithoides,* which had been established by Osborn in 1924 for small dinosaurs from Mongolia, but later shifted it to Sternberg's genus *Stenonychosaurus.* There were no teeth, but the skull cap showed the same type of small dinosaur with a large brain that Russell was looking for. He considered it to be easily as intelligent as the birds and mammals of that time.

In 1969 and 1982, Russell published detailed studies of *Stenonychosaurus,* the most complete small carnivorous dinosaur known from Dinosaur Provincial Park. The little dinosaur was about 6 feet (1.8 m) long, and if it reared up vertically it would have been about the size of a man. Its front toes seemed to have grasping powers. The large eyes, which apparently had stereoscopic vision, led to an interpretation of *Stenonychosaurus* as either nocturnal, or dependent on its good eyesight for catching small and elusive prey, such as small mammals. Russell considered that *Stenonychosaurus* had a brain much larger in proportion than those of other dinosaurs, about as much as a guinea fowl, armadillo, or primitive insectivore—a remarkable amount for a reptile. Russell collaborated with taxidermist and sculptor Ron Séguin to make a model of the appearance of the living animal. After a model of the skeleton had been reconstructed, the muscles were modelled directly onto the bones. A glass-fiber cast of the resulting model could then be colored in hues typical of large reptiles in forested environments.

Russell then proceeded to ask what would have happened to descendants of this (relatively) intelligent beast if dinosaurs had not become extinct? If there had been a continued trend toward increased brain, an adjustment of the skull shape to cope with it, and evolution of an upright posture with shortening of the neck and disappearance of the tail. This led him to develop with the sculptor a model of a hypothetical "dinosauroid," a rather humanlike biped.

❖ ❖ ❖

Although busy in British Columbia and a number of newer Alberta sites, Currie also brought fresh eyes to Dinosaur Provincial Park, the area that Weston had once called "the most important field in Canada." Since Fowler and Sternberg started developing the park in the 1950s, funding had been minimal, and it was little known to the public, even though it was only a short distance from the Trans-Canada Highway. Provincial Museum staff had done some limited exploration, but the park authorities had for a while been uncertain about their policy on paleontology and were keeping a relatively low profile. However, in the 1970s the Provincial Parks Branch decided that Dinosaur Park was a major asset which should be properly preserved, studied, and interpreted. They asked for an opinion on the importance of the site with its 73-million-year-old resources from Dale Russell, and were told that "Dinosaur Provincial Park represents the most important remaining fragment of the dinosaurian world known to mankind." In 1979, the park was made a World Heritage Site—part of an international program run by UNESCO that recognizes sites of unique importance to mankind, such as the pyramids of Egypt and the Galápagos Islands. Dinosaur Provincial Park was the first such site to be selected for its fossil resources, and the selection was celebrated with a 1980 ceremony at the park, at which a special tribute was given to C.M. Sternberg.

Park policies were developed encouraging partnerships with professional paleontologists, and when for the first time it was possible for Provincial Museum staff to undertake serious research in the park, Currie had his plans ready. Within a short time, helped by an increase in budget and staff, Currie had established an interdisciplinary project with representation from the Research Council of Alberta, the University of Calgary, Peter Dodson of the University of Pennsylvania, and Dale Russell and his colleagues at the National Museum. Dodson continued his interests in taphonomy, and Russell continued his broad view of the park, and his interest in small reptiles. The Research Council's scientists paid particular attention to the stratigraphy. Currie himself approached the park with a number of questions in mind.

Almost all the earlier fieldwork in the park had concentrated on finding the complete and nearly complete skeletons that made this park such a special place. Although Currie did not neglect these, collecting around three or four a year, nothing dinosaurian escaped his eye, and he was anxious to build up an objective body of data, which would balance the inconsistencies of earlier years. There were uncertainties about how far the described material (summarized by Russell) could be taken as representative of the park dinosaurs — how important, for instance, was the bias in favor of carnivores, which were rare and therefore almost certain to be collected.

A well-known phenomenon was that of bone beds, layers of rock in which frequent single bones were concentrated. In the park as many as ten bone beds were known for each individual articulated skeleton. In some parts of the world, bone beds provide the only available evidence of dinosaurs, yet they had been ignored in Dinosaur Provincial Park because they had not yielded skeletons, and had scarcely been studied elsewhere in Canada. Langston's earlier work at Scabby Butte was the only recent instance of systematic study of a bone bed in Canada.

Each bone bed often implied the former existence of many individual dinosaurs, but the bones were so scattered that it was usually impossible to tell which bones belong to which individual.

Currie and his staff began to map the distribution of the bone beds, and to sample the bones they contained. A wider survey in 1980 located and documented fifty bone beds, one covering more than 100 acres (40 ha). Many bone beds included a mix of all the species to be expected, but some had only bones of a single species, of which at least nine belonged to horned dinosaurs (ceratopsians), including *Anchiceratops*, *Centrosaurus*, *Chasmosaurus*, *Monoclonius*, *Pachyrhinosaurus*, and *Styracosaurus*.

In 1977 park naturalists came across a particularly rich bone bed, and in 1978 reported it to Provincial Museum paleontologists, who called it Quarry 143. "It was difficult to walk anywhere without stepping on bone," reported Currie. Larger than a football field when first found, it proved to be substantially larger when systematic excavation started in 1979. The bone bed was easily accessible, not covered by other beds, and the bones in it seemed to be all ceratopsian. As only a quarter of the park fauna represented by complete skeletons belonged to the ceratopsiais, it seemed a good opportunity to learn more about a neglected group, and to see what information could be derived from a bone bed.

Using a meter grid for recording, the paleontologists began their excavation. The bed was only 6 to 8 inches (15 to 20 cm) thick, so it was easy to expose most of the bones. Once the scrap bone had been removed, there were between twenty and sixty bones per square metre. At least 85 percent of the bones were ceratopsian, and all of these proved to belong to *Centrosaurus* (now sometimes referred to as *Eucentrosaurus*). Bones of duckbill dinosaurs, which normally provide 40 percent of the park fossils, accounted for only 3 percent of those in the bone bed.

An ingenious method of counting individuals had been worked out, which involved looking for a characteristic bone, only one of which was present in each animal. The bone chosen was the upper rim of the left eye socket, which also bore the base of a horn. By the end of

1980, less than 10 percent of the deposit had been worked, which represented a minimum count of 38 individuals. By 1985, at least 50 individuals had been counted in the area excavated, which if extrapolated to the exposed areas of the bone bed suggested the whole thing could contain remains of between 300 and 400 animals. Eventually, the excavated area was about 30 percent of the bone bed, and represented about 80 individuals.

Measurements of numbers of the diagnostic eye-socket bones provided more information. The majority of the bones represented medium-sized individuals, apparently mature adults. However, the bones—and therefore the *Centrosaurus* individuals—fell into three size classes. There were three small individuals probably less than a year old; more than twice the number in the next size class representing juveniles; and the majority were adults, 50 percent larger in size. Although the adults were of different sizes, growth was presumably now slow enough that it could be masked by the differences between individuals—three-year-old males were perhaps the same size as four-year-old females. These *Centrosaurus* remains, however, clearly represented a herd of young, juvenile, and middle-aged animals. The gaps between the sizes suggest that breeding took place at one time of year, and that the young of each year traveled with the herd as they grew. Rapid growth obviously took place between one-year-old and two-year-old animals, which then slowed down until it becomes impossible to recognize distinct age classes.

Well-grown adults in their prime are usually the least vulnerable to sudden death. It is clear here that all the individuals died at same time. Many of the bones show "green" breaks, suggesting that they were still fresh when trampled by a heavy animal. Carnivore teeth suggests feeding had been going on, as loose ones break when the animals are eating. Later, the bones had been washed over by the river so that each of the skeletons had become completely separated, and the smaller bones washed away entirely.

The bone bed seems to represent the sort of situation in which a flash flood has killed a single herd, in the way buffalo have been recorded to have died in historic times on the prairies. In the winter of 1984 to 1985, more than 10,000 caribou were killed in a similar tragedy in Quebec. Herding animals have behavior patterns in which they follow leaders, usually to safety, but occasionally to disaster. The carcasses were cast up on a sandbank where they were scavenged by carnivores, who tore apart and trampled the skeletons, broke and tooth-scarred the bones, losing some of their own teeth in the process. After the carcasses had decayed for some time, the next flood scattered the bones and bone fragments, and redeposited them downstream in a single layer, which has eventually become the bone bed.

The *Centrosaurus* bone bed is in an area of Dinosaur Park that is not open to the public, but the interpretive naturalists who originally found the site have reaped other benefits. A bus tour has been regularly led by park naturalists, from which it is easy to hike into the bone-bed site. In just one year—1988—50,000 people visited the park, of whom 1,600 took the *Centrosaurus* bone-bed hike.

❖ ❖ ❖

In the summer of 1977, John (usually called Jack) Horner was out collecting fossils with his father. They were in the Late Cretaceous Two Medicine Formation, which is widely exposed in western Montana, east of Glacier National Park, and is about the same age as the Judith River Formation, which has produced dinosaur fossils so richly in eastern Montana and Alberta's Dinosaur Provincial Park. Noticing what seemed to be a crushed lump of dinosaur bone, Horner picked it up and took it home. While checking over his collections during the following winter, he realized that it was a dinosaur egg. He well knew that this was a special discovery, but the Two Medicine Formation was not known for rich fossil deposits and the chance of a further find was slim, so he made no immediate plans to search further in the area.

Horner had been with his father when he collected his first fossil in the same area at the age of seven. He grew up in Shelby, close to the Alberta border of thinly populated Montana. He not only collected fossils, but catalogued his collection, and eventually went to Montana State University at Bozeman with a practical background in paleontology that is not available to many undergraduates. Although he took all the available courses in geology and paleontology, he failed to complete a number of other academic requirements and did not graduate. It was not until he was thirty-one that Horner learned he was, in fact, struggling with a learning disability (dyslexia), and he could hardly have imagined that he would one day be given an honorary doctorate by the same university.

While he was a student at the university, Horner was startled one day to see a young man without protective clothing casually carry a live gila monster—a poisonous lizard—into his herpetology class. Horner became friendly with fellow student Bob Makela, an outgoing enthusiast for fossil and living reptiles. The two continued collecting fossils together after Makela graduated and went on to become a high-school teacher. Horner had a stint with the family sand-and-gravel business, but felt it was not for him. He found another route into paleontology by haunting the meetings of the Society of Vertebrate Paleontology until in 1975 he was offered a job as a preparator at Princeton. There he had the chance to work with vertebrate paleontologist Donald Baird, and to see many of the collections of the established museums in the east.

In trips in his home state and across the border to Alberta, Horner had become particularly interested in duck-billed dinosaurs. In 1978, Donald Baird encouraged Horner to undertake a research project, and drew his attention to some neglected specimens that had been collected in 1900 by Earl Douglass (developer of the Carnegie Quarry) in Bearpaw deposits in Montana. The Bearpaw is a marine formation, which normally does not contain fossils of land animals. Dinosaurs seem to have occasionally been washed out to sea by rivers, or drowned while feeding in shallow water, and a number of other marine deposits contain occasional dinosaurs. When Horner looked into known dinosaur remains from marine deposits, he found that at least half of them were juveniles. Juvenile dinosaurs of any kind were rare, and (apart from the *Protoceratops* nests from Mongolia) baby dinosaurs were almost unknown. Various theories had been advanced for this, of which the most likely was C.M. Sternberg's idea that the young dinosaurs had been hatched in upland areas away from the sea, where erosion was more likely to destroy any young ones that died. In 1978,

Horner went off for his vacation (his only collecting opportunity) with the intention of looking for baby dinosaurs in Montana.

Horner and Makela drove east to show a fossil mammal site to a University of California crew led by William Clemens. In turn they were told of a rock shop in the tiny town of Bynum, whose owner wanted a dinosaur fossil identified. Eventually they visited the shop, and, after dealing with the problematic fossil (which was not unusual), they poked around the shop, identifying other items. One of the owners, Marion Brandvold, fetched two other specimens from her house. Horner later recalled his reactions:

> They weren't much to look at, just two dusty pieces of grey bone, but it was immediately obvious to me that they were the hip end of a duckbill thighbone and a bit of a rib—except that they were the wrong size. The femur, or thighbone, of a typical duckbill might be four feet high and as thick as a fencepost. The femur that Mrs. Brandvold handed me, if the bone had been whole, would have been the size of my thumb. . . . What I had in my hand was a bone from a baby dinosaur, a duckbill—exactly what I wanted, in a place I never expected to find it.

The two came away with a coffee can full of tiny bones representing the remains of at least four baby dinosaurs, including a jawbone 2 inches (5 cm) long, and instructions for locating the site where they had been found. It was back in the Two Medicine Formation, where his egg had come from the previous summer. Horner's vacation was nearly over, and he wondered if further exploration was justified. A quick call to Princeton secured not only permission for extended leave, but five hundred dollars for expenses. It was just over a century earlier that C.H. Sternberg had received a similar amount from Cope, and this advance also led to spectacular results.

The bones had come from a "bump in the landscape" on a cattle ranch owned by the Peebles family near Choteau. The first excavation showed a green mudstone filling in a hollow bowl in red mudstone. The mudstone bowl was about 6 feet (2 m) in diameter and 3 feet

(1 m) deep, and was filled with tiny bones. In Bob Makela's backyard, the two set up a makeshift screening device, using window screens and a garden hose. A sharp-eared neighbor in the local bar had tipped off the media, so that the television crews were on hand as the first material was checked.

The bones of fifteen 3-foot (1-m) dinosaurs were carefully washed from the matrix of mudstone. The bones were not articulated, so the babies had died on the spot and then their bodies had decayed. However, the bones had not been chewed, so predators and scavengers had not disturbed them. At some point after they had decayed, a nearby stream had flooded the area, filling it with mud. The bones of the little dinosaurs had later become fossilized, as silica filled the pores and hollows in the bone. The bones were incompletely fused, showing that they had belonged to quite young animals. There were no skulls (which must have been very fragile) but there were lower jaws, and Horner was intrigued to find that the tiny batteries of teeth were partly worn. It seemed likely that the hollow was actually a nest, and the worn teeth showed that the young had stayed in it for a while. This could only mean that they were being fed by a parent, in the same way as many birds do today. There had been no previous evidence of such behavior among dinosaurs anywhere, but if one dinosaur did this, why not others? A few days' work at the right site was to change our whole understanding of dinosaurs. As Horner said, "Marion Brandvold had discovered a lovely little window on the late Cretaceous. What we did was to open that window and climb through it."

While Makela and Horner were busy with the first pit, the Brandvolds were busy opening another window. They had started work on an adjacent exposure, where they found a skull of an adult dinosaur. Although skulls could not be compared, it seemed likely that this represented one of the adults that had cared for the young. It proved to be a new kind of duckbill, and was eventually named *Maiasaura peeblesorum*. The trivial name was a tribute to the Peebles family who owned the ranch, but the name of the genus was chosen to illustrate the most striking feature of the discovery. *Maiasaura* means "good mother lizard."

Once the find had been made, it was easy to uncover earlier evidence that had been ignored or misinterpreted. Charles Gilmore of the U.S. National Museum had found a quantity of eggshell in his Montana work in 1928, but had not reported it. Glenn Jepsen of Princeton had found eggs in Montana in 1930. Existing finds from the Two Medicine Formation were 80 percent juveniles, but many had been mistakenly described as adults of new kinds of small dinosaurs. In the 1930s, Charles Gilmore had even found seven or eight duck-bills in one pit, but had not realized they were young in a nest.

For a while, Horner and Makela found themselves launched on a new sideline. Makela continued as a teacher, but pitched his teepee in the camp and took charge of important aspects of the dig each summer until he died while working in the field in 1987. Horner continued at Princeton for a while, and was able to secure some support for the work from the university. In 1980 the National Science Foundation took over the funding, and in 1982 he moved closer to his fieldwork, becoming curator of vertebrate paleontology in the Museum of the Rockies, where he was also an adjunct professor at Montana State University. In 1986, he was given an honorary doctorate, and also won a major grant from the MacArthur Foundation. (Two years later, Princeton closed down its entire vertebrate paleontology program and gave its fossil collection to Yale.)

Tentative interpretations of the first discoveries were impressively validated by later work. As news spread, volunteers offered their services. By a policy of initial discouragement, Horner selected a team that was really keen and willing to put up with the discomfort of crawling on hands and knees over rough ground, looking for tiny bones and egg fragments. With an ever-increasing crew, the site and then adjacent areas were studied in detail. One site even turned up when a new recruit had trouble pitching his tent for the bones in the ground, and then had a "princess and the pea" experience that night because of the bones under his bed. After he had shifted his tent, an excavation started that ended up 20 feet (6 m) by 30 feet (9 m) and produced 4,500 maiasaur bones, representing at least 27 individual older dinosaurs. A layer of volcanic ash a little higher in the sequence suggested the possibility of a Mount St. Helens–type of eruption, poisoning dinosaurs by the thousands on their nesting grounds.

Another site in the Two Medicine Formation was discovered when a survey crew came through plotting the locations of explosive charges for seismic exploration. After a whole egg was found beside a marker peg, the oil company was persuaded to choose a new location, and the egg site became known as Egg Mountain. Its eggs proved to belong to at least two different kinds of dinosaurs, one a relative of *Hypsilophodon*, and the other still unknown. The nests were in different layers, suggesting use of the same site in successive years.

Between 1978 and 1983, the team found fourteen nests, forty-two eggs, at least three nesting grounds, and thirty-one babies. Eight of the nests were in the same layer, spaced evenly about 20 feet (6 m) away from each other, and so must have been made in the same year. In 1979, skulls of babies were found, which could be compared directly with the adult skull. Whatever other dinosaurs might have done, there was no doubt that *Maiasaura* gathered in colonies to nest, and cared for its young. They probably did so for the same reason as colonial birds, for mutual protection from predators. Instead of the foxes and skunks that will raid a gull colony today, *Maiasaura* had to defend itself from egg-eating lizards and packs of small carnivorous dinosaurs anxious to snatch a nestling or two. The nests were about 6 feet (2 m) across, and were perhaps covered with rotting vegetation to provide heat, like those of some birds today. One or both of the parents perhaps mounted guard like crocodiles do, and fed the crow-sized hatchlings with regurgitated materials after they hatched. The young may have remained in the nest as long as two months. Their instinct to stay in the nest was so strong that, if the parents were killed, the young would stay in the nest and starve to death. Jack Horner had no doubt that the dinosaurs he was finding were warm-blooded: "The fact that numerous baby hadrosaurs had been eating and staying together suggests the presence of extended parental care comparable to that practiced by warm-blooded mammals. If food was being brought to the nest, someone had to do it. And if the babies ranged out of the nest, it's unlikely they would find their way back without parental supervision."

By the time Horner's work on the Egg Mountain area was finished in 1984. Horner felt the bone bed contained remains of as many as 10,000 maiasaurs. After 1984, Horner looked farther afield, though the museum continues work at Egg Mountain with volunteer support. In recent years, he has started work on Gilmore's old site at Landslide Butte, where there are several bone beds estimated to include 53 million bone pieces within a few square miles. Significant finds include a ceratopsian nesting ground, and a hadrosaur nesting ground 1 by 3 miles (1.6 by 5 km), with at least three horizons of nests. Horner also worked with David Weishampel of Johns Hopkins Medical School on another first—the CAT scanning of dinosaur eggs. Within, they found fully formed fetuses of the previously unknown relative of *Hypsilophodon*. It was called *Orodromeus makeli,* in tribute to Bob Makela.

❖ ❖ ❖

Drumheller had worked hard to establish itself in the tourist mind as the "dinosaur capital" of Alberta, and its homegrown dinosaur museum had been a considerable success. The economic value of coal was declining, and in 1978 three city councillors asked the government for funding for a $5-million fossil museum, as a boost to the tourist trade. In the following year, Alberta minister of culture Horst Schmid announced that a new museum would be built in the city. By November 1980, a planning document for a Palaeontological Museum and Research Institute had been prepared, with a projected $14-million budget. By the time of the site dedication on May 15, 1982, the capital cost had grown to $27 million, and it was announced that it would be named after Canadian geologist Joseph Burr Tyrrell, on the strength of his discovery of one dinosaur skull in the vicinity. Although the building and location were new, the Tyrrell Museum's program was actually an expansion of the paleontology program already under way at the Provincial Museum of Alberta in Edmonton. The staff and collections were initially based in Edmonton, together with ongoing programs which are now usually credited only to the Tyrrell Museum.

In 1982, its first independent year, the Tyrrell was able to put into the field eighteen staff, three professional associates, and fifty-four volunteers. They collected 3,000 catalogued specimens, including 5 dinosaur skeletons. The interdisciplinary approach started at the Provincial Museum was extended by employing three vertebrate paleontologists with different specialities, an invertebrate paleontologist, a sedimentologist, a paleobotanist, and a palynologist. A site for the museum was selected in the badlands of Midland Provincial Park, originally the site of the Midland Coal Mine.

In 1982 the staff and collections moved to Drumheller, and occupied temporary quarters in the town while the building was constructed. Five thousand people came to the opening in September 1985. The museum exhibits include fossil life from the earliest to most recent times, but its major attraction is the huge dinosaur hall. Here, computer enlargements of oil paintings, 430 feet (131 m) wide and 20 feet (6 m) high, by Czech-born artist Vladimir Krb, show life-sized restorations of the dinosaurs that are displayed as skeletons in the foreground. The dinosaurs in the hall include examples of Jurassic (Morrison) species from the western United States and the three major Alberta assemblages of dinosaurs. A life-sized model of the carnivore *Albertosaurus* is particularly striking. Visitors to the galleries can see work going on in the large preparation laboratory. Some surviving species characteristic of the plant life of dinosaur times are shown as living plants in a "palaeoconservatory."

The museum attracted almost 600,000 visitors in its first year, and over half a million in succeeding years. The two-millionth visitor was recorded in August 1989. In May 1987, a field station was opened in Dinosaur Provincial Park, where C.M. Sternberg at last received token recognition, coupled with the name of local doctor and dinosaur booster Anderson in the audiovisual theater. In 1990, during a visit from Queen Elizabeth II the museum became the Royal Tyrrell Museum of Palaeontology. Administration of the field station has subsequently been transferred to the park.

❖ ❖ ❖

Although the Tyrrell Museum is the most striking development in the early 1980s, there were many other manifestations of a remarkable dedication to the dinosaurs. The cumulative efforts of a number of unrelated programs, coupled with increasing press and public interest in dinosaurs, have created a heady climate that some Canadians refer to as Dinomania. Calgary Zoo, whose life-sized dinosaur models were discussed in Chapter 10, developed a new Prehistoric Park which was started in the late 1970s and opened in 1983. There, many new life-sized dinosaurs stand misleadingly within a constructed badlands landscape.

"Death of the Dinosaurs" was prepared by the Vancouver Planetarium as a presentation in 1981, integrating dinosaur illustrations with cosmic aspects of the new theories of dinosaur extinction demonstrated with the planetarium apparatus. In 1983-84 the National Museum of Natural Sciences in Ottawa mounted a dinosaur extravaganza. Life-sized *Styracosaurus* models flanked Alberta's pavilion in Vancouver's Expo '86. In 1987, student Wendy Sloboda from Warner found a site that eventually produced embryo dinosaurs in Devil's Coulee, on the Alberta side of the border, across from Horner's egg sites in Montana. The Alberta government moved fast to secure the site, but the world press moved even faster, and Phil Currie, by now the Tyrrell's assistant director, could hardly get away from the phone for a week.

In 1990, the Hitachi Dinoventure-90 was mounted in Japan by a joint effort between the Hitachi Sales Corporation and Alberta Culture and Multiculturalism. Although the exhibit cost over $1 million, it attracted over 2 million visitors in two months and was estimated to generate $50 million dollars worth of publicity for Alberta's tourist trade. A century before, Henry Fairfield Osborn had started marketing dinosaurs to generate support for less-popular museum programs. Now, for the first time, dinosaurs were beginning to mean dollars in a big way, and not just for science.

"An adventure of the mind, the imagination, and the human spirit." That is the way its originator described the Canada–China Dinosaur Project, one of the most remarkable developments in dinosaur study of the last decade. Brian Noble had training in anthropology, and had worked as an interpreter in Dinosaur Provincial Park and photographed a book on the badlands before becoming a communications officer during the early days of the Tyrrell Museum. During conversations with Philip Currie in 1982, he conceived the idea of linking the dinosaur specialists of Canada and Asia in a collaborative effort, which would also involve the public in a major way. The two areas had remarkably similar dinosaur remains, and yet the fossils of Mongolia and China had not been extensively studied by scientists from outside the communist world since the late twenties.

After leaving the Tyrrell staff, Noble started a feasibility study exploring possible connections with Mongolia in 1983 with an eight-thousand dollar grant from the Canada Council. The original idea was to develop a Canada–Mongolia Dinosaur Project. Although the Mongolians expressed enthusiasm, there was no follow-through, and Noble suspected the Soviets were preventing any action. He managed to make a connection with China through an Alberta businessman.

The Ex Terra Foundation (its name is Latin for "from the Earth") was set up in 1984 in Edmonton as a nonprofit foundation. It developed links with the National Museum of Natural Sciences, the Tyrrell Museum, and Academia Sinica (the senior scientific body in China). Dale Russell and Philip Currie served as scientific advisers. In April 1985 there was a positive response from the Chinese, and in November 1985 paleontologists Sun Ailing and Dong Zhiming visited Alberta.

In May 1986, an agreement was signed with the Chinese for the Canada–China Dinosaur Project to include joint work in Inner Mongolia and Canada. Funding for the visiting scientists was provided by the Canadian and Alberta governments. Almost as soon as the agreement was signed, joint fieldwork began. In the spring of 1986, Dale Russell, Philip Currie, Brian Noble, and Dong Zhiming traveled to survey possible sites in northwestern China. The summer of 1986 brought five Chinese researchers to Canada. Currie was apprehensive about bringing the Chinese to Drumheller so early in the project, as he was afraid the $2 million annual budget of the museum would overawe them, but relations were cordial, and each agency contributed according to its resources. During the next few years, major expeditions were held, producing some remarkable results. (The Asian expeditions are discussed in Chapter 17.) In July 1989, Dale Russell, Philip Currie, and Dong Zhiming traveled to the south coast of Bylot Island in the Canadian Arctic. In 1987, this area was the site of the discovery of a juvenile hadrosaur toe bone by an Inuit, Joshua Enookalook. He was part of a team from Memorial University in Newfoundland, studying the Upper Cretaceous rocks in an area now called Dinosaur Valley. In the summer of 1988, a National Museum of Natural Sciences party had found more remains of plant-eating duck-bills, and teeth of small predatory dinosaurs. The 1989 Dinosaur Project expedition made discoveries of the Cretaceous flightless bird *Hesperornis*. Traveling north to Bay Fiord of west central Ellesmere, they found bones of marine reptiles, and fragmentary ones that may be from dinosaurs. There was evidence that the climate was more moderate then, supporting the idea that dinosaurs could have migrated between Canada and China across the Arctic.

The three- to four-year scientific program was intended to lead to a major international exhibit, with a $20-million budget, which was envisaged to tour for at least three years. The program has been funded by $7.3 million loans from the Alberta and federal governments, but ran into a number of difficulties along the way. Although the exhibition was originally planned for 1989, the starting date has gradually receded as the project got bigger and more complex. However, more than thirty museums expressed interest world wide, and the exhibit has been projected to travel to at least twelve museums, and be seen by 12 million visitors.

❖ ❖ ❖

One of the earliest vertebrate fossils from western North America was *Troodon* ("wounding tooth"), described in 1856 by Joseph Leidy (who thought it was a lizard) from a discovery made by Hayden in Montana. The specimen was a single, small saw-edged tooth, and although more teeth were found in Alberta and Montana, they were never associated with enough bones to give a convincing view of the obviously carnivorous animal. Although it was soon regarded as a dinosaur, there was no agreement as to how it was related, and it received little attention for more than a century. Horner's crew, working on Egg Mountain, found *Troodon* teeth and wondered if they related to the hypsilophodont dinosaurs, but no jaws were found with *Troödon* teeth in place.

In 1983 Jack Horner was visiting the construction site of the new Tyrrell Museum with Philip Currie, when he found a piece of the jaw of a small carnivorous dinosaur. The rest of the small jaw—only a few inches long—was still in the ground, and Currie decided to dig it up later. Unfortunately, the crew could not find the site again, and the rest of the jaw was not recovered until Horner returned two years later. The result was exciting to Currie. "For the first time we had a *Stenonychosaurus* jaw with *Troodon* teeth in it. So we were able to show *Stenonychosaurus* and *Troodon* were one and the same dinosaurs." Clearly, *Troödon* was a little carnivore, as had been supposed; Dale Russell has nicknamed it the "Cretaceous coyote." The teeth in Montana egg sites were probably lost when *Troodon* raided the hadrosaur colonies.

In 1983, Linda Strong-Watson of the Tyrrell staff discovered and collected a partial skull and brain case of *Stenonychosaurus-Troodon* in Dinosaur Provincial Park, which was studied by Philip Currie. The more complete skull showed some other remarkable features. "Many of these animals, including *Stenonychosaurus*, are so birdlike that you look at one and say, 'Well, was this a bird or a dinosaur?' My own studies and those of others have me wondering if many of the features we associate with birds aren't primitive dinosaur features as well." By 1985 Currie was ready to explain the detailed resemblances between *Stenonychosaurus* and the birds. He pointed out that some details of the dinosaur skull are closer to modern birds than to *Archaeopteryx*, long considered the first bird.

During the first China expedition in Alberta, in August 1986, Tang Zhilu, head technician with the Institute of Vertebrate Paleontology, found what seemed to be a crocodile braincase in Dinosaur Provincial Park. However, on closer examination it proved to be an even better braincase of *Troodon formosus*. It was compared to a man-sized ostrich with teeth. Currie arranged to have CAT-scans of the delicate internal structures of the skull, and found a passage across the roof of the skull, connecting the inner ears. This feature is known in birds, but had not been described in dinosaurs. After this, Currie no longer had any real doubt that little dinosaurs like these were close to the origin of birds: "What's interesting about the whole concept of birds coming from dinosaurs is suddenly you're dealing with an animal that isn't extinct any more. The dinosaurs are still alive."

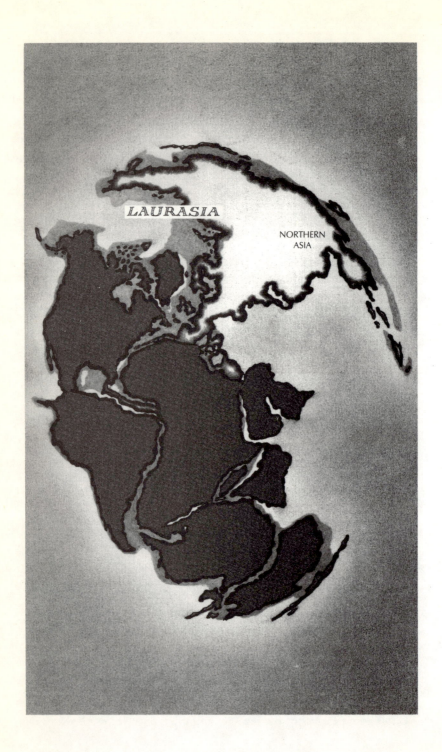

LAURASIA/
NORTHERN ASIA

NORTHERN ASIA HAS BEEN PERHAPS THE MOST COMPLEX CONTINENT on which to search for dinosaurs. Asia includes pieces of two different Mesozoic continents; the part of Asia north of the Himalayas (here called northern Asia) was part of Laurasia, while the Indian subcontinent was part of Gondwanaland. The rapid growth of dinosaur study in northern Asia is discussed in Chapters 13 to 16, and that in India in Chapter 17.

Northern Asian geology includes many areas of Mesozoic rocks, but these are widely scattered and often obscured by superficial deposits. Its geography provides abundant obstacles to paleontological exploration in the form of mountain ranges, deserts, and forests. Lastly, there is enormous cultural diversity which (with some exceptions) has both inhibited the development of home-grown paleontological research, and often discouraged fossil exploration by non-Asians.

As a home for dinosaurs, ancient northern Asia had much in common with the other parts of Laurasia: Europe and North America. Northern Asia had dinosaur faunas generally similar to those in other parts of Laurasia, though there were times when it developed its own unique forms. Dinosaur remains are embedded in deposits of every Mesozoic age. Far from the sea, central Asia developed huge desert areas which expose bones, but which are not easily traveled. Mongolia and China have extensive badland landscapes which are familiar to those who have hunted for dinosaurs in the North American west. Farther south, large areas of outcrop were buried by loess, the windblown detritus of the ice age, and provide fewer exposures.

Chinese culture developed an early interest in scientific matters, and recorded probable dinosaur bones in the Jin dynasty. The culture later became less questioning, and the Chinese simply associated fossil bones with mythical dragons, although the belief in dragons may have originated in an attempt to explain large fossil bones.

Apart from a few early explorations by travelers such as Marco Polo, the West was slow to infiltrate the inland region. In this century, northern Asia was potentially accessible from both west and east, but Russian dominance guarded the west, and the fiercely defensive Chinese protected the east. The Russians made the first scientific explorations, but the 1917 revolution stopped further development for a long time. Many nations were active in China, but it was the Americans who made a dramatic leap overland through China to Mongolia in the 1920s. In the rest of this century, the Chinese, and then the Mongolians have developed scientific expertise, and made remarkable discoveries. Political accessibility has determined who from the rest of the world could work in China and Mongolia, and Russians, Poles, Britons, Americans, and Canadians have all worked there since the early 1970s.

13

THESE MUST BE DINOSAUR EGGS

"This fine specimen of an egg is sold to Colonel Austin Colgate—for $5,000." In the winter of 1923–24, $5,000 was a large price to pay, but it was no ordinary egg, for it predated the first domestic chicken by at least 65 million years. The American Museum of Natural History was raising funds for its next expedition to Mongolia, and as a publicity stunt, sold one of the dinosaur eggs it had found the previous year. The colonel was not after a tough breakfast, for he donated his purchase to Colgate University. As a publicity stunt it was an inspired gesture, and $250,000 was successfully raised for the next expedition. Unfortunately, the museum underestimated the power of the modern press. The Chinese and Mongolians got wind of the event, and not unreasonably interpreted it to mean that each egg the Americans had already collected was worth $5,000. There was already an anti-foreign movement, whose desire to keep Asian treasures at home was only pacified by the assurances of the Americans that the fossils were of scientific value only. The news led to increasing problems with the Chinese authorities for the American expeditions, and eventually fieldwork became impossible. "They never could be made to understand that that was a purely fictitious price," regretted the leader, "based on carefully prepared publicity; that actually the eggs had no commercial value."

The story highlights both the amazing successes and the enormous difficulties the Americans faced in the Gobi Desert. The incident is only slightly less bizarre than the train of events that led the Americans to find dinosaur eggs in the inhospitable Gobi. Leader Roy Chapman Andrews made sure Americans were aware of the difficulties the expedition faced: "It came like a cyclone bringing a swirling red cloud of dust. In less than ten minutes the temperature dropped at least thirty degrees. A thousand shrieking demons seemed to be pelting my face with sand and gravel. . . . We could not see twenty feet, but we heard the clatter of tins, the sharp rip of canvas, and then a tumbled mass of camp beds, tables, chairs, bags, and pails swept down the hill. Lying flat on the ground with our faces buried in wet clothes we at least could breathe."

This desert storm in the Gobi Desert was a typical part of the life of the American expeditions. Another storm sandblasted windshields of the expedition's cars so that they were useless. In the summer the desert, an area measuring 2,000 miles (3200 km) by 1,000 miles (1600 km), can be incredibly hot, for it is in the rain shadow of Earth's highest mountains, the Himalayas, and other ranges. On July 1, 1928, the expedition recorded a temperature of 140° F (60° C) in the sun, and 110° F (43° C) in the shade, yet it could fall to 50° below zero (-46° C) or more in winter. Despite the extreme climate, the desert was not devoid of life. Large desert sheep, gazelle (often known as antelope), and bustards provided food for the expedition, but other species were less welcome. One site had more living reptiles than fossil ones: "the men were annoyed by the brown pit viper, *Agkistrodon halys intermedius*, which was present there in numbers. When the sun began to warm the rocks near noon, these extremely poisonous reptiles would crawl out from their nests among the rocks, and prevent the fossil collectors from becoming drowsy over their work. Each man usually accounted for five or ten during the day."

From the east, the Gobi Desert stretches beyond the Great Wall of China, which was built to keep out the inhabitants of the desert. For the Gobi and the steppe beyond it were the birthplace of the Mongols, whose troops led by Ghengis Khan and other leaders carried out invasions west to Moscow and Hungary, south to Baghdad and Burma, and east to Beijing. More recently, Mongolia has been politically dominated by China and Russia, first by imperialist regimes and later by communist states.

During the 1920s, when the American expeditions were active, it seemed that no one was really in charge. Outer Mongolia was nominally controlled by Russia, which was still torn by internal conflict. Inner Mongolia was loosely controlled by China, but that great country was also in turmoil. Not unnaturally, Mongolian officials were suspicious of the purpose of the expedition, and in customary fashion required substantial bribes to allow free passage. More honest thieves were the brigands—usually deserting soldiers from unpaid and defeated armies. "I am without money—will you not lend me your purse?" was their courteous invitation. Several times when largesse was refused, small parties of brigands attacked the expedition's cars.

The American Museum interest in the Gobi was part theoretical, part practical. As the rest of the world was explored for fossils, the ancestral lines of the mammals could be traced back to the dinosaur age. European and North American fossils were becoming relatively well known and were strongly similar in many ways, yet almost nothing was known of central Asia, which lies between them. In 1900 Osborn suggested that perhaps the evidence for the origin of placental mammals (the majority of living species) might be found in the Gobi Desert. Since the discovery of Java Man in the 1890s, the press took more interest in the possibility that Asia could also be a potential source of fossils of early men, including what they regarded as the "missing link" in human evolution. A rhinoceros tooth found by Vladimir Afanas'evich Obruchev (1863–1956) in 1892 had been the only hint that fossils were to be found in Mongolia, but around 1920 another Russian, Borissyak, found mammals of the Tertiary era (after the dinosaurs) in Kazakhstan.

The Gobi expeditions were devised and led by Roy Chapman Andrews, an employee of the American Museum. Andrews is not well known today, but we can get a rough idea of him from the film character Indiana Jones, who is alleged to have been based partly on Andrews. Certainly Andrews, posed in the desert with his broad-brimmed hat and 6.5-mm Mannlicher rifle, looks the part. His unfailing zest for exploration and his frank enjoyment of dramatic encounters with brigands support the identification, though Jones purports to be an archaeologist rather than a paleontologist and zoologist. Jones has a casual approach to his science, and Andrews too was impatient and often damaged fossils in his haste to get them out. In fact, his fellow workers referred to an injured fossil as having "been RCA 'd."

Born in Beloit, Wisconsin, Andrews (1884–1960) planned to be a naturalist from childhood. "Nothing else ever had a place in my mind . . . to enter the American Museum of Natural History was my life ambition." After attending college in Wisconsin, he headed to New York in 1906 with money he had made by taxidermy. When he was told at the museum that there was no work, Andrews offered to scrub floors until there were other jobs available. He was soon assigned to making a life-sized papier-mâché model of a whale for exhibition, and graduated to collecting whale skeletons, first in New England, then in British Columbia and Alaska, and later in Japan, Korea, and China. Between expeditions, Andrews published papers in mammalogy, and studied at Columbia University, eventually earning his master's degree and doctorate. However, he was not just a scientist. Slide lectures were his strength, and he wrote many popular articles and in later years a number of popular books.

In 1919, Andrews managed to visit the Gobi with his wife, Yvette Borup Andrews. They were on a mammal-hunting expedition, and got as far as the capital city of Urga (now Ulan Bator). By Western standards the country was appallingly barbaric—they were shown the jail at Urga where prisoners, some of them heavily manacled, were confined for years to boxes too small to allow them to sit up or stretch out. On this trip, Andrews saw rocks he thought might be fossiliferous. More important, as Andrews reported: "I had found my country. The one I had been born to know and love." When he was back in New York early in 1920, he invited the museum's president to lunch.

The president of the museum was Henry Fairfield Osborn, eminent paleontologist and architect of the museum's "lots of dinosaurs" policy. When Andrews explained that he wanted to make a complete scientific survey of a hitherto unknown area, he had a sympathetic listener.

> The main problem was to discover the geologic and palaeontologic history of Central Asia; to find whether or not it had been the nursery of many of the dominant groups of animals, including the human race, and to reconstruct its past climate, vegetation and general phys-

ical conditions. . . . It was necessary that a group of highly trained specialists be taken together into Central Asia in order that the knowledge of each man might supplement that of his colleagues. . . . The fossil history of Central Asia was completely unknown.

Andrews's team approach was a major advance over that of most previous expeditions, which had been typically led by one scientist or explorer with a variety of more or less technical or unskilled help. Andrews had also worked out the logistics of a new kind of expedition. During the last decade, while Andrews had largely been abroad, Henry Ford had pioneered the production line and revolutionized the production of vehicles. Andrews proposed using a fleet of Dodge automobiles and Fulton trucks (for the first time in Asian scientific exploration), supported by a caravan of 125 camels to keep the autos supplied with fuel and the expedition with food. As it was impossible to work in winter, the expedition would use Beijing as a base, and the whole enterprise would run for a minimum of five years.

Osborn was convinced, but the museum could not embark on such a venture without special funding. Andrews set out to raise funds for the expedition, embarking on the New York social whirl and telling his story wherever he went. He was fortunate in raising $50,000 from a visit to millionaire J. Pierpont Morgan (who just happened to be Osborn's uncle), and soon got together the quarter of a million dollars needed to start. By now, the press had caught on to the missing-link idea, and covered every detail of the expedition. Andrews received thousands of telegrams from people offering their services for every imaginable duty. Clairvoyants offered to turn their attention to finding bones, young women offered everything from cookery to marriage, and hundreds of boys were willing to undertake any duties whatsoever to get on the expedition.

Critics suggested that "they might as well look for fossils in the Pacific Ocean as in the Gobi." But Osborn sent Andrews's party off on the day of departure with a resounding gesture of confidence: "The fossils are there. I know they are. Go and find them." If they weren't, after all the money, effort, and publicity sunk into the expedition,

Andrews probably wondered how many heads would roll.

If there was no guarantee of fossils, at least Andrews had everything else in hand. He believed with Arctic explorer Vilhjalmur Stefansson that "adventures are a mark of incompetence." Andrews suggested that "eat well, dress well, and sleep well is a pretty good rule for everyday use. Don't court hardship."

He had already seen that vehicles could move with ease over the rocky desert, though the sandy stretches were much harder to negotiate. His plan of combining camels with vehicles worked well, and he stuck to it for each succeeding expedition. The scientists traveled in the vehicles, which could cover "as much in one season as others have done in ten years." Andrews estimated it would only take six days to cross the Gobi in a car.

On April 21, 1922, the "biggest scientific expedition ever to leave the United States" passed through a gate in the Great Wall at the town of Kalgan, northwest of Beijing. Seventy-five camels had gone ahead, each carrying 400 pounds (180 kg) of gasoline and other supplies. Three Dodge cars and two Fulton trucks headed off into the Gobi. The cars amply justified expectations, as they traveled 265 miles (426 km) in four days. Most Mongols had never seen cars before, but Andrews had thought of a dramatic way to soften the shock. His personal tent was colored dark blue and marked with a design of yellow bats, a symbol of good fortune in Mongolia.

The experienced staff of the museum were used to the badlands of the western United States, and could be counted on to make good use of their time if they could find suitable localities. A wealthy young man, Bayard Colgate, who was on a trip around the world, took charge of the motor transport. (Like Osborn, he had a rich uncle, who was later to purchase the auctioned egg.) The expedition included two geologists, as well as Davidson Black (a Canadian doctor and anthropologist from the Peking Union Medical College), and paleontologist Walter Granger (1872–1941), who had achieved considerable stature since his early work at Como Bluff and Bone Cabin Quarry, and had replaced Jacob Wortman at the Museum in 1899. For the early years of the new century, Granger had worked mainly on early mammals. Andrews justified Granger's presence "partly as a gamble, and partly because the man chosen . . . could be counted on to pull more than his own weight whether he had any fossils to collect or not." He was also remembered as a jovial man, who combined a remarkable knowledge of fossils with good humor. He was, in fact, not only chief paleontologist of the expedition but also its second in command. The expedition was fortunate, too, in its Asiatic staff. Merin, the leader of the camel caravan, had already led two other expeditions, and was a tower of strength, usually arriving where and when he had promised, despite all obstacles.

After four days, Andrews "heard from the Mongols of a region where bones were to be found; bones 'as big as a man's body' they said." The area, known as Iren Dabasu, was on their way to Urga, and on arrival they dropped Granger off to examine an outcrop, while the others pitched their tents.

> We were hardly settled before Granger's car roared into camp. The men were obviously excited when I went out to meet them. No one said a word. Granger's eyes were shining and he was puffing violently at his pipe. Silently he dug into his pockets and produced a handful of bone fragments; out of his shirt came a rhinoceros tooth, and the various folds of his upper garments yielded other fossils. He held out his hand: "Well, Roy, we've done it. The stuff is here. We picked up fifty pounds of bone in an hour."

While dinner was being cooked, Granger found the tibia of a dinosaur, the first in Inner Mongolia. No more Cretaceous deposits were found until late in August, but then they reached a badland basin of Cretaceous rocks that had a dinosaur "under every bush": "From our tents, we looked down into a vast pink basin, studded with giant buttes like strange beasts, carved from sandstone. One of them we named 'the dinosaur,' for it resembles a huge Brontosaurus sitting on its haunches. . . . caverns run deep into the rock, and a labyrinth of ravines and gorges studded with fossil bones makes a paradise for the paleontologist."

In the distance a beautiful flat-topped mesa was capped by black lava, but in the sunset its sides glowed blood red. They named the site the Flaming Cliffs of Shabarakh Usu. Although they did not intend to visit the area, a futile search for an expected trail led them to the vicinity. On September 2, J.B. Shackelford, the expedition photographer, walked out to a pinnacle of rock on which he picked up a small white bone. It was a reptilian skull. But the area yielded little else; there were only what appeared to be a few fragments of eggshell, perhaps of some giant Tertiary bird. The expedition camped overnight, but then headed back to base. "We could hardly suspect," said Andrews in later years, "that we should consider it the most important deposit in Asia, if not in the entire world."

When the expedition returned to Beijing at the end of September, the skull was sent to New York. Osborn cabled, "You have made a very important discovery. The reptile is a long sought ancestor of *Triceratops*. It has been named *Protoceratops andrewsi* in your honor. Go back and get more." Andrews, pleased to have the "First horned face" named after him, was delighted to oblige. The name had been chosen by Granger's colleagues William King Gregory and C.C. Mook, and the new dinosaur was later described by Granger and Gregory.

❖ ❖ ❖

By 1923, the conflict between China and Mongolia that presented such a hazard to the first expedition was less active, and the country was more prosperous as the second expedition headed out. However, it was still dangerous—one member of the 1922 expedition had been murdered during the winter, and bandits and discharged soldiers were everywhere. On a solo trip Andrews was threatened by three mounted bandits, but charged them with his car and escaped as the horses panicked.

There were three new collectors, George Olsen, Peter C. Kaisen, and Albert F. Johnson (who had been with Brown in Alberta). Liu and "Buckshot," Chinese servants from the previous trip, were promoted from "mess boy" to paleontological assistant. The expedition returned to Iren Dabasu, where bones of carnivorous and herbivorous dinosaurs were excavated. By July 8, they had returned to the Flaming Cliffs (Shabarakh Usu) locality, which was about 300 miles (480 km) south of Urga. By the time the party sat down for dinner on the first night, enough dinosaur skulls had been located to allow each collector to begin his own excavation. On July 13, George Olsen told his colleagues that he had found what seemed to be fossil eggs.

Every paleontologist has found or been shown concretions (rock structures of inorganic origin) that look like eggs. "We did not take his story very seriously," said Andrews later. "In a small sandstone ledge were lying three eggs partly broken. The brown shell was so egg-like that there could be no mistake." The elongate oval objects were about 8 inches (20 cm) long, and measured nearly 7 inches (18 cm) round the middle. The thin shells had a corrugated pattern. The men stared at them for a while in silence, until Granger could no longer doubt what they had found. "No dinosaur eggs have ever been found, but the reptiles probably did lay eggs. These must be dinosaur eggs, they can't be anything else." Despite Granger's confidence, they couldn't believe their luck. "The prospect was thrilling," recalled Andrews, "but we would not let ourselves think of it too seriously, and continued to criticize the supposition from every possible standpoint. Finally we had to admit that we could make them out to be nothing else."

What are now known to be dinosaur-egg fragments had in fact been found in France as far back as 1869, but at that time no one had taken them seriously or related them to dinosaurs. It was now clear that the fragments of other years and other sites were also dinosaur eggs, and for the first time there was clear confirmation that dinosaurs, like many modern reptiles, had laid eggs. The assumption was made that the eggs belonged to the previous year's find, *Protoceratops*, as most of the seventy skulls and fourteen skeletons found at the site that year were of that genus.

Even more remarkable, the three eggs were not the only ones to be found. Granger found another five, and then Johnson found a group of nine, two of which were cracked, showing what seemed to be tiny skeletons that were interpreted as embryonic young; and proof positive that they really had been laid by *Protoceratops*. (These retained their status as the only known embryo dinosaurs until John Horner of Montana looked at them critically after finding embryos in Montana, and found the supposed bones were calcite crystals.) One block of sandstone was sent back intact to the museum, and was found to contain thirteen eggs in two layers. Andrews visualized the mother laying them, turning in concentric circles, then covering them with sand like a turtle does today. It is not known whether the eggs were buried by a sandstorm, or the embryos died during a cold spell, but certainly the eggs had never hatched.

Crocodiles and turtles were found in the area; sure signs that there were streams and ponds where the dinosaurs lived. The scientists were more excited by other dinosaurs. A small genus was named *Saurornithoides*, or "birdlike reptile," and another, *Velociraptor*, or the "fast-running robber." One small skeleton was found on top of a cluster of eggs, and the collectors envisaged it in the act of plundering a *Protoceratops* nest when it met its fate, perhaps overcome by a sandstorm. The following year Osborn named it *Oviraptor philoceratops*, or "the egg stealer that loves horned dinosaurs." Some tiny skulls were taken back for study, labeled by Granger as "unidentified reptile." So many fossils were found that the last of the flour was used for paste to protect them, and the burlap supplies ran out and had to be supplemented by the team's underwear, shirts, and pajamas.

Another strange dinosaur came from the Oshih Formation. *Psittacosaurus*, or "parrot reptile," is named for its toothless beak. It was at first thought to be an ancestral duckbill, but although there is no neck frill it has more recently been interpreted as an ancestral ceratopsian.

Osborn and his wife came out to visit the team at the tail end of the second expedition, narrowly escaping the Yokohama earthquake. To be in Mongolia was, he said, "the high spot of my scientific life." After its second season, the expedition was clearly successful. It was obvious that the originally planned five years would be inadequate. Another eight were envisaged. All the expedition staff would return to New York to start the study of the collections, and Andrews would embark on fresh fund-raising efforts.

In October, Andrews returned with the Osborns to the United States, where (thanks to the skilled publicity of the museum) news of the egg discovery had been leaked. As he docked in Victoria, reporters from Seattle besieged him, offering to pay thousands of dollars for exclusive rights to photograph the eggs. As they crossed the continent by train, they were met by reporters at every stop. When Andrews gave his first lecture at the museum, 4,000 people fought for 1,400 seats, and the lecture had to be given twice.

During 1924 the scientists described the most important parts of the material that had been found. With the help of the much-publicized egg auction, Andrews, who was by now more involved with marketing and managing the expeditions than their scientific results, raised $280,000 in preparing for the next expedition.

In May 1925, the largest of all the Mongolian expeditions set out from Peking. Forty men and their vehicles were supported by 125 camels, which carried 4,000 gallons (15 000 l) of gasoline, 100 gallons (380 l) of oil, 3 tons (2.7 t) of flour, and 1.8 tons (1.6 t) of rice and other supplies.

Andrews attempted to improve the political climate by visiting Urga with casts of dinosaur eggs and other fossils. Before he left, he received word from Osborn that the tiny skulls found in 1923 and thought to be reptilian had been identified as the remains of the oldest known mammals. At the time Andrews knew only of a similar South African find, though a few others had been made by that date in different parts of the world. It proved that small mammals—perhaps our own remote ancestors—had lived at the same time as the dinosaurs. The expedition returned in great haste to the Flaming Cliffs, where they found more dinosaur eggs extending through 200 feet (60 m) of sediment, as well as more tiny skulls. The association of mammals with eggs suggested to Osborn the possibility that dinosaurs had eventually become extinct because mammals had eaten their eggs. As mammals have since been shown to coexist with dinosaurs for most of their long career, this theory has long been abandoned by scientists, but is still resurrected from time to time in the popular press.

Andrews was twice called out of the field to deal with further red tape in Urga: "The officials seemed to feel it was not reasonable that an expedition with so many camels and motor cars, and obviously costing such a large sum of money, could be coming to Mongolia merely for scientific work. We were under constant surveillance."

Andrews reluctantly decided that further expeditions would be confined to China. During 1926 and 1927, there was armed conflict in north China, in which foreign visitors were being attacked. Most expedition staff were sent back to North America, though Andrews and a colleague remained in Beijing. The only field trip was made to Yunnan province. An intense social round of polo, tennis, and elaborate dinners kept the foreign residents entertained, as did an endless stream of visiting celebrities, including Noël Coward, Douglas Fairbanks, and Lord Northcliffe. At one point there was fighting nearby, and the foreign community gathered for Bombing Breakfasts on the roof of the hotel, where they could watch the single plane of the opposing forces fly over and drop a few small bombs on the city.

The situation continued to deteriorate, and the Chinese government was increasingly pressured by an ultranationalist "Society for the Preservation of Cultural Objects" to resist foreign exploration and removal of material overseas. In 1928, Andrews had to bribe both politicians and bandits before an expedition could even leave for the field. Some fossils were found, but the Chinese would not let Andrews take them out of the country. His collection was seized by soldiers, and he was accused of spying and opium smuggling. It took six weeks of negotiation before the fossils were returned. In 1929, a list of demands from the same group made an expedition impossible. In 1930, the last American expedition included in its personnel two Chinese scientists and Pierre Teilhard de Chardin, the French priest and anthropologist who was much involved with Peking Man. This expedition was attacked by bandits who were only driven away by gunfire. Andrews tried to set up an International Institution for Asiatic Research and secured a million-dollar endowment, but without Chinese cooperation nothing could be done. Although J.P. Morgan was persuaded to threaten to withhold funding from the Nationalist Chinese, President Hoover felt unable to intervene. In 1931 Andrews gave up the unequal struggle, and the American Museum of Natural History expeditions to China and Mongolia came to an end. However, he stayed in China, writing a major book about the expeditions, before returning to New York in 1932.

❖ ❖ ❖

The expeditions had cost more than $1 million. There were many important fossil finds, from a number of different periods, and research and publishing their results continued for years. Although the press had dramatized the expeditions as a search for a human "missing link," no human fossils had been found, though by remarkable coincidence Peking Man was discovered close to the expedition's base in 1929. Ironically, rich deposits of dinosaur eggs were discovered in North America in the 1980s, which may well have been discovered much earlier if a similar effort had been put into systematic exploration of the American West.

As a result of the expeditions, *Protoceratops* had become perhaps the best-known dinosaur in the world. It was known from more than a hundred skeletons—far more than the iguanodons of Bernissart. This was the first collection to represent a cross section of a population, in which all growth stages could be seen, from eggs and hatchlings to adults. The association of the eggs with adults had provided both scientists and the public with a vivid picture of the dinosaurs as they must have been when alive.

Osborn retired as president of the American Museum in 1932, and died in 1935. Besides being a paleontologist of remarkable breadth, he was also something of a showman. He not only employed a large number of talented fossil collectors and paleontologists, but also hired painter Charles Robert Knight (1875–1953) to paint murals of dinosaurs as they might have been in life. With the mounted skeletons of dinosaurs in front of the paintings, the museum set a new standard of liveliness for dinosaur displays.

Andrews had gone through a period of disillusion after his return to America. No longer the center of a major enterprise, he considered making a movie in China with Douglas Fairbanks, toured Europe, and tried to launch an expedition to Russian Turkestan. When American Museum director George Sherwood became ill, Andrews first became acting director in 1934, and later assumed the position. It was the height of the depression, and Andrews continued to travel extensively. He stayed until 1941, when he was somewhat unfairly blamed for the museum's ills and asked to resign from the position. He spent the rest of his life reliving his career as the great explorer, and writing books about dinosaurs and the Gobi Desert which inspired many of the next generation of dinosaur collectors. He died in 1960 at the age of seventy-six.

New discoveries of importance continue to be made as the Gobi fossils are studied and restudied in the light of later research. Barnum

Brown and Erich Maren Schlaikjer (1905–72) did a study of *Protoceratops* which was published in 1940. In 1976, Peter Dodson published further work in which he has been able to distinguish between the different skull shapes of male and female *Protoceratops* by making careful measurements of a number of skulls. New discoveries have not been confined to analysis of well-known material. As recently as 1980, Walter Coombs, Jr., reported finding undescribed baby *Psittacosaurus* fossils in the expedition collections. As the two tiny skulls were under 1.6 inches (4 cm) and thus as small as those of the mammals that caused so much excitement, it seems strange that they should have been neglected. They represent individuals only 16 inches (40 cm) and 10 inches (25 cm) in length. It is clear that they were hatchlings, yet (like the baby *Maiasaura* of Montana), the teeth were worn, suggesting they had been eating abrasive plant food.

Osborn was well aware that the scientific success of the expeditions was limited. Even where the expedition had been most successful, the story of the Gobi dinosaurs was still incomplete: "There are still great unknown or unfossiliferous gaps to be filled in the prehistory of the ancient life of the Gobi Desert. Our explorations have as yet not revealed the closing periods of the Lower Cretaceous nor the closing period of the Upper Cretaceous, in which large ceratopsians like *Triceratops*, as well as large iguanodonts, like *Trachodon*, will doubtless be found."

These gaps in knowledge of the ancient Gobi were to be filled, first by the Russians and Poles, and then the Mongolians and Chinese themselves, with a variety of partners from elsewhere in the world.

14

DRAGONS' TOMBS IN THE DESERT

THE AMERICAN MUSEUM EXPEDITIONS TO MONGOLIA made the primitive ceratopsian *Protoceratops* one of the world's best-known dinosaurs—the only one for half a century that was known through all its life stages: eggs, young, and adults. A further discovery in 1971 added significant information not only about *Protoceratops*, but also about a contemporary carnivore *Velociraptor*, also first discovered by the Americans. Conflicts between carnivorous dinosaurs and their herbivorous prey have been envisaged since the first two dinosaurs were described, and dramatic confrontations have become a cliché of dinosaur illustration. Yet there had never been any direct fossil evidence of such an incident.

In 1971 fossil skeletons of two dinosaurs, about the same size, were found in close association. As they were excavated, it became clear that when the *Velociraptor* had died it was actually holding the head of the *Protoceratops* with one of its clawed forefeet, while the other had been gripped in the ceratopsian dinosaur's powerful beak. Its hind feet were touching the neck and belly of the ceratopsian, and although the bones do not prove it, one of the talons might actually have been embedded in the *Protoceratops'* disemboweled belly. While it is less evident how the *Velociraptor* met its death, a strong butt in the chest from the ceratopsian could well have caused enough damage to kill the animal. With this dramatic evidence it is not difficult to imagine a violent moment in the past, when the *Velociraptor* tried a surprise attack which failed, and perhaps receiving a crushing blow from the bony-headed *Protoceratops*. A renewed attack was fumbled as the ceratopsian seized one of its attacker's forefeet in its mouth, and held on while flailing claws ripped into its vulnerable belly. Collapsing in death, the two bodies were covered by blowing sand before scavengers could find the bodies and tear them apart.

The personnel of the original American expedition would no doubt have been pleasantly surprised by this remarkable discovery. However, they might well have been astonished by the discoverer. In the 1920s, the Americans had found the Mongolians to be mainly priests, bandits, sheepherders, or corrupt officials, yet the new fossil find was described by a Mongolian-born vertebrate paleontologist, Rinchen Barsbold. How could such a change happen in only a few decades?

After the American expeditions were ended in 1931 by growing instability in Asia, the wealthy American fossil enthusiast Childs Frick hired Chinese fossil collectors to bring in fossils. The Chinese revolution of 1949 left Asia and its dinosaurs shut in behind what came to be known as the Iron and Bamboo curtains—the cultural (and sometimes physical) barriers that isolated the U.S.S.R. and China from the rest of the world. The revolutions and Russian involvement in the Second World War left much of the two continents of Europe and Asia ruled by communist regimes, whose behavior toward each other was sometimes friendly, sometimes as hostile as they were to the outside world. For example, a defended border separating China and the U.S.S.R. ran between Inner and Outer Mongolia. In each region, a new stability gradually developed. In a sometimes hesitant, sometimes confident way, these regimes embarked on a political, economic, social, and educational experiment on an enormous scale. Although the dismantling of some of the political and economic structures fills our daily news, other parts of the experiment were remarkably successful.

The spread of literacy and the establishment of universities and research programs produced remarkable technical and scientific growth. State-supported programs for vertebrate paleontology were developed, first in the European countries (particularly Poland, Czechoslovakia, and Russia), and later in the Asian countries of Mongolia and China. This chapter tells the story of the paleontological exploration of Soviet-controlled Asia by scientists from Eastern Europe, while the next concentrates on the Chinese story.

❖ ❖ ❖

Little more than a decade after the last American expedition, the Scientific Commission of the Mongolian People's Republic took the initiative and asked the Soviet Academy of Sciences to send an expedition to explore Mongolian fossil resources. Although preparations for an expedition were actually started in 1941, the U.S.S.R. was soon embroiled in the Second World War. Despite the enormous devastation of the war, discussions reopened in 1945, and in the following year the Paleontological Institute of the Soviet Academy of Sciences was able to send its first expedition. It was led by Professor Ivan Antonovich Efremov (1907–72), who was well known as a novelist as well as for his scientific work. Others on the expedition included Professor Uri Alexsandrovich Orlov (director of the Institute), second-in-command Anatole K. Rozhdestvensky (who, like Efremov, wrote a book about the expeditions), and six other scientists and technicians.

The expedition lasted for two months, and was an attempt to assess the fossil potential of the region. Two traverses of the Gobi Desert were made, one of which was in the southeast and the other to the south. The second produced a major find of large dinosaurs in the Cretaceous deposits of the Nemegt Valley, providing ample justification for further work.

A second expedition took place in 1948, again headed by Efremov and supported by Rozhdestvensky. This time there were fifteen scientific members of the expedition, supported by fourteen laborers. A base was available for two months of preparation, for the place that Andrews had known as Urga was now Ulan Bator, a thriving city in which a university had been founded in 1941.

The party left on March 18, with five scout cars. They first worked south of Saynshand in the southeast Gobi. Moving westward to the south Gobi, the party visited the American dinosaur egg locality of the Flaming Cliffs 300 miles (480 km) south of Ulan Bator. The site had formerly been known as Shabarakh Usu but was now called Bain-Dzak. Here, more *Protoceratops* skeletons and eggs were found.

In the Nemegt Valley area, 180 miles (290 km) southwest of Bain-Dzak, many dinosaur skeletons were found. At one point the expedition driver Pronin found a 7-foot (2-m) thick slab of very hard sandstone, which proved to contain the remains of seven incomplete duck-billed dinosaurs, *Saurolophus*. The site (and its adjacent camp) was named the Dragon's Tomb. Upper Cretaceous dinosaurs were scattered over a region more than 60 miles (100 km) long, and extensive excavations produced a complete, 25-foot (7.6-m) duckbill, and skeletons of a large new carnivore. Lastly, at Bain-Chiré, several hundred miles northwest of Iren Dabasu, a skeleton of an armored dinosaur was discovered, which was equated with a Canadian genus, *Dyoplosaurus* (later merged with *Euoplocephalus*).

When Efremov led a third expedition in 1949 he had an even larger staff of thirty-three, but concentrated substantially on more recent deposits after the age of dinosaurs. However, more work was done in the Nemegt Valley, where the geologists Efremov and N.I. Novojilov analyzed the deposits as the remains of the delta of an enormous ancient river.

The expeditions were remarkably successful in collecting fossils, returning with 460 crates (120 tons; 108 t) of bones to Moscow. The Nemegt Valley alone had produced ten skeletons of the large carnivore and a big duck-billed dinosaur. Further expeditions followed in 1959 and 1960, when a bulldozer was used to dig up some of Andrews's sites.

As the material was studied over the next few years, the new finds were identified, and eventually the best specimens were displayed in the Paleontological Museum of the Academy of Sciences, Moscow. The Russian scientists had access to the literature from the rest of the world, and realized that some of their finds were remarkably similar to Upper Cretaceous dinosaurs that had already been described from North America. A large duckbill was placed in the Canadian genus *Saurolophus*, but in a new species *angustirostris*, or "narrow beaked." The huge carnivore specimen was 23 feet (7 m) high at the hips, with a skull 4 feet (1.2 m) long. It was named *Tarbosaurus bataar* by E.A. Maleev in 1955. This dinosaur is very similar to the North American *Tyrannosaurus*; in fact, some paleontologists feel they are so close that they should bear the same name.

Others presented more difficulty in interpretation. An intriguing

1948 find from the Nemegt Valley seemed to combine the largest known claws, up to 28 inches (71 cm) long, with large flat bones. As some turtles have such claws and the flat bones seemed to be plates from a turtle shell, in 1954 Maleev named the creature *Therizinosaurus cheloniformis*, or "turtle-like scythe reptile." In 1957, 1959, and 1960 similar claws to those of *Therizinosaurus* were found with arm bones attached, making it clear they belonged to a carnivorous dinosaur of some kind. It was then realized that the flat bones were ribs of a sauropod. Although some scientists regard *Therizinosaurus* as a dangerous predator, it has also been suggested that the huge claws were used to open mounds of ants or termites.

❖ ❖ ❖

Zofia Kielan-Jaworowska was a student at the University of Warsaw just after the Second World War when she first heard of the Gobi Desert. The Institute of Paleontology lay in ruins with most of the rest of Warsaw, so the class was held in a room in the apartment of Professor Roman Kozlowski (1889–1977), an invertebrate paleontologist of broad experience. He had painted a blackboard on the wall, and in a bookshelf was the entire paleontology library destined for the new institute. Six students attended the first postwar paleontology class, and, in the Eastern European style, female students were not discouraged from undertaking such traditionally male activities. Kielan-Jaworowska was fascinated when her professor described the American expeditions. She managed to find an article about them, and then a Polish translation of one of Andrews's books. As her work in paleontology continued, Kielan-Jaworowska heard of the Russian expeditions. On a visit to Moscow in 1955, she saw fossils of *Tarbosaurus* and *Saurolophus* in the museum, and Rozhdestvensky showed her his expedition photographs.

At a 1961 meeting of representatives of the Eastern Bloc Academies of Sciences, there was representation from a new Academy from Mongolia. Kielan-Jaworowska's former professor Kozlowski suggested a joint Polish-Mongolian program in the Gobi, and at a 1962 meeting in Ulan Bator an agreement for a three-year expedition was ratified. Kielan-Jaworowska (who was by then at the Paleozoological Institute of the Polish Academy of Sciences) was put in charge of the organization and preparation of the scientific program for the expeditions. The experience of the Institute was largely with invertebrate fossils, and the only vertebrate fossils Poland had to offer were ancient fish and Ice Age mammals—neither providing good training for Mesozoic reptiles. There was not a single dinosaur bone, or even a cast of one, in any museum in Poland. Most of the scientific books and papers had been destroyed during the war, and many of the 200 publications which referred to the Gobi were available only on microfilm. The scientists split the information resources, mastered their content, and shared the important information with the others.

Technical support was another problem. Although there was by now a railway connecting Irkutsk, Ulan Bator, and Beijing, most of the Gobi was still remote and without facilities of any kind. Fortunately, a technician who had managed other expeditions was found, and a list of several thousand items of equipment was prepared, discussed, and acquired in four months. The equipment (including a new Polish Star truck) left by train, and in May the expedition staff flew to Ulan Bator.

The Polish team of five (not including Kielan-Jaworowska) was led by Dr. Julian Kulczycki, and in Ulan Bator they were joined by five Mongolian participants, including two paleontologists, Dovchin and Dashzeveg. (Mongolians do not use first names in their own country, though to simplify relations with Europeans they often take their father's name and use it as a first name.)

Like the first Russian expedition, this was to be a reconnaissance of the southeastern and southern Gobi, locating major outcrops. The Polish Star 25 truck was found to be fine on the stony desert, but it bogged down readily in the soft sandy areas. Fortunately they had added another vehicle, a Mongolian Gaz 63, and the party members were able to cover over 5,000 miles (8045 km) before September. They also found that the Polish and Mongolian tents could not withstand high winds and sandstorms and had to be replaced the following year. Only the traditional felt yurts would have worked, and they were too heavy to carry, though on subsequent expeditions the Mongolian team members borrowed them locally when they could.

The team worked mainly in the Nemegt Basin and at Bain-Dzak (Flaming Cliffs), where they collected a few eggs from the surface, and a number of mammal and dinosaur bones.

The winter was spent in preparations for the full-scale expedition in 1964. The two Mongolian paleontologists came to Warsaw in December 1963 for a training course, where they assisted in the language and the interpretation of maps and place names, and helped prepare the itinerary. A few months before the expedition was due to start, Kulczycki fell ill, and as Kielan-Jaworowska was completing an extensive study of Paleozoic invertebrates, she was unable to be present for more than the month of July. At relatively short notice Professor Kazimierz Kowalski, who was head of the Institute for Systematic Zoology in Cracow, took over the leadership of the expedition. Kielan-Jaworowska did the scientific preparation for the expedition with a member of the previous expedition, Dr. Andrzej Sulimski, an assistant at the Institute. Two more women, Teresa Maryanska (an assistant at the Museum of Earth) and Magdalena Borsuk-Bialynicka (also of the Paleozoological Institute of the University of Warsaw) were also included, with two geologists and a chief technician.

In March 1964 the equipment was sent off by train, and in mid-May the eleven participants flew to Ulan Bator, stopping to see the Russian Gobi collections in Moscow on their way. The 1964 trip was four months long, three of which were spent in the field. The unsatisfactory Star 25 truck from the previous year had been left in Ulan Bator and was used for deliveries between the capital and the field camps. A six-wheel-drive Star 66 proved far more suitable for the rough desert conditions. The expedition had also designed new tents without floors, which were cooler, as the sides could be rolled up in hot weather.

Kielan-Jaworowska arrived in July, and was able to see a *Tarbosaurus* from the Russian expeditions mounted in the Municipal Museum of Ulan Bator. She was supplied with a Gaz 69 field car and, accompanied by a Polish-speaking employee of the Academy and a Russian-speaking driver, set off for the field camp in the Nemegt Valley. The driver sang Mongolian folksongs in a falsetto voice, and was able to dodge the many camels and select the right set of vehicle tracks to follow across the roadless steppe. The journey involved two overnight stops (one in a hotel of yurts) and a 7,000-foot (2100-m) mountain pass.

The Nemegt Valley is a closed basin, its sides scarred by ravines, and its bottom containing salt lakes which dry up as the summer advances. Spiny and scented shrubs are browsed by gazelles, mountain sheep, and ibexes. Geologically it contained outcrops both of the Cretaceous (the last dinosaur age) and the post-dinosaur Paleocene. In the Cretaceous site at Tsagan Khushu the paleontologists had found dozens of small turtles, fossil tree trunks and single dinosaur bones. Kielan-Jaworowska later recalled an important find: "While I was walking with Gwidon Jakubowski and looking at the exposed light-colored and red Cretaceous sandstone strata, he showed me a place where bones were showing through a wall about 7 feet down. These bones were about 8 feet apart, and it could be assumed that they belonged to a single skeleton."

The bones proved to be part of a small *Tarbosaurus* skull, so the excavation continued.

> After a few days we were able to gaze at an almost complete, excellently preserved tarbosaur skeleton lying on its side with its head thrown back, its legs drawn up, and its tail bent. The bones protruding from the other spot in the wall formed part of the tail, which was arched back with its tip close to its head. The skeleton . . . had been preserved in the exact position in which the animal had met its death 80 million years ago. Dead camels are often found in the desert in the same posture of agony, head thrown back and legs drawn up.

Only the end of the tail, part of the lower jaw, and the right forelimb were missing. The animal was about 25 feet (7.6 m) long, and was eventually transported in 16 crates. It was the first dinosaur ever collected by the Polish expeditions, and the first to be mounted in Warsaw, where a cast was made of the animal as it was found before it was fully removed from its rock matrix.

Nearby, a smaller dinosaur was found, which seemed to be one of the bird mimics so well known from North America. The Russians had found fragments of these, but no complete skeletons, and when its finder, Wojciech Skarzynski, announced at dinner that he had found the skull, everyone went up to the site to have a look. It was the first ornithomimid (bird mimic) skull from Asia. Unfortunately the 8-foot (2.4 m) animal was short its forelimbs and neck vertebrae. Even so, this news was so exciting that, in the absence of any vehicles, Teresa Maryanska walked the 5 miles (8 km) to the other camp to pass on the news. Kielan-Jaworowska later found a much bigger ornithomimid, about 17 feet (5 m) long.

Short trips were planned to other sites that had been visited by the Russians, including the Dragon's Tomb at Altan Ula. Kielan-Jaworowska and her colleagues hunted through the wilderness of badlands until she noticed a broken board. She soon located further wooden fragments, marking the place where bones had been crated, and then recognized the Dragon's Tomb from Russian photographs. Calling from the highest point, she attracted the attention of her colleagues, who arrived fifteen minutes later. Some bones were still there, but they were fragmentary, the sandstone was too hard, and the distances too great to allow any more to be collected. However, another fossiliferous locality had been noted for the following season.

The success of a two-day reconnaissance trip to Nemegt depended on finding the Russian camp to locate the fossiliferous beds. Again there was a large area of badlands to search. Toward evening, the setting sun revealed faint impressions in the gravel. These proved to be old vehicle tracks which led them to a camp site, where a small amount of debris and a carved sign in Russian marked the place where fossils could be found in abundance.

Although Kielan-Jaworowska had to return, the rest of the expedition continued and made a final reconnaissance further west in the Altan Ula outcrops, before moving on to Bain-Dzak. There they collected *Protoceratops* skulls and eggs, the first complete skeleton with skull of the armored dinosaur *Pinacosaurus*, and some Cretaceous mammal skulls. A final trip led into the Trans-Altaian Gobi before returning to Ulan Bator on September 10.

❖ ❖ ❖

After two expeditions, the Polish–Mongolian program already had much of the equipment needed in Mongolia for the third. In 1965, another six-wheel-drive Star 66 came with a bonus—a mechanic who wanted to see the vehicle in action in severe conditions. More visitors from Mongolia helped with the preparations in Poland, while the Polish Institute acquired scientific equipment it had promised to donate to the Mongolian Academy. A doctor was persuaded to come along for emergencies, and (since he could expect to be unemployed most of the time) to act as cook. The 1964 expedition had been well supplied with canned meat, vegetables, fruits, and preserves, but no condiments had been provided, and the meals had been insipid. Even though they were geologists and paleontologists, the "expedition's ladies" (this time including Kielan-Jaworowska on a full-time basis) planned the food with care. They listed bay leaves, marjoram, cinnamon, and other flavorings, but the shopping was delegated to students, so that the exhibition members found a large oversupply of spices when the packages were eventually opened. There was enough yeast to stock a dozen expeditions, and the residue was presented to a Mongolian bakery when the expedition ended. Although ready to handle the food when necessary, Kielan-Jaworowska could hold her own in tougher circumstances. In an incident which is not in the official account of the expeditions, her Mongolian guide once became very drunk on vodka, and she promptly took charge and drove the heavy truck.

The expedition planned to work in two groups with several additional vehicles. One would work at Bain-Dzak and look for more tiny mammals. (The Americans had had no doubt that these were contemporaries of the dinosaurs, but Russian scientists had disagreed, and the question had to be resolved.) The larger group would continue work in the Nemegt Valley, and later, the two groups would combine and move on to Tertiary deposits.

The combined parties set off on June 1. The weather was wetter than usual, but was still very hot. The camp routine involved rising at 6:30, eating breakfast at 7:00, and heading for the field at 7:30. A midday break was extended for several hours in the hottest weather, when temperatures were often over 100° F (37° C), and expedition members rested on their mattresses in the shade of the trucks. Then an evening work session from about 5:00 to 8:00 was followed by supper at 8:30. Water had to be brought from a distance, not only for drinking and washing, but for the plaster used in the excavations. The expedition recruited six laborers from the area, four men and two women.

The Poles and Mongols had separate camps close together, and despite language difficulties, relations were good. Some of the Poles had tried to learn Mongolian, but with little success. However, Dovchin, and later in July the geologist Barsbold, had languages in common with the Poles, which made communication practical.

The first few days at Altan Ula were frustrating, as a number of dinosaurs were found that were so eroded that they were uncollectable. Others were in better shape, but were showing in the sides of ravines, 30 feet (9 m) or more below the surface, so that it was impractical to excavate them. The first significant discovery was the pelvis of a quadrupedal dinosaur, which was so big that it ended up in a box weighing 2.5 tons (2.25 t), while the spinal column of a duck-bill, *Saurolophus*, was the best find.

There was more excitement on the fifth day, at a site about an hour's walk from camp.

> The bones looked very interesting. Lying in a patch of shifting sand on the surface was a long, dark, thick bone over 3 feet long. . . . About 10 feet away was another large flat bone, with rounded edges, perhaps a part of the scapula. As soon as the covering sand had been removed . . . we saw that there were more bones a little further down, and that these were whiter and in a better state of preservation. . . . The arrangement of the bones indicated that the skeleton had been preserved almost intact.

Unfortunately it was on a high rocky plateau some way from the nearest possible approach by truck. Despite the difficulties, most of the workers were on the site the next day. They started to trench down toward the bones, repairing the fragile ones near the surface by gluing with polystyrene, and finding the lower ones firmly embedded in hard rock. The weather was at its hottest, and a single parasol provided the only shade.

As the skeleton became clearly outlined, a ditch was dug around it. The only accident occurred when one of the Mongolian laborers, a sixteen-year-old woman, had a pick driven into her hand. Although she wanted to continue working, she was sent back to camp, where the surgeon was faced with his first patient. Later, another pick crunched through bone, but it was the dinosaur's—the line drawn for the trench was by no means big enough to enclose the entire animal.

With the new perception of its size, the puzzle of identification deepened. Elsewhere, only sauropods were as large as this, but these beds were Late Cretaceous, and there were no certain reports of sauropods from these beds, though occasional bones that might be sauropod had been found by the Soviet paleontologists. However, once an enormous femur and 5-foot (1.5-m) ribs had been uncovered, it was clear that it could not be anything else. The largest limb bones had to be broken in several pieces before they could be moved, but the backbone and pelvis were embedded in hard rock, and had to be moved intact. As if to confirm the diagnosis, a sauropod skull was found at a different site.

While the big dinosaur was being excavated, Kielan-Jaworowska traveled over to the other camp at Bain-Dzak. A bottle cap printed in English was the only debris found from the American expedition, but it was enough to confirm the site location, with the help of a local man who had worked for the Americans forty-three years earlier. The expedition had found more mammal skulls, and some of them were definitely associated with the dinosaurs, so their age was no longer in doubt.

Back at Altan Ula, the sauropod excavation was completed, and a tarbosaur skeleton was being excavated. At another locality, Kielan-Jaworowska found some other bones with a 12-inch (30-cm) claw. With help, she excavated the forelimbs and shoulder girdle of an amazing animal, and found the rest had long disappeared. Each clawed forelimb was 8 feet, 6 inches (2.6 m) long, and the fossil seemed to represent an entirely new group of carnivorous dinosaurs. Although the season was winding down, two more tarbosaur skeletons were found, one of which had to be excavated and packed in four days. In the last few days, Kielan-Jaworowska was begging her colleagues not to find any more large skeletons, but an ornithomimid skeleton (without a skull), a tarbosaur pelvis, and a skull 30 feet (9 m) up a cliff were all found and collected. As the field season was nearing its end, there was time for celebration. Late in July the Polish party invited their Mongolian colleagues to celebrate a Polish national holiday, with games round the bonfire. A few days later, local Mongols invited the party to a traditional dinner. In a yurt, twenty Poles and Mongolians were entertained to a dinner of boiled mutton with macaroni, washed down with kumiss (fermented mare's milk) and tea.

Finally, at the end of July, the group moved on to Nemegt, where ostrich dinosaurs and more *Tarbosaurus* remains were found. Kielan-Jaworowska also located a 10-inch (25-cm) skull, which seemed to be related to the Canadian bone-headed dinosaur *Pachycephalosaurus*. The expedition left the valley on August 17, and caught up with the sauropod at the depot in Dalan Dzadgad. It was now completely packed in 35 crates, of which the largest weighed more than a ton. Although many specimens had gone forward to Ulan Bator, 100 crates, weighing more than 20 tons (18 t), had to be transported. After several months in the desert, the Polish males had grown impressive beards, which they considered as big an achievement as the fossils that had been discovered. A committee of three Poles and three Mongolians divided the fossil material between the two Institutes, and the personnel of the expeditions finally parted company at the beginning of September.

❖ ❖ ❖

The Polish and Mongolian academies have maintained an ongoing relationship, and paleontologists from both have continued to study the new material that emerged from the three expeditions, and others in the late 1960s and early 1970s. The mysterious animal with the huge forearms was given the apt name *Deinocheirus*, or "terrible hand," by Polish paleontologists Halzska Osmolska and Ewa Roniewicz in 1967. Without new material, its relationships and behavior remain obscure, though startling interpretations have been made from time to time, such as the idea that it had habits like a sloth's and hung from trees. The huge sauropod (missing mainly its head and neck) was named in 1977 by Kielan-Jaworowska's colleague Magdalena Borsuk-Bialynicka. She called it *Opisthocoelicaudia*, which means "tail vertebrae cupped at the back."

In 1972 the Soviets apparently intervened to prevent further Polish fieldwork in Mongolia, and a Soviet–Mongolian expedition found some exciting material, including five new skeletons of the "egg stealer" *Oviraptor*. Dr. Rinchen Barsbold has published preliminary accounts showing the presence of collar bones that are combined to form a birdlike furcula, or wishbone. This bone had been thought to be absent in dinosaurs, which obscured the otherwise close relationships between dinosaurs and birds. Another dinosaur-bird link was provided by *Avimimus*, described by the Russian Sergei Mikhailovich Kurzanov in 1981, which seems to have signs of feather attachments on the bones of the forearm.

Mongolia has now produced more kinds of dinosaurs than any other nation but China and the United States. Russian and Polish paleontologists have described many of them. The Polish team are perhaps the strongest group of women vertebrate paleontologists anywhere in the world, and they have continued to work on Mongolian material from the earlier expeditions even though new fieldwork has been impracticable. New genera of dinosaurs from Mongolia are now being regularly described by the Mongolians themselves, particularly Altangerel Perle and Rinchen Barsbold. In a remarkably short time, outside exploration of what were locally regarded as tombs of the dragons have been replaced by a systematic study of the dinosaurs by locally born paleontologists.

15

DRAGONS OF CHINA AND JAPAN

THE FIRST SERIOUS MODERN WORK ON CHINESE vertebrate fossils was not based on scientific excavation, but on a collection of "dragon bones" purchased from drugstores. In 1899 German naturalist K.A. Haberer went to China, intending to explore the interior. The Boxer Rebellion was raging, and Haberer was unable to travel beyond the ports, so he acquired a large collection of bones from Chinese apothecaries. In 1903 Max Schlosser of Munich recognized ninety different fossil mammals from the collection.

The Boxer Rebellion was only one of many episodes of great political and military unrest in East Asia, which have continued throughout the twentieth century. Until the establishment of the People's Republic in 1949, mainland China was frequently embroiled in social and political upheaval, civil war, and foreign occupation. During the Cultural Revolution (1966–69) intellectuals and other experts came under attack, and many had to spend time in labor camps, and Chinese universities, museums, and research institutes closed down for a decade. Even after the Cultural Revolution, fluctuations in China's political climate have continued to affect the freedom with which Chinese scientists can pursue their work, and the accessibility of China to foreigners.

In the early years of the twentieth century, Europeans who ventured into the Orient were mainly traders and missionaries, but there has been a long tradition of European and American Orientalists who lived or traveled in China and Japan, learned Eastern languages, and collected specimens and works of art and interpreted science, history, and culture. As the century continued, many foreign professors were appointed to Chinese colleges and universities, and they formed a community of international scholars. So international was this colony that a story is told of a dinner party at the home of Canadian doctor Davidson Black in which the male scientists (whose education included several languages) withdrew to one room and talked, while Mrs. Black found herself hostess to a group of wives who found they did not have a single language in common.

Some Chinese received scientific education at home or abroad, so that when the Geological Survey of China was established it was possible to appoint a Chinese director, Dr. Wong Wen-hao. Gradually, the developing picture of Chinese geology showed the presence of extensive deposits of Mesozoic rocks, often covered in some areas by thick, windblown loess deposits. There were fossils to be found, but the earliest discoveries had been removed from China and were not studied or described until later years.

❖ ❖ ❖

The first dinosaur finds had been made early in the century, but were not recognized until the 1930s. A Russian, Colonel Manakin, was traveling along the Amur River between Russia and the Chinese province of Manchuria in 1902, when he collected some large fossils that had been discovered by local fishermen on the Chinese side of the river. They were thought at first to be bones of a Siberian mammoth, and the news led to an expedition by Ukrainian paleobotanist Afrikan Nikolaevich Kryshtofovitch (1885–1953) and Russian V.P. Renngarten during 1915 to 1917. They excavated the site at a place called Yuliangzi. The fossils were taken to St. Petersburg in 1917, the year of the Russian Revolution, so it is not surprising that the fossil was not named until 1935. Anatoliy N. Riabinin found it was a flat-headed hadrosaur, and named it *Mandschurosaurus amurensis*, or "Manchurian reptile from the Amur." The skeleton went on display in the Central Geological Museum, Leningrad, as St. Petersburg was by then called.

An American paleontologist, George Davis Louderback (1874–1957) from the University of California at Berkeley, was prospecting for oil when he found fossil remains in the Sichuan (Szechuan) Basin in 1913. He took a tooth and thighbone back to Berkeley, but they were not studied until 1935, when they were identified as belonging to a carnivorous dinosaur.

Also in 1913, a German missionary, Brother R. Mertens, found a large partial skeleton of a dinosaur in China's Shandong Province, but it was not reported to professional paleontologists. From the same area, a German mining engineer, W. Behagel, contributed a block of sandstone containing three fossil vertebrae to the Chinese Geological Survey.

After travels to both the Arctic and Antarctic, Swedish geologist Johann Gunnar Andersson (1874–1960) had been hired by the Chinese Geological Survey to search for coal and ores, and between 1914 and 1924 he traveled widely through China. Andersson's interests ranged beyond economic minerals, and when he asked about fossils, he found "dragon stories" everywhere he went.

He was aware that the "dragon bones" which were available for purchase in every drugstore in China were in fact the fossil bones and teeth of a wide range of extinct animals, but found the sources of the bones were kept secret by the pharmacists. However, Andersson began inquiring about bones from missionaries, and had begun to have some success at locating fossil sites, but had too many other duties to successfully pursue the leads. He approached Professor Carl Wiman of the University of Uppsala, who persuaded a young Austrian paleontologist, Otto Zdansky, to spend two years in China helping Andersson with fossil work. Zdansky succeeded in locating some of the sources of dragon bones, and provided the first account of their mining to the Western world. He found that the miners understood that they were excavating fossil bones, and by paying more than the druggists, he managed to secure new collections.

When he saw the vertebrae Behagel had given to the Geological Survey, Zdansky thought they were from a dinosaur, and called in Walter Granger of the American expedition to confirm the opinion. In 1922 Andersson and Chinese geologist H.C. T'an followed the clue, traveling to Shandong by railway and then push-cart, powered by a tough peasant, assisted by a sail in suitable weather. T'an located bones near the village of Ning Chia Kou, and only then did local missionaries tell them of Mertens's earlier find. Andersson encouraged cooperation between T'an (the "field worker and pioneer") and Zdansky (the "highly trained paleontologist . . . [and] incomparable technical expert"), and in the following year, both continued to work in the area. The bones had just been wrapped with bandages dipped in gum when a band of robbers attacked the neighboring town, causing the collectors to seek refuge When Zdansky returned to the site, he found that the curious robbers had stripped the bandages off the bones, but done no other damage.

The main find was a partial vertebral column about 29 feet (8.8 m) long, representing an animal at least 60 feet (18.3 m) long. Andersson sent the bones to Wiman at Uppsala, and he named a new species of dinosaur in 1929. Wiman was fascinated by its large feet, which he considered to have been an adaptation to walking in soft ground, like the mud shoes used by Swedish travelers. He called it *Helopus zdanskyi,* but when the generic name proved to have been used before, it was renamed *Euhelopus* in 1956 by the eminent vertebrate paleontologist Alfred Sherwood Romer (1894-1973). The full name now means "Zdansky's good marsh foot," and it is a late Jurassic sauropod, which may be related to *Brachiosaurus* or *Camarasaurus.* T'an also found stegosaur bones, the first from Asia. In the following year, 1923, T'an found and Zdansky collected a duckbill from the same area. Wiman named it *Tanius sinensis* in honor of the Chinese geologist.

Paleontology in China got great impetus from a fossil site at Choukoutien (southwest of Beijing) known as Chicken Bone Hill. It was known as a source of mammal bones from 1918, but became famous after 1926 as the source of Peking Man. Work at this site was internationally supported by the Rockefeller Foundation, and research was concentrated in the Institute of Vertebrate Paleontology in Beijing. At this institution, international paleontologists and paleoanthropologists, such as Canadian surgeon Davidson Black (1884–1934) and the French priest Pierre Teilhard de Chardin (1881–1955), made their reputations, and the first Chinese paleontologists were trained. So small was the paleontological community that many of those involved with Peking Man also worked on dinosaurs. A particularly important figure at the Institute was C.C. Young (1897–1979). (Chinese personal names differ from Western ones in that the surname comes first. In the early part of the century, Chinese scientists who associated with Western scholars sometimes anglicized their names. Young, for instance is also known as Young Chung Chien and Yang Zhong-jian.)

Young (who had been at school with Mao Tse-tung) studied in the United States, Canada, and England, and also with German paleontologist von Huene. He returned to China in 1928, went on an expedition with Andrews, and worked on the fossil mammals of the Peking Man site as assistant director and paleontologist of the Cenozoic Research Laboratory. In 1936 he led a joint Sino-American expedition to Sichuan, where Young and Californian Charles Lewis Camp (1893–1975) found a sauropod which Young named *Omeisaurus* in 1939. The name is derived from the nearby sacred mountain, Mount Omei, and the dinosaur is notable for a remarkably long, lightly constructed neck.

Between 1927 and 1931 China and Sweden jointly sponsored the German-funded Sino–Swedish Northwest China Expeditions, led by Swede Sven Hedin and Chinese geologist F. Yuan. A good many fragmentary remains of dinosaurs were collected, but they were not described until Swedish paleontologist Anders Birger Bohlin studied them in 1953.

❖ ❖ ❖

By the 1930s the Chinese were playing a major role in the scientific exploration of their country. In 1929 a Cenozoic Research Laboratory was set up to deal with the work at the Peking Man site, with Canadian Davidson Black as honorary director. Later, a German, Franz Weidenreich (1873–1947), ran the laboratory for some years before leaving for the American Museum of Natural History in 1941. C.C. Young then took charge, evacuated the laboratory to southwest China during wartime, and, in 1959, became director of a new Institute of Vertebrate Paleontology and Paleoanthropology, with interests in vertebrate fossils of all ages throughout China.

Late in the decade, the geologist and paleontologist M.N. Bien (Bien Meinian, who was also one of the discoverers of Peking Man) recognized fossiliferous rocks near the city of Lufeng, 40 miles (64 km) northwest of Kunming, capital of the southwestern province of Yunnan. He named them the Lufeng Series in 1941, and regarded them as late Triassic, though they are now considered Lower Jurassic. Bien called in Professor Young, and the two opened quarries on a large scale before the Second World War, and revealed a rich variety of fossils. Notable was a large series of saurischian dinosaurs of different types, but there were also some mammal-like reptiles. In 1941 Young named one of the commoner dinosaurs *Lufengosaurus huenei*, after his old teacher von Huene. Appropriately, the dinosaur was a plateosaur, much like von Huene's *Plateosaurus*. A postage stamp was issued in 1958 to mark the first dinosaur skeleton mounted in China—the first time a dinosaur had appeared on a stamp anywhere in the world. (There have been so many since that a book has just been published about them.) *Lufengosaurus* was about 20 feet (6 m) long and stood 10 feet (3 m) high, and probably walked on both two and four legs at different times. It had sharp claws on its forelimbs, which might have been used for gathering vegetation, or for defense.

By the time the postage stamp was issued, Young had other dinosaurs to think about. In 1950 a large spike-headed duckbill was located in Shandong Province, which in 1958 he described as *Tsingtaosaurus*. In 1952 a new sauropod was found near the Mamenchi Ferry in Sichuan. In 1954 Young named it *Mamenchisaurus*, from "a site by a stream (chi in Chinese) called Mamen." In 1957 a joint team of the Sichuan and Chonquing museums spent three months excavating a single skeleton of the new dinosaur. It had been found in Upper Jurassic beds at Taihezhen, Hochuan County, in a site that had long produced "dragon bones" for drugstores. The skeleton not only proved to be remarkably complete (with only the forelimbs, skull, and part of the tail missing), but was also the largest dinosaur found in Asia. Even without all the tail, the biggest *Mamenchisaurus* skeleton was 72 feet (22 m) long. The neck alone accounts for 49 feet (15 m), more than half the length of the animal; each vertebra is very long and supported by overlapping bony struts, and its neck has an extra vertebra not found in any other dinosaur. The full skeleton is estimated to have been up to 80 feet (24 m), and may have weighed as much as 30 tons (27 t) when living. It was relatively lightly built, resembling *Diplodocus*.

❖ ❖ ❖

Longgujian in the province of Shandong (a peninsula in northeastern China) yielded another new dinosaur in 1964. A mass of unarticulated bones was excavated by the Beijing Geology Museum during a four-year program, and they proved to belong to a duck-billed dinosaur 51 feet (15.5 m) long, as large as some sauropods. In 1973 it was named *Shantungosaurus giganteus* by C.C. Hu. It was without a crest, and the forefeet had hooves, suggesting that it walked on all fours.

In 1976, excavators returned to the original site of the first dinosaur found in China, *Mandschurosaurus*. At Yuliangzi, a new skeleton of *Mandschurosaurus amurensis* was collected for the Museum of Heilongjiang Province.

❖ ❖ ❖

During the Cultural Revolution some paleontologists were sent to the farms for years or placed under house arrest, but despite this and other dislocations a new generation of paleontologists had been trained and a vigorous program of activity was under way by the time C.C. Young died in 1979. Sichuan, in south-central China had been the source of the first Chinese dinosaur discovery. In the 1970s, the area of Zigong in south-eastern Sichuan was explored. In 1974, the Wujiaba Quarry produced a complete 23-foot (7-m) skeleton of a new stegosaur, which was named *Tuojiangosaurus multispinus* by Dong, Li, Zhou, and Chang in 1977. Dong Zhiming, who has become the leading Chinese dinosaur special-ist of the present generation, was at school when Young's *Tsingtaosaurus* was excavated nearby, and was inspired by the experience to study pale-ontology at Fudan University. When he graduated in 1962, he joined the Institute of Vertebrate Paleontology and Paleoanthropology, where he studied with Professor Young.

In 1979 an industrial plant was being constructed at Dashanpu when excavations struck dinosaur bones. Dong Zhiming was called in, and with colleagues developed the rich Middle Jurassic Dashanpu Quarry in the Lower Shaximiao Formation. It has since produced more than 100 dinosaur skeletons, as well as those of fish, amphibians, and pterosaurs. *Shunosaurus* is now known from twenty skeletons, including at least five skulls. It is a primitive sauropod about 40 feet (12 m) long whose tail ends in a club, with two pairs of sharp spikes. Another primitive sauropod, *Datousaurus*, is known from two incomplete skeletons with skulls and, at 50 feet (15 m), is even larger. It was named by Dong Zhiming and Tang Zhilu in 1984.

A new primitive stegosaur, *Huayangosaurus taibaii*, was named in 1982 by Dong Zhiming. It was based on remains of twelve skeletons from the quarry, was about 15 feet (4.5 m) long, and seems to be the oldest stegosaur known. A number of new carnivores and hypsilophodonts have also been described from the quarry. When high levels of arsenic were found in the bones, there was a suggestion that the well-preserved dinosaurs had died in a mass poisoning by toxic vegetation, but it seems more likely that they had died over a long period and the arsenic seeped into the bones afterwards.

The small town of Zigong, near the quarry, is the home of a spring festival that brings a million tourists to buy and sell silk dragon-shaped or -decorated lamps. In 1987, the Zigong Dinosaur Museum opened in Sichuan, it is the first museum in Asia to specialize in dinosaurs. The large museum is actually built over the fossil-bearing beds, and a substantial section of the beds with dinosaur fossils intact is exposed in the Burial Hall. With these finds the Sichuan basin now provides the longest continuous record of Jurassic dinosaurs anywhere in the world. From the *Lufengosaurus* fauna of Lower Jurassic, through the Middle Jurassic *Shunosaurus* fauna, to the *Mamenchisaurus* fauna of the Upper Jurassic, a remarkably complete succession of dinosaur faunas has emerged.

Sichuan was the scene of a joint British-Chinese expedition in the fall of 1982. British Museum staff, including paleontologists Alan Charig, Angela Milner, and Ron Croucher (Head of the Paleontological Laboratory) were working with the Institute of Vertebrate Paleontology and Paleoanthropology. Contact had first been made when a delegation from China visited the British Museum in 1977. Some members of the delegation spoke English, and their hosts noted that "all four of the delegates were relaxed and charming." They traveled widely to museums, and visited Darwin's house in Kent. The following year, the Chinese invited four British vertebrate paleontologists to visit China, and Charig (who had had a Chinese student in Britain for two years) visited Sichuan for ten days. He tried to arrange a field trip, but first ill health, and then major flooding of the Yangtzi River held up the expedition. In 1982, the expedition was finally possible, and the party flew via Hong Kong to Beijing. The base in Sichuan was a coal town called Wangcang, which had never before been visited by foreigners; two guards had to be assigned to protect the English party from the "intense yet friendly" curiosity of the locals. The party were accommodated in the VIP block of the government hostel, in clean but primitive conditions.

They excavated a site about twenty-five minutes' drive from the town, in the Upper Shaximiao Formation (Upper Jurassic). The site had been found by a miner who noticed bones sticking up in a sweet-potato field. It was a bone bed which dipped at about twenty degrees, so that the overburden rapidly increased to about 6 feet (2 m). A gang of fifteen peasants were hired by the day to do the heavy work, with the help of a gas-powered drill supplied by the British. The drill was used to make holes for dynamite, which was exploded by the Chinese with what seemed to the British like gay abandon.

Gradually, they uncovered a mass of bones which were not artic-ulated. The bones were three or four deep, and varied from a 5-foot (1.5-m) thighbone to a tiny tooth 3/4 inch (1.9 cm) long. They proved to be largely from sauropods that had decayed and washed up on an ancient sandbank. While collecting together, the parties exchanged ideas about field techniques. The British demonstrated the use of glass fiber, and fast-setting polyurethane foam, which does not need water and so can be used in desert conditions. The Chinese not only did not have access to these materials, but the local plaster was of poor quality, and sackcloth (burlap) commonly used for plastering was quite unobtainable, so that they improvised with old mosquito net-ting. The Chinese built boxes around the plastered bones and filled them with a mix of plaster and sawdust. This made a strong but extreme-ly heavy jacket, so they were interested to learn the technique of fas-tening wooden splints to the bones used by the British team. In five and a half weeks the party amassed 220 loads of bones. Crates were built and the bones packed in rice straw, then carried a quarter-mile (400 m) to the road. All the bones went to Beijing, but casts were promised to the British party.

Up to this time, Chinese dinosaurs had been relatively little known in the Western world, although some had been mentioned in general surveys of the dinosaurs. The first popular book to tell Westerners about Chinese dinosaurs was an English edition of *Dinosaurs from China*, written by Dong Zhiming in collaboration with Angela Milner of the British Museum in 1987.

❖ ❖ ❖

In the summer of 1988 two paleontologists were prospecting a site in Inner Mongolia. One of them picked up a shiny object, and showed it to the other. It was a battered tin flask, bearing a picture of a 1920s car and labeled "Spirits" in English. The Dodge Motor company, supporting Andrews's American expeditions, had supplied the team with hip flasks, and this was clearly one of them. The finder was Dong Zhiming, of the Institute of Vertebrate Paleontology and Paleoanthropology (IVPP) in Beijing, and his companion was Philip Currie of the Tyrrell Museum of Palaeontology in Alberta, Canada. The discovery was of more than historical significance, for it confirmed that the locality they were visiting at Iren Dabasu was the same site the Americans had studied.

The origins of the Canada–China Dinosaur Project have been discussed in Chapter 12. As far back as 1982, Currie, Noble, and other colleagues had compiled a list of all the genera that seemed to occur both in China and Canada, and the list showed many similarities between the dinosaurs of the two countries. Furthermore, the Chinese record of dinosaurs is extensive, filling many gaps where dinosaurs cannot be found in the rest of world. In the spring of 1986, Dale Russell of Canada's National Museum of Natural Sciences, Philip Currie, Brian Noble, and Dong Zhiming surveyed possible sites in northwestern China, which now included the area of Inner Mongolia that the Americans had explored.

Serious joint research started in 1987, when eleven Canadian scientists went on the first trip to China with more than twenty-five Chinese, in what was claimed to be the largest international paleontological expedition to date. *Life* magazine has called it "the most expensive dinosaur field trip ever." Noble and the Ex Terra Foundation have raised more than $7 million for the project, from government and private sources, and $100,000 a year has gone into two-month research expeditions to Inner Mongolia. Equipment came from a variety of sources; for instance, the Donner Canadian Foundation provided five jeeps.

The Canadian scientists flew 1,500 miles (2400 km) from Beijing to Urumqi, on the southern boundary of the Junggar Basin. Two months were spent working in Jurassic deposits in northwest Xinjiang, in the Gobi, near the town of Jiangjunmiao. The Canadian contingent were struck by the resemblance of the landscape to the Alberta badlands, but found it even drier and harsher. The area yielded about a dozen large dinosaur skeletons, including a skeleton that may be a new species of *Jiangjunmiaosaurus*, a large megalosaurid carnivore first discovered in 1983. Another was the largest sauropod ever found in Asia, estimated at 90 feet (27 m) long. It was at first compared to *Mamenchisaurus*, but further work suggests it is a *Titanosaurus*. The Canadian scientists were impressed by the skill with which the Chinese used dynamite to remove surplus rock without damaging the bones.

At the end of the field season some of the group traveled 3,000 miles (4800 km) across northern China to Inner Mongolia to identify potential sites for the expeditions of 1988 and 1989.

❖ ❖ ❖

In July 1988, the Chinese year of the dragon, Brian Noble found a number of tiny teeth. Currie recognized that they belonged to an anky- losaur called *Pinacosaurus grangeri*, discovered by the American expeditions, but the size was puzzling. They returned to the site, and excavated a series of tiny skeletons. Six baby *Pinacosaurus*, each about the size of a sheep, had died in windblown sand deposits, much like those at the site today. Here was proof that yet another kind of dinosaur had lived a social life.

The 1988 expedition completed its excavation of the most impor- tant 1987 finds and then headed to new sites. Its members included Zheng Jiajiang, Brian Noble, Philip Currie, and Tom Jerzykiewicz (a geologist now with the Geological Survey of Canada who had been in the area from the other side with the 1971 Polish Mongolian expe- dition to the Gobi). At Bayan Manduhau they found the richest Mesozoic vertebrate site in China. There were 125 significant finds, including 40 dinosaurs and 5 kinds of unhatched dinosaur eggs. As well as the baby *Pinacosaurus*, there was a similar group of young *Protoceratops*.

In 1989 a Canadian and Chinese joint party were working in Xinjiang, and had completed collection of the titanosaur. When the tanks rolled into Tiananmen Square in June, several members of the

Ex Terra expedition were in China, but all got out safely. Fieldwork in China was put on hold, though other aspects of the program continued. Eleven new kinds of dinosaur have been documented, of which the first, to be called *Sinornithoides*, is being described by Dale Russell and Dong Zhiming. It is a small carnivore, heron-sized at 4 feet (1.2 m) long, and has a large brain and sickle claws on the hind feet.

As tensions quietened down, fieldwork has been resumed, and has already produced valuable scientific results. Philip Currie has summed up the impact of the research program: "We had to bring this project up to speed quickly, but what we've found has justified the effort; we'll probably spend years and years analyzing what we have found in the desert in just these few trips."

The joint project has also raised the profile of vertebrate paleontology in China, where the Institute had been achieving amazing results on a budget of about quarter of a million dollars (U.S.) a year. A new headquarters is planned for downtown Beijing, which will be on the same scale as the Tyrrell Museum, but the financial support is only partially committed. Some of the new generation of Chinese paleontologists is being trained in the United States, where they will have better access to new ideas and techniques, and if adequate resources can be made available, the amazing dinosaurs of China will become even better known.

❖ ❖ ❖

Japan, too, had a long period of isolation which ended in the late nineteenth century. Though Japan fought with Eastern and Western powers, since the Second World War it has embraced many Western ways with enthusiasm. However, a country subject to frequent earthquakes, volcanic eruptions, and tsunamis (waves caused by submarine earthquakes) has other priorities in its geological research than looking for rare fossils of dinosaurs.

In the 1930s a partial skull, vertebrae, pelvis, and leg bones of a juvenile lambeosaur were found in a coal mine in Late Cretaceous rocks on Sakhalin Island, north of Japan. A Japanese scientist, T. Nagao, from the faculty of Science at Hokkaido University, named the fossil in 1936. He chose the name *Nipponosaurus sachalinensis* (Japanese reptile from Sakhalin). No further Japanese research followed, as these islands ended up in the hands of the Soviet Union after the Second World War.

In the 1980s, new work was under way on Japanese dinosaurs, as Professor Yoshikazu Hasegawa of Yokohama National University describes a number of finds that have been made. Reports include carnosaur teeth from Kumamoto Prefecture and Ishikawa Prefecture, the latter found by high-school students. Other records include remains of *Edmontosaurus*, a vertebra of the bird mimic *Gallimimus*, and a partial leg bone from marine deposits of the Chinese sauropod *Mamenchisaurus* from Iwate Prefecture. The Japanese scientists use a custom of naming significant fossils informally while they are being described, and to provide a convenient name for public use. Intriguingly, the names all end in -*ryu* the Japanese word for dragon. In the modern study of ancient animals, traditional beliefs continue to have relevance. Though some of the finds may prove to belong to existing genera, if these Japanese names become in due course the basis for formal scientific names, the literature will be enlivened with up to nine genera bearing such names as "Katsuyamasaurus" and "Hisanohamasaurus." Dinosaur footprints have also been found in a number of localities, including Seboyashi in the Gumma Prefecture. These are exposed on a steeply dipping surface, which provided a challenge when casts were made. Scaffolding had to be erected up the whole slope to provide a footing for the workers, who worked in temperatures down to 50° F (10° C). The site has been interpreted through signs and also made the basis for the Nakasato Dinosaur Museum.

Though actual dinosaur discoveries in Japan have been relatively few, there has been enormous popular interest in discoveries elsewhere in the world. In 1990, the Hitachi Dinoventure was launched and was expected to attract two million visitors. This Tokyo exhibit was prepared as a joint venture between Alberta's Tyrrell Museum and the Hitachi educational publishing organization and other corporations in Japan. Extensive funding was placed into the advanced preparation of new specimens, and twenty-one skeletons and casts were flown across the Pacific in a Boeing 747 to provide the core of the exhibit. Could they have been aware of it, the dinosaurs whose ancestors had evolved in Asia and slowly walked across the continent of Laurasia might have appreciated the convenience of the trip in the opposite direction.

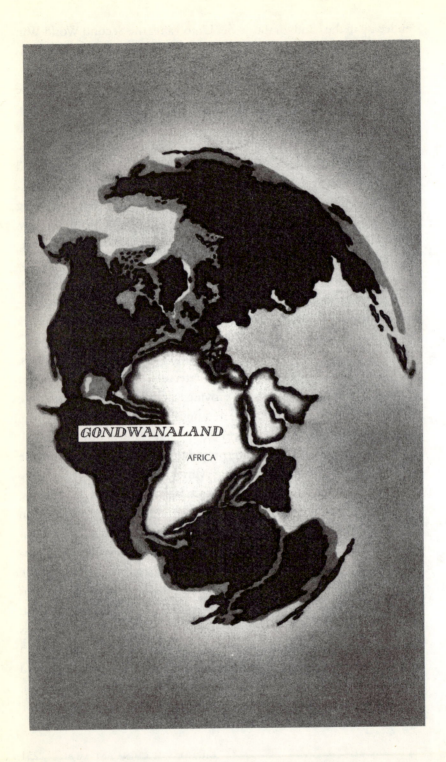

GONDWANALAND

AFRICA

GONDWANALAND

THE SOUTHERN CONTINENT, GONDWANALAND, STARTED TO SEPARATE from Laurasia as an embryo North Atlantic–Mediterranean Ocean began to open in the Late Triassic. The ancestral cores of South America, Africa, Antarctica, India, Australia, and New Zealand drifted off together, and by the Late Cretaceous Gondwanaland had fragmented into three or four sections roughly corresponding to the modern continental and subcontinental blocks. Since the dinosaurs died, these gradually drifted to their present positions, with South America in contact with North America, Africa in touch with southwestern Asia, and India in slow collision with the Laurasian block to form what is now Asia, while New Zealand still drifts far from other land.

The ancient southern continents were thus closely linked at first, so that dinosaurs could travel easily between them when not impeded by climatic or topographic barriers. The early dinosaurs of the Late Triassic are similar in all continents. During the Jurassic, links were so close that a major African site has a fauna closely similar to the Morrison Formation of the western United States. In the Late Jurassic and Early Cretaceous, the more distinct continents developed their own faunas.

Where their remains are present, dinosaurs are not easy to find in the remains of Gondwanaland, as much of the landscape is covered by dense tropical forest, or (in Antarctica) under permanent ice. Only in the relatively lightly vegetated areas of North, East, and South Africa, Patagonia in southern Argentina, and parts of Australia have dinosaurs been found with relative ease.

Apart from Antarctica, each southern continent has had its own human populations. Although all had ancient cultural traditions, these were generally not oriented to science. Despite its closeness to Europe, Africa long resisted penetration by peoples other than the Arabs. Other southern continents could only be reached after long sea voyages from Europe. Indigenous peoples were displaced or killed, or mingled with settlers primarily from northern continents. Some parts were (or became) densely populated; some (such as Australia) remained very sparsely populated. Antarctica has been peopled only as a result of geographical exploration in the present century. In general, Western science has gone to the southern continents as an innovative venture, and has been much better supported in some areas than others.

European explorers brought the first southern dinosaur finds back to Europe for description by scientists there. As North America became dominant in the paleontological scene, it too sent out expeditions and brought back collections. Homegrown dinosaur specialists have also developed in the southern continents, and though they have often been handicapped by the poverty of their countries, they have done important work.

The southern continents are characterized by comparatively few and late dinosaur discoveries, and a relative scarcity of information, which is often published in unfamiliar languages or inaccessible periodicals. The dinosaur story of these continents is treated here in only two chapters. One of the major sites from Africa is presented first, then those of the other continents are grouped within a single chapter.

GONDWANALAND/AFRICA

Africa provided a home in the Mesozoic for a great range of dinosaurs, whose remains have been found in the Sahara Desert countries of Algeria, Morocco, Libya, Mali, Niger, and Egypt; in South Africa; and in the East African countries of Madagascar, Zimbabwe, and Tanzania. A major east African site from Tanzania forms the subject of Chapter 16.

Africa has been at the root of some Western traditions, through Egypt, Coptic Christianity, and then the Arab world, which gave us such scientific disciplines as algebra and chemistry. The rest of Africa was to Europeans a dark continent. It was closest to Europe of the southern continents, and voyages nibbled at the coasts, but the unhealthy and dangerous nature of travel held back much exploration until the mid-nineteenth century. As the country was penetrated, the abundance and richness of living wildlife focused attention away from the fossils of past wildlife until well into this century. Now that Africa has become famous as the source of the earliest fossil hominids, its dinosaurs are overshadowed by dramatic finds in the only other area of vertebrate paleontology to capture the public imagination.

Scientific discovery has been largely at the hands of scientists from various European countries, some of whom became residents of African countries. The story of Tendaguru shows how political changes far away had a major effect on the study of an important site. As in other countries, natives of the African countries assisted in the discovery of the remains of fossils and are beginning to play a more significant part in recent years.

16

ASTONISHING CREATURE

ALTHOUGH THE CONTINENT OF AFRICA WAS LARGELY unknown to the outside world until well into the nineteenth century, three kinds of dinosaurs had been found in Africa before Stanley met Livingstone at Ujiji in 1871, symbolically ending the period of primary exploration. In 1854, less than a decade after he named the dinosaurs, Richard Owen described *Massospondylus* from the Stormberg beds of South Africa. Two other Triassic dinosaurs were described by his rival Thomas Henry Huxley in 1866 and 1867. All were medium-sized prosauropods from South Africa, and each was known from only a few bones. Although more important dinosaurs were to be found later in these beds, the most glorious find of African dinosaurs comes from another site. It is more recent in date, as it is Jurassic (about the same age as Como Bluff in Wyoming), and lies in a part of east Africa that has in this century been known successively as German East Africa, Tanganyika Territory, and Tanzania. Its name is Tendaguru.

Mention Tendaguru to dinosaur enthusiasts, and their eyes are likely to sparkle. Over a period of more than twenty years in the first quarter of this century, the site yielded remarkable dinosaurs, including one that was for a long time the biggest dinosaur known. For part of this time, the site probably had the largest labor force ever to collect dinosaurs, people who worked against extraordinary odds. The area is one of those parts of Africa where disease-carrying flies made it impossible to keep livestock, so that every huge bone had to be carried by porters over rough country to the sea. It may be the experience of walking in hot weather or the varying routes through the rough country, but in different accounts the distance from Tendaguru to Lindi varies from 40 to 70 miles (64 to 113 km).

Two major expeditions worked the site, first from Germany, then from England. Both were relatively well funded, and each worked the area for several years. The main differences were in style and leadership—and in the results that each achieved.

v   v   v

No one in the scientific world had heard of Tendaguru until Herr Sattler banged his shin on a fossil bone in 1907. W.B. Sattler was a geologist with Der Lindi-Schürfgesellschaft (the Lindi Prospecting Company), which was exploring inland for semiprecious minerals. About 40 miles (64 km) inland from the port of Lindi, he was working a scrubbily wooded country near a low hill, where there is a village called Tendaguru. The site is now near the southern boundary of Tanzania, just ten degrees below the equator.

Sattler knew enough to recognize that (in every sense) he had stumbled onto something big, and he reported the discovery to the governor of the colony in Dar es Salaam. By chance, a well-known German paleontologist was visiting the colony at the time. Professor Eberhard Fraas (1862–1915) was an authority on fossil reptiles (particularly ichthyosaurs, crocodiles, and plesiosaurs), and had published on German dinosaurs. Visiting the German Club in the capital, he heard about Sattler's find and was able to visit the site. Although he fell ill and had to cut short his visit, he took back some souvenirs to his home in Stuttgart. He used the bones to support his contention that the world's biggest dinosaur was waiting to be dug up at the site. Unfortunately, he had also taken home the dysentery germ.

Fraas was an eminent scientist, and he also knew how to work on the national pride. As he published articles and talked about his finds, he made it a matter of national honor to develop this important site in German East Africa, and to disseminate the results to the scientific world. As public enthusiasm for the site grew, his illness developed, and it soon became clear that someone else would have to lead the planned expedition. The disease lingered in his body for eight years of increasing disability, but before it killed him he must have rejoiced to see some of the results that followed his African discovery.

Among the people who were impressed by Fraas was Dr. Wilhelm von Branca (1844–1928), then director of the Geological and Paleontological University Institute and Museum in Berlin. He started to raise funds, with a committee chaired by the Duke of Mecklenburg, Regent of Brunswick. The influential committee was able to tap a variety of funding sources, including the Imperial Government, the City of Berlin, the Academy of Learning, and almost a hundred private citizens. It was estimated that 180,000 marks would be needed for the first three years' work, and an additional sum of 50,000 marks was granted by the Prussian State in 1912. This was worth in total more than $50,000 U.S., a considerable sum before the First World War.

The personnel of the expedition were chosen from the academic staff of the museum and University of Berlin. In charge was Werner Janensch (1878–1969), curator of fossil reptiles at the Berlin Museum, Frederick Wilhelm University, Berlin. Janensch had been at the museum since 1901, and had studied invertebrate fossils as well as vertebrates. As second in command, Janensch took Edwin Hennig, who had been born in 1882 and was twenty-seven when the expedition started. He was also a paleontologist with expertise in both invertebrate and vertebrate fossils, and had knowledge of geomorphology. Hans von Staff (1883–1915), who was a lecturer and worker on stratigraphy and invertebrate fossils at the University of Berlin, and a year younger than Hennig, also joined the expedition. To complete the team, Herr Sattler, the original finder, accompanied them to Tendaguru. Over the years, other German paleontologists shared in the work.

If Herr Sattler had revisited the site after the expedition settled in, he would have remembered with amazement the quiet forest where he had once bruised his shin on a fossil bone. The gently rising Tendaguru Hill was still there, with Tendaguru village at its foot. But the quiet bush gradually became noisily active, as huts were built, sites located, helpers hired, and excavations developed in all directions. Few bones were visible at the surface, but random excavations produced bones in many places. In 1909, its first year, the expedition employed 170 native laborers. Supervised by the scientists dressed in their semiformal field clothes, including broad-brimmed hats and shirts with wide collars, the diversely dressed laborers dug with spades, and were taught to plaster the bones that were exposed. The laborers in turn brought their families, so that a whole village developed just for the expedition and its camp followers. Much of the food for this multitude had to be brought in on a four-day march from the port of Lindi, and as domestic animals could not live in the area, all the food was carried by porters. On their return trips, the plastered bones were carried back to the coast by the same porters, slung from poles carried by one, two, or four men.

In the second year, 1910, the labor force escalated to 400 men, with a corresponding increase in the village. By 1911, 500 men were working, (almost certainly the largest force ever used to excavate dinosaurs) and the population of the village fluctuated between 700 and 900 people. A native *Oberaufseher* (overseer), Boheti bin Amrani, had developed into an expert excavator. The expedition had worked sites in every direction up to a kilometer from Tendaguru Hill. As the excavations were pushed back into the hillsides, huge wooden walls were constructed from branches to prevent the cliffs from collapsing into the bottom of the pit. The traffic along the trail to the coast was almost constant. In the first three years it is recorded that 4,300 loads of bones were carried out, in 5,400 trips. At Lindi, the bones were packed in 800 boxes, weighing 400,000 pounds (180,000 kg) or around 200 tons (180 t).

Even though the mechanics of the expedition were enough of a challenge, the scientists had other problems to discuss over their evening meals. The bones were often huge, broken into pieces, and sometimes heavily encrusted with lime. Worse, they were not arranged neatly in skeletons, but scattered as if they had been toys in a giant's game.

Edwin Hennig later described the struggle to make sense of the gargantuan jigsaw.

> The remains of our giants, that is the bones of the legs, the vertebra, and the teeth, were almost without exception strewn around confusedly in the embedding rock. Whenever we thought we were gradually assembling the parts of an animal, some saurian goblin would play us a trick: three like thighbones, two pelvises, or something of the sort would almost always suggest the presence of the same species on one spot—but for ever so long the skull, which we particularly wanted, would not turn up. Gradually however, the legendary creatures beginning to arise from the graves became stranger and stranger; they kept us constantly in suspense. Thus several elements of legs appeared, and before we could properly free the joints they looked like strong femurs. After days of widening the shaft, a considerably larger piece would be added, and then it would turn out that what we had been dealing with was only the metacarpal bone. Quite a glove those hands would have worn! These bones would now be joined by the tibia. Then after a while the humerus belonging to the same animal would turn up.

Although the scientists had some idea what kinds of dinosaurs they were dealing with, most of their discoveries had not been described before. The scientific value of the expedition was all the greater, but not too much work on identification could be done until the bones were freed from their plaster jackets in Berlin and painstakingly described. After three years, most of the expedition team returned to Berlin to get on with the work of description.

It was felt that one more year was needed, and Hans Reck (1886–1937), who was only in his mid-twenties, found himself in charge of the Tendaguru excavation. He was already knowledgeable in geology, and had traveled to Iceland in 1908 to study volcanoes. During 1912, he and his men produced another 50 tons (45 t) of bones. Excavations now lay in a strip 3.5 miles (5.6 km) north–south and

1.5 miles (2.4 km) east-west. An adjacent area at Kindope had also produced important results. After four years, the fieldwork alone had cost 136,000 marks—more than half the money collected for the expedition.

Before any detailed scientific work of describing the dinosaurs could commence, an immense amount of preparation was necessary. Branca records that a single dinosaur shoulder blade 6 feet (1.8 m) long was in 80 pieces, requiring 160 hours to clean, stick together, and harden. One vertebra alone used 450 hours of preparation time.

While the research was still continuing, publication commenced. The major part of the work was published in series of volumes resoundingly entitled *Wissenschaftliche Ergebnisse der Tendaguru-Expedition, 1909-1912* (The Results of Study of the Tendaguru Expedition), and many papers were published in a variety of journals.

By this time, the area around Tendaguru was riddled with holes. There were fifty excavations with sauropod bones, and at least thirteen with stegosaur remains. Three saurian beds, one above the other, were traced. They were separated by marine sediments with seashells, in all about 250 feet (76 m) thick.

Sauropods dominated the dinosaur fauna, and some had left their leg bones upright in a clay bed, while the rest of the skeleton lay dismembered close by. Janensch interpreted this situation as reflecting sauropods that had been caught in quicksand and then drowned by the incoming tide. Certainly the sites had been close to the sea, as fossil marine shells such as belemnites were found with the bones, and one large skeleton at Kindele actually had sea shells inside its body cavity.

This interesting association makes Tendaguru one of the rare sites where marine and terrestrial deposits can be closely correlated, and the beds have been found to extend from Middle Jurassic into Lower Cretaceous. The dinosaurs seem to have lived along the course of one or more rivers near the ocean, where a sand bar may have normally prevented the mixing of marine and fresh water. As the dinosaurs died, their skeletons were deposited in river sediments, and periodically the sea would invade and cover the land, leaving marine fossils.

As well as dinosaurs, there were pterodactyls—*Rhamphorynchus* and *Pterodactylus*—and a crocodile—*Steneosaurus*, also known from sites in Europe. A mammal was found, a bone of a bird, and some fish, while plants included conifers, ferns, and cycads.

❖ ❖ ❖

The first dinosaur from the site, *Gigantosaurus*, was described by Fraas in 1908. Unfortunately the name had already been used, and it was renamed *Tornieria* by R. Sternfeld in 1911. There were only a few leg bones, including a right tibia 2 feet, 6 inches (76 cm) long, of a large sauropod. Branca worried about the discrepancy between the huge body and the "inadequate size of the masticatory apparatus," and assumed that it must have been exceptionally voracious to sustain itself. *Tornieria* is now considered to be quite close to the English whale lizard, *Cetiosaurus*.

Another sauropod, *Dicraeosaurus*, was described by Janensch in 1914. It resembled a small *Diplodocus*, with a very long tail and a relatively short neck. The specimen was 43 feet (13 m) long, and its weight is estimated at 6.5 tons (5.9 t). By this time, the First World War was raging, but the scientific work continued for some time.

A stegosaur, *Kentrosaurus aethiopicus*, was described by Hennig in 1915. It was like the American *Stegosaurus* but had smaller plates on its neck and the fore part of the back, and the rest was covered with sharp spines, some more than 2 feet (60 cm) long. Two more spines stuck out from the hips and from the end of the tail. It was smaller than *Stegosaurus*, at about 16 feet (4.9 m) long. *Kentrosaurus* was particularly abundant at Kindope, where disjointed remains of about fifty animals were found in a pit 50 to 60 feet (15 to 18 m) deep, and 3,000 feet (915 m) square.

It was not until 1919 that Rudolf Virchow described *Dysalotosaurus lettowvorbecki* from incomplete skulls and numerous bones from Tanzania. This slender hypsilophodont has since been equated with Marsh's *Dryosaurus* from Como Bluff.

In 1920 Janensch described *Elaphrosaurus* from an incomplete skeleton without a skull. He regarded it as a small carnivore and the only good theropod skeleton from Tendaguru, but it is now often regarded as an ancestral ornithomimid. It was about 20 feet (6 m) long, and had relatively short hind limbs.

Some flat-bladed teeth, nearly 6 inches (15 cm) long, suggested the presence of a large carnivore, regarded as *Ceratosaurus* known from the Morrison Formation. Each weighing about 5 tons (4.5 t), a pack of these carnivores could have brought down the largest sauropod from the site—*Brachiosaurus*.

Brachiosaurus or "arm reptile," was first known from a very incomplete skeleton from Colorado in the western United States Its name refers to the forelegs, which are longer than the hind legs—unlike those of most sauropods—and it was regarded as the largest known dinosaur at the time. Elmer Riggs, its finder, suggested it was not amphibious (as sauropods were generally regarded to be at the time) but a terrestrial animal with a lifestyle like that of an elephant.

When the African site produced a virtually complete skeleton of the same animal, it could finally be appreciated to the full. Hennig described the process of preparation.

> Only in Berlin could the last delicate excavation be done: complete cleansing from adhering soil, soaking of the bones, joining of the fragments, and so on. In 1911 all the pieces had finally been gathered together in the Berlin Museum of Natural History. But for the preparation and mounting of this giant—which went on despite the First World War—no less than twenty-six years were needed! Not until 1937 was the astonishing creature stationed in the great hall of the museum, which was barely large enough for it. Its spinal column measured seventy-five feet in length, its ribs alone eight feet; the neck was over forty feet long.

This impressive skeleton of *Brachiosaurus* still stands in the Humboldt Museum in what was until recently East Berlin. The skeleton as mounted is 39 feet (12 m) tall and 74 feet (23 m) long. It is the tallest, and most massive, but not the longest mounted dinosaur skeleton in the world. In life it was estimated to have weighed as much as 80 to 90 tons (72 to 81 t), but more recent work suggests these estimates are too high. The huge beast raised many questions. The nostrils were on top of its head, so it was suggested it did live in deep water after all. It is now thought that if the neck was fully stretched its lungs would not have survived the water pressure. How could its heart pump blood all the way up to the head? How could it find and consume enough to eat through a relatively tiny mouth? Since *Brachiosaurus* lived, it must have managed to solve these problems, but it is not always easy to understand how.

Two species were named, the larger *Brachiosaurus fraasi*, and the smaller *B. brancai*. Hennig remarked that *Diplodocus* would look like their chick. Commentators were also baffled by the presence of the same animal in Africa and North America, and postulated an Antarctic route to connect the two places. Although no new skeletons have been collected, fragments of bones half as large again as the largest described have been informally reported from Tanzania.

Janensch stayed on at the museum until 1953, and he died in 1969. Hennig did important work in other parts of Africa, including the mammals of Olduvai Gorge. But the Germans had lost their access to Tendaguru, for in the land deals that followed the First World War, German East Africa became British East Africa, and was split into Tanganyika and other territories.

❖ ❖ ❖

William Edmund Cutler (whose adventures in western Canada are mentioned in Chapter 8) clung firmly to his short period in a nonacademic position in the University at Winnipeg, for it is recorded that the first British expedition to Tendaguru was "under Mr. W.E. Cutler of Manitoba University." In 1924, Cutler was about forty-six, and had never been to Africa before. The British Museum (who wanted to find a complete *Brachiosaurus* of their own) sensibly arranged for Cutler to be "accompanied by Mr. L.S.B. Leakey of St. John's College, Cambridge". The young Louis Seymour Bazett Leakey (1923–72) had been born in Kenya, spoke a number of African languages, and was now completing his academic education in England. The governor of Tanganyika, Sir Horace Byatt, approved of the Tendaguru expedition being considered a special commission, so that its members were allowed to import ammunition and arms for their personal use, and "such material as is requisite for the conduct of their work, including spirit, and plaster of Paris for preservation purposes."

The expedition left London in February 1924. Leakey left Lindi on April 16 to look for the German camp.

> After four strenuous days of "safari" trying to follow the ten-year-old German trail through elephant grass anything from six to twelve feet high, thorn-bush, scrub, and patches of bamboo, with here and there a small native village, we reached the hillock on which the last German camp had been pitched. . . . The area was wild. . . . Lions, leopards and elephants roam at large, and there are innumerable snakes. One night Mr. Leakey's pet monkey fell a victim to a leopard, and he himself has had narrow escapes from snake-bite.

While Leakey hired native help, built a camp, and organized construction of an 8-foot (2.4 m) road for the entire distance to Lindi, Cutler waited at the port for the arrival of the equipment, and finally arrived at the camp on May 24. Leakey was quickly relegated to the "making and labelling of parcels . . . [which] consisted of carefully wrapping up, first in some soft paper and then in brown paper, all small hard bones" while "plastering was never done by anyone but Mr. Cutler himself, as several years' practical experience are needed to make a successful plasterer." Leakey proceeds to explain, step by step, how it is done, making it clear that he was quite as capable as his leader. The expedition collected about 600 bones, including a shoulder blade 74 inches (188 cm) long, but there were no complete skeletons. Although few dinosaurs were collected, at least Leakey picked up enough technique to start his career as a paleoanthropologist.

Cutler seemed interested in everything but dinosaurs, being a particularly ardent butterfly collector. He also conducted sadistic experiments on pythons and hornbills. Cutler tried to stop Leakey from writing anything about the expedition. Unfortunately, he did not take Leakey's advice about the local diseases seriously, and soon suffered from malaria and dysentery. After a few months, he became too ill to leave his tent, and died of blackwater fever in Lindi in 1925.

Meanwhile, Leakey had written articles for the *Illustrated London News*, describing the expedition, and the British Museum wrote to *The Times*, asking for public support: "Its primary object is to obtain the bones of *Gigantosaurus,* a Dinosaurian reptile of stupendous size, which was discovered by the Germans a few years before the war."

After Cutler's death, the expedition came under the leadership of Frederick William Hugh Migeod (1872–1952), who in the English amateur tradition is described as an English civil servant, linguist, and vertebrate paleontologist, "an African traveller of many years experience and an authority on native languages." He was assisted by Major T. Deacon, and they made a number of finds, including limb bones of a large theropod, and published a number of articles on this and later British expeditions.

In April 1927, John Parkinson (1872–1947) took over responsibility for the expeditions, assisted by Deacon. Parkinson was an economic geologist, vertebrate paleontologist, and novelist who had worked in industry in Nigeria, Liberia, Kenya, Tanganyika, India, Burma, Abyssinia, Ceylon, and Venezuela. He led expeditions to Tendaguru through 1927–29, and extended the work to cover invertebrate fossils.

Parkinson describes the process of traveling by steamer to Dar es Salaam, capital of Tanganyika Territory, then by the British-Indian fortnightly coastal steamer *The Dumra,* to Lindi, a "straggling, lost, but harmless looking place occupying the west side of a considerable estuary." Here "quinine can be bought at the post office." Fortunately, technology had by now come to the rescue of the traveler. "The days of the 'foot-safari' are past. . . . Nowadays you load up a lorry . . . you can get the lorry up all the hills if now and again you partially unload it and then push; rocks may outcrop from side to side, delightful to the geological eye, though bad for tyres; but during the dry weather the odds are distinctly in favour of your final and safe arrival."

The roads were poor, and flimsy bridges were a problem. Apart from the trucks, "all transport was by natives: fly prevents donkeys or mules living in the neighbourhood." Parkinson noted that women near the coast still used the *pelele*, a wooden disc inserted into the lower lip, which is said to have been a device to render them hideous in the eyes of the slave traders who used to pillage the coast. Moving away from the sea, "the land becomes less populated, less fertile, and much more tedious." Accommodation was supplied by crude rest houses, and eventually Tendaguru came into sight: "one arrives at a point where Tendaguru Hill, with a large grass hut or 'banda' near its summit, can be seen from afar, standing low enough, it is true, but sufficiently conspicuous to form a landmark above the drab expanse of tree-tops which intervene."

The countryside was hilly and forested, with little game, as poisoned arrows and traps were in use everywhere. Fortunately, Boheti, who had helped the Germans, was still available. "Without Boheti, the element of chance involved in the question, 'Where shall we dig next?' would have assumed almost overwhelming proportions. At first, as far as we could see, bones might be anywhere, only they weren't."

The party found similar bones to the German discoveries in similar sites, and then developed a relatively new site at Kindope, which proved to be "astoundingly rich in bones": "In some cases . . . a small patch of sand is almost a bone breccia, and has then to be uncovered rather in the same sort of way that one would dissect out a nerve of a dogfish or rabbit. This is accomplished by means of an awl, the particles of sand being swept off by a broad, soft brush. The work requires much time, and in a pit is a somewhat hot task, so that we rigged a tarpaulin on sticks to afford shelter from the sun and the heavy dew at night."

The working season was from June to November, and the numbers of workers averaged fifty-one, not counting casual labor hired to carry fossils to Lindi. The cost of an overseer and two headmen was £43 per month, and they supervised much of the excavation. In the patronizing way of the period, Parkinson weighs up his labor force: "Taken as a whole, the men were surprisingly intelligent. Now and again, of course . . . a boy would show no aptitude; he despised collecting shells or even bones, a mental attitude not uncommon among the adult population of England." He is less lukewarm about his chief overseer:

> Boheti, formerly Oberaufseher to the German expedition, was and is an enthusiast and a master in the craft. . . . he could be trusted to continue carefully and painstakingly throughout the day and produce the best possible results at the end of it with well earned pride. His memory retained the smallest details relevant to the past, and with a few chosen helpers (his own selection, of course) could be left to carry on. . . . In the evening he returned triumphant or despondent as the case may be, followed by his assistants, each with a "karai" [large iron basin] poised on his head full of potential treasures.

The men responsible for carrying the bones could also be trusted: "Only once since 1903 have I known a carrier unintentionally drop a load and that was because he was cannoned into unexpectedly by another member of the caravan. . . . So the bones were carried on heads."

Carriers were used even when they reached the road, as the bones would have suffered too much bouncing in the back of a truck: "A heavy bone, over 60 lbs, would be slung on a pole and carried by two men, a very heavy bone by four."

❖ ❖ ❖

The readers of *The Times* had clearly not responded with enthusiasm to the appeal, for in 1925 funds ran out. A grant of £1,000 was made in April by the Tanganyika government with nominal support from Nyasaland. Migeod took over again until mid-November 1929, and work was concentrated at Nguruwe. In total to 1929, £10,680 ($50,000 U.S.) was spent. This was about the same amount as the Germans had spent, but produced significantly less results.

About 1928, Francis Arthur Bather (1863–1934) of the Natural History Museum arranged to have the area around Tendaguru designated a "fossil reserve." This must be the first fossil game park in Africa.

In 1930, Parkinson wrote *The Dinosaur in East Africa*, a book summarizing his experiences. In this book he imaginatively re-created the ancient scene:

> the long lagoon, separated from the open water by a foam-edged bank of sand, was there, with a big river . . . probably terminating in a delta, opening by various mouths, shifting, silting up, and changing behind its sand bank as does the Niger. One can realize dinosaurs, drowsily reposing or ponderously wading in the wide expanses of hot shallow water, the lagoons which stretch unsuspected behind the sand banks, mile after mile of tributary creeks. . . . At the entrance to the lagoon, pebbles and the larger grains of rock would settle downward, but the rotting carcasses, buoyed up by the gases of decomposition, float onwards to slow dismemberment. Doubtless many animals were caught and entombed in the lagoons themselves, many more swept seaward when the sandy barriers shutting out the sea were broken through.

Parkinson's view of the lifestyle of the large sauropods is less modern than that expressed by Riggs in 1903. Parkinson criticized restorations of *Diplodocus* that showed the animal walking on land, suggesting instead that "a lizard-like attitude may be more probable, the abdomen and tail touching the ground in rest, grazing it in ordinary motion, the knees widespread and pointed obliquely forwards."

However, he was perceptive about gizzard stones, finding "very smooth pebbles, of an old, hard rock, . . . the largest 45 mm long. . . . The writer permitted his imagination rein enough to permit a speculation about whether a dinosaur could swallow pebbles, as do birds, to aid the trituration of food in a gizzard-like receptacle of his digestive system." The British collections were largely of single bones, and have never been described.

In total, the German and British expeditions located and removed nearly 100 articulated specimens and hundreds of isolated bones. The total labor was estimated later at 225,000 man days (no attempt has been made to estimate the extensive support work provided by the many women who also lived at the camp, though Parkinson points out the importance of their role in providing water and firewood and preparing food). Even that total is more than twelve times the effort that had gone into collecting dinosaurs in Canada, another rich area, up to the late 1970s. The comparison with Canada is appropriate in that a later reexamination of the fossils of Tendaguru was made by two Canadian paleontologists (Dale Russell and Pierre Béland) working with John McIntosh from the United States. The Canadian paleontologists were invited to visit the site, and did so in 1977 and 1978. McIntosh provided measurements and identifications of the bones in the Berlin collections, 40 percent of which had not been discussed in the published accounts of the site and its dinosaurs. Ongoing geological work in the country and studies of the fossils other than dinosaurs were also available to make possible a new synthesis of the Tendaguru story.

Recent work confirms the Upper Jurassic age of the principal deposits, which were laid down in a latitude about that of modern Cape Town. The area seems to have been generally warm and wet, though periodic droughts may have been responsible for mass deaths of dinosaurs. The margin of the sea was at that time around Tendaguru Hill, resulting in the overlap of marine and terrestrial rocks. Russell, Béland and McIntosh drastically reduce the previously estimated weight of the large sauropods; for instance, *Brachiosaurus* is thought to have weighed 15 tons (13.5 t), not 85 (76.5 t). Estimates by other specialists lie between 35 and 52 tons (32 and 47 t). This has implications for the brain size in relation to the body size—if bodies were smaller, then the brains were not so small in proportion.

Detailed analysis yields intriguing information; for instance, limb bones of the sauropod *Barosaurus* are mainly from the left side, leading to the suggestion that the majority of them died lying on their left sides, perhaps because they were migrating along the shore. The Upper Saurian Bed contains isolated feet of sauropods in an upright position—the only surviving remains of animals that were mired, while the upper part of the skeleton was destroyed on the surface.

Separated in time by a bitter war, British and Germans separately achieved a remarkable understanding of an astonishing site. Both were aided by the same dedicated local inhabitants, whose descendants may even now be preparing to grapple with the new significance the site might have. Parkinson truly remarked that, "Tendaguru is not finished yet," but Russell and his colleagues also pointed out that "to be comparably successful to the German expedition, a new programme of excavations would have to be at least as ambitious."

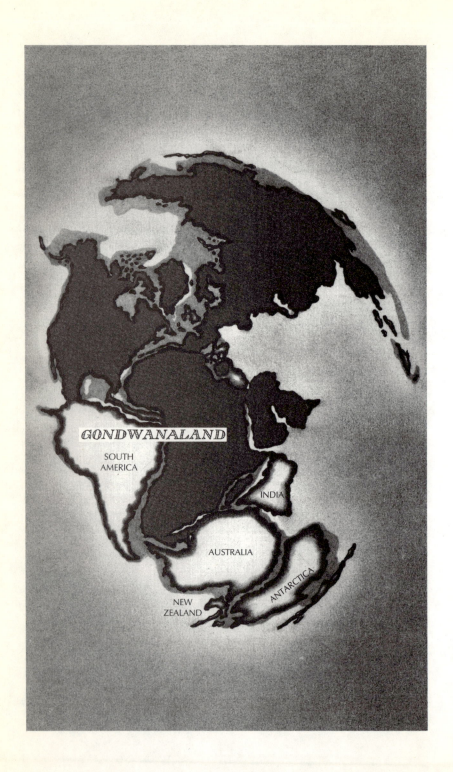

GONDWANALAND
India, South America, Australia, New Zealand, Antarctica

GONDWANALAND REMAINED MORE OR LESS INTACT UNTIL THE END OF
the Jurassic. Then the section that is now India drifted until it collid-
ed with the south coast of northern Asia and forced up the Himalayan
Mountains. (Some evidence suggests that it was an island for a while,
other evidence—including that of the dinosaurs—suggests it
remained in close touch with Africa during its drift.) Australia and
Antarctica remained in contact with each other until the end of the
Cretaceous, while South America moved away from Africa as an embryo
South Atlantic opened up, but remained in tenuous contact with North
America.

The rocks in which many southern dinosaurs are exposed outcrop
in areas covered by jungles, such as central and southern India, and Brazil.
In these areas, discoveries were infrequent. Where they occur in regions
of steppe and desert, such as central Argentina and the southern province
of Patagonia, discoveries were made earlier, unless the area was
sparsely settled, as in parts of Australia. Antarctica is so densely covered by ice that, although everything pointed to the presence of dinosaurs,
the first discoveries were made only very recently.

The ancient kingdom of the Gonds in southern India gave
Gondwanaland its name. The ancient Indian culture of meditation
and transcendence did not lend itself to scientific study, so discoveries
came with colonial settlement and exploration. However, the Indians

have since produced many paleontologists to deal with their discoveries, initially in collaboration with colleagues from other countries. Australia had very few discoveries until a recent renaissance of scientific exploration brought some exciting finds, and New Zealand was not known to have dinosaurs at all until a decade ago. South America has a complex colonial history, with scientific exploration by expeditions from Europe and later North America being supplemented and replaced by increasing local scientific expertise. The rocks and fossils of Antarctica have been extensively explored only in recent years, by international scientific surveys.

17

REUNITE GONDWANALAND

IN THE EARLY DAYS OF BUMPER STICKERS, A PARTICULARLY obscure one read: "Reunite Gondwanaland." It seemed to be a political slogan for some country in Africa one feels one has heard of but cannot quite place. To geologists, of course, it was a highly entertaining "in" joke, for it would take more than the united political power of the all nations to reunite the Mesozoic southern continent.

For a while, even comprehending Gondwanaland defeated the geologists of the world, for, until the 1970s, continental drift was a theory for which no possible mechanism could be conceived. The chief student of how the vertebrate fossils link the southern continents has been Edwin Colbert from the American Museum of Natural History. Early in his professional career, he had seen the ocean-basin surveys at Columbia University, which were beginning to provide stronger support for the continental-drift idea. Naturally, his attention turned to the implications of the theory for fossil vertebrates.

Accounts of his travels to each of the southern continents give valuable glimpses of the progress of vertebrate paleontology in different continents, and are referred to here partly in order to create some unity in this diverse chapter. For, in some ways, this chapter attempts (on paper at least) the impossible feat of reuniting Gondwanaland by showing how the dinosaurs of the different sections of Gondwanaland were discovered, and how the links between the sections of the ancient southern continent then became apparent.

Dinosaurs in the Land of the Gonds

The first report of dinosaurs in India comes from the travels of Captain Sleeman, in 1828. The remains came from what is now known as the Upper Cretaceous Lameta Formation, in the central areas of peninsular India. Captain Sleeman was perhaps more famous for his suppression of the celebrated cult of Thuggee, in which strangers were murdered as a religious offering.

India under the British had an early Geological Survey, and it was perhaps in connection with geological explorations that a partial femur and vertebrae were found in the same area. They were made the basis of a species called *Titanosaurus indicus* in 1877. Despite its impressive name, it is a relatively slender *Diplodocus*-like sauropod. It was named by Richard Lydekker (1849–1915), who was with the Geological Survey of India from 1874 to 1882, publishing a number of papers on dinosaurs and other fossils before moving to the British Museum in 1883, where he catalogued the entire collection of fossil vertebrates. He continued to take an interest in Indian fossil reptiles, and in 1887 recorded *Megalosaurus* from the Ariyalur beds of Tiruchiapalli on the strength of a single tooth.

❖ ❖ ❖

Charles Alfred Matley (1866–1947) was an English accountant in India with a strong amateur interest in rocks and fossils. In 1921 he found bones, a tail club, and armor plating of what seemed to be an armored dinosaur from the Lameta limestone, high in the Cretaceous. In 1923, he named it *Lametasaurus indicus*. The bones later proved to belong to a theropod, leaving only the tail club, and scutes as evidence of the ankylosaur. Since armored sauropods have recently been found in South America, the armor plating, too, may be from another animal.

Matley collaborated with the German paleontologist von Huene in a detailed study of the Lameta beds of Bara Simla Hill at Jabalpur, published in 1933. They identified three beds with dinosaur remains. At the bottom, a carnosaur bed (containing carnosaur, coelurosaur, stegosaur, and sauropod bones) was separated by the Main Limestone from the Ossiferous Conglomerate, with some sauropod remains, and 4 feet (1.2 m) higher, the sauropod bed. At least eight genera have been named by Matley and von Huene from the carnosaur bed, most on very fragmentary evidence such as a few vertebrae. The best represented is *Indosaurus*, a heavily built megalosaur represented by a braincase with suggestions of horns behind the eyes. In the sauropod bed was found *Titanosaurus*, and remains of another sauropod, *Antarctosaurus*, first named by von Huene from South America. More recently, the rocks have been shown to be formed in a shallow lake environment alternating with soils, and nests and eggs of sauropod dinosaurs have been found in the area.

It has been suggested that one of these eggs contains a partial skeleton of a baby titanosaur, and the unfortunate baby has been pictured as about to hatch on a world in which the dinosaurs were about to become extinct. Unfortunately, this tender moment may not have happened, for another paleontologist thinks the remains are actually of a snake.

Barnum Brown worked the Lameta beds in the 1920s, and his material in the American Museum collection has recently been studied by an Indian scientist who identified several carnosaurs. The first dinosaur described by an Indian scientist was a leg of a stegosaur by Dhirendra K. Chakravarthy in 1934.

❖ ❖ ❖

In 1964 Edwin Colbert made his first visit to India. The invitation came via Pamela Lamplugh Robinson of the University of London. Dr. Robinson had trained a number of Indian paleontologists who were later employed at the Indian Statistical Institute in Calcutta. Colbert travelled with Dr. Robinson and a group of Indian paleontologists. At this time, the idea of continental drift was regarded as eccentric by most geologists, but Colbert had become interested in the similarities between the predinosaur mammal-like reptiles of the Lower Triassic in the southern continents, particularly one called *Lystrosaurus*. As opportunity offered, he visited each of the southern continents to see the evidence of these reptiles that could be found, both in museums and in the field. Ned Colbert had already published his first book on dinosaurs in 1945, and done research on them at the Ghost Ranch in 1947, but though he had not yet developed the strong special interest in dinosaurs which is now associated with his name, he did take the opportunity to see dinosaur material as well. In his entertaining autobiography *Digging into the Past*, he has described many of his museum visits and field trips, which give an interesting picture of the contrasting stages of development in the different southern continents during the 1950s and 1960s.

Colbert describes the experience of staying in rest houses dating back to British India, where the building is free but the traveler must provide his or her own bedding and food, and be prepared to be displaced by travelers of higher status. Once in the field, he had the strange experience of having an assistant to carry his geological hammer. Although his field experiences were without danger, another geologist had the experience of walking a circuit in the bush completely unaware that he was being followed by a curious tiger.

At Sironcha, there was something special to see. India's first Jurassic dinosaur and the earliest known sauropod at the time—about 200 million years old—was being excavated in a shallow quarry. It was so hot that a brush shelter was necessary to protect the workers. Villagers were hired to dispose of the surplus rock, which they carried in baskets and dumped a few hundred feet away. The rock layer was called the Kota Formation, after the village of Kota on the east bank of the River Pranhita, a tributary of the River Godavari. The rocks included continental deposits (sands and clays), and thin limestones which had been deposited in lakes.

Fossil fish of the same types as European early Jurassic had been found there in the nineteenth century, but the dinosaurs were not found until 1958, when a rich layer of bones was discovered at the junction of a sandstone with a clay lens. About 300 bones were excavated from an area 92 by 36 feet (28 by 11 m) during the 1960–61 field season. Although there was no complete skeleton, some of the bones were articulated, and included a sauropod femur almost 5 feet (1.5 m) long. There was no skull, but there were loose teeth. Work continued over a number of years, and by 1979, the site had yielded 800 sauropod bones.

The dinosaur was named *Barapasaurus* in 1975 by four Indian paleontologists: Sohan Lal Jain, T.S. Kutty, Tappan K. Roy-Chowdhury, and Sankar Chatterjee (whose later work in Texas is discussed in Chapter 11). The name comes from the word for "big leg" in the local language. It was a large, slender-limbed sauropod with spoon-shaped teeth. Although so early, it was already giant-sized, as it is only a little smaller than the American *Diplodocus*. The dinosaur was being mounted (the first in India) in the Geology Museum of the Indian Statistical Institute in 1977 when Colbert returned to India for the second time. He was then keynote speaker at the Fourth International Gondwana Symposium, and outlined the growing contribution of vertebrate fossils to the understanding of the links between the different territories of Gondwanaland—and the support they gave to the idea of continental drift.

Mouse Reptiles and Plated Sauropods

South America was opened up scientifically by voyages and overland expeditions by a number of great scientists, including Darwin and Humboldt. Although fossils were found by these early expeditions, they were of the strange mammals that occupied South America during the long period after the dinosaurs, when it was completely isolated from the rest of the world.

The first documented dinosaur discovery from South America came from Argentina in 1882, when Commandante Buratovich discovered some large fossil bones near the city of Neuquén, where the Neuquén and Limay rivers join to become the Río Negro. They were sent to Florentino Ameghino, as were five boxes more discovered by Captain G. Rhode shortly afterward. Florentino (1854–1911) was the oldest and the best known of three remarkable brothers born to Italian-born parents. He became the scientific paleontologist of the three, while the middle brother, Juan, became a successful bookseller and helped to support the other two. The youngest, Carlos (1865–1936), was a great fossil collector. Florentino studied to be a teacher, and began to publish articles on fossil mammals at the age of twenty-one. In 1878, he had the chance to go to an Exposition in Paris, where he exhibited a number of his fossils and sold some of them to the American paleontologist Cope. Florentino stayed on in Paris, acquiring a French wife and publishing some books. He returned to Argentina after four years and was surprised to find his teaching job had gone to another, but he soon opened a bookshop named after the *Glyptodon* (a fossil mammal) and studied fossils in his spare time. When he received the Neuquén fossils, he recognized them as Upper Cretaceous dinosaurs.

A contemporary of the Ameghinos, Santiago Roth (1850–1924)

had been born in Switzerland but settled in Argentina, where he became director of the Paleontological Section of the Museum of La Plata. He went searching for the Neuquén dinosaurs soon after 1882, and found more material. This he sent to Richard Lydekker, who had just left the Indian Geological Survey for the British Museum in London.

In 1884, Florentino Ameghino became a professor at the University of Córdoba, and two years later was appointed to the La Plata Museum, where he quarrelled with the director and resigned within a year. He maintained his research with another bookshop, describing his only two dinosaurs in 1899. *Clasmodosaurus* was a sauropod based on fossil teeth from Santa Cruz, and *Loncosaurus* a carnivore based on teeth and a femur (which recent investigation has suggested do not belong together). In 1902, he at last received a post worthy of his talents, when he became director of the National Museum in Buenos Aires. In his long scientific career, he named more than 6,000 fossil species, mainly mammals.

About the late 1880s Roth searched the province of Chubut, finding more dinosaurs, also from the Upper Cretaceous, which he sent to Lydekker and Arthur Smith Woodward of the British Natural History Museum. Lydekker described *Argyrosaurus*, one of the largest sauropods, from a left leg and foot in 1893. The femur is 6 feet, 6 inches (2.0 m) long. Woodward published a series of papers on South American reptiles from 1901 onward, describing *Genyodectes*, a carnivorous dinosaur, from a jaw with teeth from Chubut.

Other attempts to gather and study fossils were less successful. John Bell Hatcher (whose dinosaur collecting in the American west has been discussed in Chapter 8) led the Princeton University expeditions to South America in 1896–99. In Entre Rios, Argentina, he made an unexpected find: "I . . . visited an old monastery, where I was much interested in a considerable collection of fossils and other objects of natural history. . . . most of these bore no labels. . . . I was chiefly interested in the remains of some fossil saurians which . . . I judged to come from Triassic deposits. The sole attendant at that time . . . seemed as ignorant as myself regarding their history. . . . His chief interest seemed to lie in a collection of the hearts of dead saints, or other worthies, preserved in alcohol."

Hatcher himself found dinosaur bones when in the Mayer Basin at the foot of the Andes on the third expedition (1899), but was not equipped to collect them: "I found fragments of the bones of dinosaurs, and occasionally a nearly complete vertebra or foot-bone. . . . near the summit I came upon a nearly complete fore-limb of a large dinosaur. The weight of the humerus alone could hardly have been less than two hundred pounds. I wished very much to take this limb, but its great size and weight would have precluded our taking it with us to the coast."

Although dinosaurs have in later years been found in other countries in South America, including Brazil and Peru, Argentina has yielded the most, and has the most coherent story of discovery.

It was R. Wichmann who undertook the first important dinosaur diggings in the southern part of the Río Negro. From several large quarries he collected more sauropod bones, and also the first armored dinosaur remains from South America.

In 1918, the Museum of La Plata undertook serious excavations east of the city of Neuquén, and found several dinosaur skeletons. In 1921 and 1922, Roth and an assistant, W. Schiller, excavated more Cretaceous dinosaurs in Patagonia. Roth was now in his seventies, so the Museum of La Plata invited von Huene from Germany to work on the dinosaur collection. The German paleontologist was by now an authority on European dinosaurs and had also published on African and North American species.

He traveled to South America, reviewed the dinosaurs in the museum, and went into the field. Back home, he completed a monograph of nearly 200 pages on Argentinian Cretaceous dinosaurs, which was published in 1919. He summarized for the first time the youngest dinosaurs of Argentina, showing that they lived in a tropical climate close to the sea, in an area shared with crocodiles, turtles, and lungfish.

Some of von Huene's South American dinosaurs include two slender sauropods, the somewhat inappropriately named *Antarctosaurus* (1929), with a 2-foot (60-cm) skull and a 7-foot (2.2-m) femur; and the similar *Laplatasaurus* (1928). *Loricosaurus* (1929) was named from bone fragments and pieces of armor plate, and was naturally assumed to be an ankylosaur. No one had yet envisaged southern dinosaurs so different from northern ones that an armored sauropod was possible. Von Huene also collected dinosaurs in Brazil.

After von Huene's work, there was little new dinosaur discovery in South America for some decades. A Spanish-born paleontologist and zoologist of considerable repute, Ãngel Cabrera (1879–1960), moved to Argentina in 1925 and joined the La Plata Museum in 1926. Although his principal work was on mammals, he did describe a fragmentary dinosaur from Chubut Province in 1947. *Amygdalodon patagonicus* ("Patagonian almond-tooth") is based on some vertebrae, ribs, leg bones, and teeth from the Jurassic Cerro Carnerero Formation, and may be a brachiosaur or cetiosaur.

Colbert's first trip to South America was in 1959, and led him first to Brazil and then to Argentina. In Brazil, he was hosted by a number of Brazilian paleontologists, including one with the decidedly un-Portuguese name of Llewellyn Ivor Price (1905–80). Price had been born in Brazil of American parents, and after studying with Romer in the United States he returned to Brazil as coleader of the Museum of Comparative Zoology (Harvard) expedition in 1936, to find fossils in the red Triassic rocks of the Santa Maria Formation in the southernmost part of Brazil, Río Grande del Sul. Price later worked for the Brazilian Geological Survey, where he has inspired a generation of Brazilian paleontologists and has found Cretaceous dinosaurs from São Paulo. Colbert's expedition was to the same beds, where an important fossil was found right beside a country road, and the paleontologists worked before a constant procession of carts and a perpetual audience.

In Argentina, after visiting museums in Buenos Aires and La Plata, Colbert headed west for the foothills of the Andes. His host and guide was a doctor with an interest in fossils. Dr. Jose Minoprio lived in the town of Mendoza, where, many years before, Darwin had recorded being bitten by a vinchuca bug. (After many years of speculation about the illness Darwin suffered from in later life, it is now often thought to have been Chagas' disease, caused by a parasite carried by the bug.) The doctor was a specialist in this disease, and although it is of interest to all paleontologists, Colbert was a little startled to be put in a white gown and escorted around the hospital wards to see the patients. With the doctor, Colbert was able to tour some of the

Triassic rocks, of which he saw more on a later trip for an international Gondwana conference.

❖ ❖ ❖

In 1959, Victorino Herrera, a goatherd in the remote desert San Juan area of central Argentina, led an Argentine paleontologist through the bone-rich badlands of the Ischigualasto Formation to a fossil he had found. The paleontologist was Osvaldo Reig, who was for a while associated with the Mar del Plata Museum, but who has lived in a number of countries on three continents and is best known for his work on the chromosomes of recent mammals. He was able to collect a pelvis and hind leg, and some vertebrae, from which in 1963 he described a new dinosaur, *Herrerasaurus*, as well as a similar dinosaur, *Ischisaurus*. Both were from rocks now known to be Upper Triassic (about 230 million years old), where there are few other dinosaurs. Both were at first thought to be primitive prosauropods. *Herrerasaurus* was small, about 10 feet (3 m) long and 5 feet (1.5 m) tall, and is thought to have been carnivorous. However, it had four toes on the hind feet, unlike all the later carnivores. In 1973, the Argentinian paleontologist Juan Luis Benedetto recognized its distinctness by creating a family for it called the Herrerasauridae. As attempts were made to fit *Herrerasaurus* into the conventional classification, it seemed that it did not clearly belong to either of the two main groups of dinosaurs, and could indeed be close to the animals that were ancestral to both groups. Clearly, more material was needed, but although there were intermittent searches, no new fossils turned up for some years.

Meanwhile in 1970, Colbert described another early dinosaur that had been found in the St. Mary's Formation he had visited in Brazil. It was named *Staurikosaurus pricei*, "Price's cross reptile" (after his friend Price and the Southern Cross). *Staurikosaurus* has been considered the earliest dinosaur known, but may not be any older than *Herrerasaurus*. It has five toes on all its feet, and so is more primitive than four-toed *Herrerasaurus*. In 1987, a second *Staurikosaurus* skeleton was described from the Ischigualasto Formation in Argentina by Don Brinkman and Hans-Dieter Sues.

In 1988, Paul Sereno of the University of Chicago went on a six-week expedition to the San Juan with Jose Bonaparte and other Argentine and American colleagues. Sereno is the son of an Illinois milkman and housewife whose plans to become an artist were abandoned after an undergraduate visit to the American Museum. In 1984, while still a student, he managed a round-the-world trip visiting fossil localities in China, Mongolia, Siberia, and Europe.

Now in the Valle de la Luna (Valley of the Moon) National Park, the landscape and Triassic rocks are similar to those of Petrified Forest National Park in the United States. They had been visited by von Huene in 1930 and Romer in 1958, who also collected from other sites in the region in 1964. A femur was found less than 20 feet (6 m) from the truck, and many other specimens were located, including a *Herrerasaurus* skeleton, complete except for the neck and skull. In the fourth week, Sereno realized a small piece of territory had been missed in their systematic search, but did not check it until the end of the expedition, when nagging doubts took him back an hour's drive for another look. Sereno tells how he laid down his pack and "walked off fifty feet, straight to the most complete early dinosaur skeleton, and the first herrerasaur skull ever discovered. . . . my eyes slowly stopped along what appeared to be elongated neck vertebrae . . . right up to the beautiful occiput [back of the skull] of a primitive dinosaur." The skull was attached to another almost complete skeleton, and was in remarkably fine condition, with tiny bones associated with the ear and eyes still in place. After a year of preparation, it was clear that the dinosaur was undoubtedly carnivorous, with finely serrated teeth and an extra jaw hinge to allow large pieces of flesh to be swallowed.

❖ ❖ ❖

Since the early 1960s, a new generation of paleontologists has emerged in Argentina, for whom dinosaurs are of particular interest and importance. More than a dozen paleontologists have named new dinosaurs in the last two decades, of whom the best known is Jose F. Bonaparte, Sereno's host in the 1988 expedition. A protégé of Romer's 1960s visits, Bonaparte was a self-taught paleontologist who took charge of the fossil collections at the University of Tucuman, and then became head of vertebrate paleontology at the Argentine Natural Sciences Museum in Buenos Aires. From 1975 he has had periodic support from the National Geographic Society.

Bonaparte has excavated in beds of all the dinosaur-bearing periods, and has described Triassic, Jurassic, and Cretaceous material. Among his important discoveries are *Riojasaurus* (1969), a huge 33-foot (10-m) Late Triassic prosauropod, based on a nearly complete skeleton from La Rioja Province. Another prosauropod was named *Coloradia* (1978), but had to be renamed *Coloradisaurus* because the first name had already been used. Particularly fascinating is *Mussaurus patagonicus,* the "Patagonian mouse-reptile," named in 1979 by Bonaparte and his colleague Martin Vince. This tiny creature was found in the Late Triassic of El Tranquillo Formation, northern Santa Cruz province. It has a body only 8 inches (20 cm) long—small enough to lie in a human hand—and a baby face with a very short snout and big eyes. Several partial skeletons in beautiful condition were found huddled together with two eggs, suggesting at first that *Mussaurus* is a hatchling of a prosauropod such as *Coloradisaurus.* Adult skeletons have now been found, confirming the prosauropod nature of this little dinosaur, but showing sauropod-like features in the skull.

New carnivores include *Piatnitzkysaurus* (1979), which is an incomplete medium-sized megalosaur that may have been ancestral to the North American *Allosaurus*, and *Unquillosaurus*, a huge Upper Cretaceous form described by Jaimé E. Powell in 1979. In 1985, *Abelisaurus* ("Abel's reptile") was also named by Bonaparte and Powell. Another late Cretaceous form, it resembles *Albertosaurus* of Canada but has some distinctive primitive features which have caused it to be placed in its own family. A related form described in the same year is *Carnotaurus,* or "carnivorous bull," based on a fairly complete skeleton (without its legs and tail tip) which was found in a very hard concretion. The skull has horns, and it is the only carnosaur with almost complete skin impressions.

Most interesting are the sauropods, some of which show the developing isolation of Gondwanaland. *Patagosaurus* (1979) is the name of a nearly complete skeleton from the Jurassic of Patagonia. It seems closest to the British *Cetiosaurus leedsi*, and shows that similar animals could move between north and south at that time. Another Jurassic form, *Volkheimeria* (1979) also resembles those of northern continents, as well as other Jurassic sauropods in India (*Baraposaurus*) and Australia (*Rhoetosaurus*).

Saltasaurus (named after Salta Province by Bonaparte and Powell in 1980) is from the Upper Cretaceous of Patagonia. By that time, Gondwanaland was clearly separated from the north, as it has an extraordinary feature not known on northern sauropods. *Saltasaurus* is known from a large number of bones from several individuals, and also has bony armor of hand-sized oval plates and small pea-sized round plates that must have been embedded in the animal's hide. This association has led to the reexamination of a number of sauropod discoveries found in other parts of the world where bony plates were considered to have belonged to an armored dinosaur related to the ankylosaurs. Apart from Argentina, such associations have been recorded from other Gondwanaland localities in India and Madagascar; the only northern record is from Spain. More recently, there have been reports of a bizarre relative of *Diplodocus*. Named *Amargasaurus*, as it was found near La Amarga, it has a short neck with tall forked spines rising from some vertebrae, which may perhaps have supported a double sail running along the neck and back.

Dinosaurs Down Under

Australia's first dinosaur discovery came in 1891, when fragmentary material from the Queensland coast was described by Harry Govier Seeley as *Agrosaurus macgillivrayi*, or "MacGillivray's Field Reptile." A tibia 8 inches (21 cm) long was the principal bone, and there was also a claw and a broken tooth. For a while it was thought to represent an Upper Jurassic coelurid, but more recently it has been regarded as a prosauropod resembling *Anchisaurus* from the Lower Jurassic or Upper Triassic; just one more instance of the world-wide distribution of these primitive dinosaurs.

The next significant find also came from Queensland, but not until 1924. Paleontologist and botanist Heber Albert Longman had been born in England, but emigrated to Queensland in 1902, and joined the Queensland Museum in 1911, where he became director and stayed until 1945. He worked on fishes and marine reptiles, but reserved particular enthusiasm for his two dinosaur finds. The first find in 1924 was a discovery in a large sandy outwash plain in Lower to Middle Jurassic rocks 170 to 180 million years old, near Roma in southeastern

Queensland. Some fragments found their way to Longman at the Queensland Museum, who recognized them and asked for more. Although 420 pounds (190 kg) of bone were collected in the next few weeks, they were badly weathered and fragmentary. In 1926, Longman described the material he had—parts of the tail, pelvis, and femur. Longman chose the name *Rhoetosaurus brownei*. The genus comes from *rhoetos*, a Greek word for giant, as the animal was the largest, living or fossil, ever to be found in Australia. A further 2,000 pounds (900 kg) were subsequently collected, including a neck vertebra and parts of the back and more of the femur, which was at least 5 feet (1.5 m) long. The site was then neglected until 1975, when Mary Wade, curator of geology at the Queensland Museum, relocated the site and found bone fragments that exactly fitted those of the original discovery. The animal is an older cetiosaur, which has been estimated to have been between 40 and 56 feet (12 and 17 m) long and 10 feet (3 m) high at the hip, and it has been suggested that it could have weighed as much as 22 tons (20 t). The skeleton was placed in the Queensland Museum, and Longman described it with enthusiasm as "Australia's largest fossil."

A small group of dinosaur remains in New South Wales went across the world to be studied. A tooth and two vertebrae from Lightning Ridge in New South Wales were described by von Huene in Germany in 1932 as representatives of three different genera. *Fulgurotherium* appropriately means "lightning beast" and is probably a hypsilophodont; *Rapator* is a medium-sized carnivore whose name means "the robber"; and *Walgettosuchus*, the "Walgett crocodile," is a spine-backed carnivore.

Longman's second dinosaur was *Austrosaurus*, described in 1933 from a few vertebrae and rib fragments from a Lower Cretaceous locality in northern Queensland. It was another sauropod, which has been thought to be either a brachiosaur like the giant from Tendaguru, or a cetiosaur. Other fragments perhaps of this species have been found from time to time. Survival of an older type of sauropod to this date is an indication that Australia had become separated from other evolutionary developments. Though this barrier might have been an ocean, Southern Australia at this time was in the vicinity of the South Pole, and a long period of winter darkness might have served to keep other species away.

Muttaburra, an area on the banks of the Thomson River, 62 miles (100 km) northeast of Longreach, was used in the 1960s for mustering cattle, and so the graziers were not surprised to see bones scattered by the hooves of the cattle. However, local residents picked some of them up, and eventually a local grazier, D. Langdon, recognized that they were perhaps of significance and reported them to the Queensland Museum in 1963. The director, Alan Bartholomai, a paleontologist, proceeded to collect as much material as he could.

In the following year, Colbert made his first visit to Australia on his way home from India, and he reports seeing the skeleton of this animal, which had been recognized as a new type of iguanodont. By end of his 1964 trip, Colbert had perceived so many similarities between the fossils of the southern continents that he was convinced that the single continent Gondwanaland had really existed, and he devoted many years to working out the implications of this in a series of books and papers.

It was nearly twenty years before the fossil was finally assembled and studied, and then it was described by Bartholomai and his American-born colleague Ralph E. Molnar in 1981 as *Muttaburrasaurus langdoni*, named after the place and its discoverer. The rocks were from the Mackunda Formation in Lower Cretaceous shallow marine deposits, and the bones were associated with fossil bivalves, gastropods, and ammonites. (Although most dinosaurs are found in fresh water or land-formed rocks, a few dinosaur carcasses were washed out to sea, so that a dinosaur in marine beds is not totally unexpected.) The skeleton was the most complete dinosaur found in Australia up to that time, and was of an animal about 23 feet (7 m) long. It has an enlarged nose like one of its Mongolian relatives, and its cheek teeth were different from those of other ornithopods, so it has been suggested that it might have been partly carnivorous, but this idea is not generally accepted. The specimen was mounted in the Queensland Museum, Brisbane.

In the early 1970s, a remarkable site was found in Queensland, near the town of Winton, some 930 miles (1500 km) from Brisbane. It was excavated by Richard A. Thulborn of the University of Queensland and Mary Wade of the Queensland Museum in 1976–77. More than 4,000 dinosaur footprints were exposed in 3,260 square feet (300 m^2). The tracks freeze a few moments in time, when a large carnivorous dinosaur about 16 feet (5 m) long stalked through mud toward a lake, and stampeded a herd of 150 smaller dinosaurs, of two kinds. Tracks show that the large dinosaur changed direction (presumably to try and catch a smaller one), so that some of the smaller dinosaurs were trapped against the water and had to run back past the predator, stepping as they did in his still soft footprints.

The site was purchased in 1978 by the state park service, a roof was constructed over the best tracks in 1979, and the area became a park and was opened to the public in 1982. While the roof was being built, straw was used for insulation, and it caught fire, causing a certain amount of damage to the rock surface. Other damage has been caused by public vandalism, but fortunately parts of the quarry have been left unexposed for later study.

❖ ❖ ❖

In 1980, Ralph Molnar named two other new dinosaurs. *Kakuru* (described with Neville Pledge) was a small theropod about 10 feet (3 m) long from South Australia, based on a tibia. *Minmi*, a small ankylosaur from the Bungil Formation in South Queensland, was the first armored dinosaur from Australia. It was based on a few vertebrae and pieces of armor plating found in 1964 at Minmi Crossing, and was only about 10 feet (3 m) long. The partial skeleton was found upside down in deposits of an inland sea, and the body had been filled with clay before the skeleton was buried. The bones were encased in calcareous concretions, which were dissolved away with acetic acid in 1970. There are only eleven vertebrae, some ribs, the right foot, and pieces of armor. Extra plates of bone 0.8 by 1.6 inches (2 by 4 cm) lay alongside the vertebrae; these have not been found in any other kind of dinosaur. A more complete skeleton has recently been found which is being described. Ankylosaurs are rare in Gondwanaland, but have also been recorded in Madagascar, and recently in Antarctica.

The State of Victoria produced its first dinosaur at the turn of the century, when government geologist William Hamilton Ferguson found a claw from a carnivorous dinosaur near Cape Paterson around the turn of the century. It was not until 1978 that the search was resumed. Tim Flannery, a graduate student at Monash University of Melbourne, with his cousin John Long, located the site of the find.

Within minutes, Flannery found a broken humerus, and over the rest of the summer found another thirty bones. For the following two summers Flannery continued the search with Ralph Molnar. Patricia Rich-Vickers (a professor at Monash University) and her husband, Thomas H. Rich (a curator at the Victoria Museum), also came along, and became hooked on dinosaurs. The couple had studied vertebrate paleontology together at Columbia University, but at that time their interests had been in birds and mammals. They had resolved to go with the first job offer either of them received, and ended up in Melbourne.

A number of sites (one of which is now named Dinosaur Cove) have now been studied in Otway National Park. Greenish rocky sandstone from the Lower Cretaceous forms rocky bluffs exposed to the cold winds from the Antarctic, and digging involves climbing and laborious tunneling. In the hard rocks, hundreds of fragments of dinosaurs have now being found by the team, who are supported by Earthwatch volunteers. Some of the bones belong to known dinosaurs, such as the latest occurrence of the North American carnivore *Allosaurus* ("different lizard") shown by a single ankle bone (which is sturdier than that of other allosaurs). More exciting are two new hypsilophodonts. *Atlascopcosaurus* is named after Atlascopco, a company that donated rock drilling equipment for their fieldwork, while *Leaellynasaura*, "Leaellyn's reptile," is named after the couple's daughter, who at the age of two had asked for a dinosaur of her own. It was a juvenile specimen of a small dinosaur, that had large eyes that may be an adaptation to the darkness of the polar situation of the south coast of Australia, which was still part of Antarctica in the Cretaceous.

Australian dinosaurs are still being documented piece by piece, and some of them seem to be as strange as the unique mammal fauna of today.

Bones in the Te Hoe Valley

The rocky core of New Zealand is thought to have separated from the rest of Gondwanaland some eighty million years ago, before the dinosaurs became extinct. Yet during many years of research, no dinosaur bones were found. Bones from the extinct giant bird, the moa, were sent to England in 1839, and T.H.D. Hood sent plesiosaur bones to Owen in 1859. Collecting continued, and Hood sent a shipload of bones to England in 1869, but the *Matoaka* went down on the way. In 1877, thirty-nine cases of bones were sent to Cope in the United States, but these also seem to have been lost. Julius von Haast, superintendant of the Canterbury Museum, employed fossil collector Alex McKay in 1871 specifically to look for dinosaur bones, but nothing was found. A further hint came when an oil geologist in the late 1950s noted reptilian bones on the North Island, but no one was then available to follow up his discovery.

The eventual discoverers of dinosaurs in New Zealand are Joan Wiffen and her husband, Pont, with the help of a few friends, all living in the Hawkes Bay region on the east side of North Island. Joan describes herself as a "typical 'non-working' wife," though she and her husband (a radio technician) also run a 10-acre (4-ha) farm. When an opportunity came to take adult education classes, Pont chose geology, and when he fell ill Joan went along to the rest of the classes. The couple became interested in minerals, and Joan was particularly inspired by fossils. In 1972 they were inspired to search for vertebrate remains in the the back country. With the oilman's map in hand, they started looking at Mangahouanga in the Te Hoe Valley, where fast-flowing streams roared over log jams between steep rocky banks. At first they found marine invertebrates and fish, but in 1973 found their first reptile bones, which proved to be plesiosaur vertebrae.

Many amateurs would have withdrawn with a feeling the mission was accomplished, but the Wiffens were inspired to redouble their efforts. They established a field camp in an old shack, and developed sophisticated methods of dealing with brittle bones in a hard-rock matrix. There was a great shortage of comparative material to identify their finds, but they obtained what books they could, and in 1974 visitor Dale Russell of Canada identified one item of their collection as a theropod toe bone. In 1975, fragments of a vertebra were collected, but it could not be identified with the information at hand. After a visit to Australia, a cast of the specimen was sent to Ralph Molnar. "About a week later, I had a phone call. 'It's a dinosaur!' " The discovery was formally announced in 1980 at the Fifth Gondwana Symposium in

Wellington, New Zealand. Since then, the search has continued, and in 1988 an ankylosaur rib was also identified.

James Ross Island and Mount Kirkpatrick

Antarctica has fascinated zoogeographers because it lies between the southern continents of Africa and South America on the one side, and Australia on the other. Before the development of the theory of continental drift, the distribution of such unusual animals as the marsupials (found living in Australia and South America) was explained by land bridges that had perhaps once connected the different continents. The idea of continental drift provided an alternative mechanism for animal dispersal, and again focused attention on Antarctica. As dinosaurs were better understood, an explanation was needed for the close similarities between sites on different continents, such as Como Bluff in the United States and Tendaguru in east Africa. Fossils critical to this question must be located in the Antarctic, but how could they be found under miles of ice? Fortunately, not all the rocks of the Antarctica are permanently hidden, and some of them contain fossils.

In 1968 Colbert was retiring from the American Museum and planning to move to Arizona, when he had a telephone call. A piece of fossil bone had been found in Triassic sediments from Antarctica, about 400 miles (643 km) from the South Pole. It was only 2 inches (5 cm) long, but could be identified as part of the jaw of an amphibian, and indicated that there was a chance of finding other vertebrates in Antarctica. Instead of retiring, Colbert found himself in the Antarctic within six months, supported by a small group of scientists, including Jim Jensen of Utah (and later *Supersaurus* fame). The trip was far from smooth, involving winds that could blow a person over, and more than one helicopter crash. One Triassic site showed coal and petrified wood, indicating vegetation at the time of the dinosaurs. Eventually, on a site known as Coalsack Bluff, abundant reptile bones turned up, including definite evidence of the characteristic mammal-like reptile, *Lystrosaurus*.

After this discovery, it seemed possible that dinosaurs could be found in Antarctica, but two decades passed before the first discovery was reported by Argentinian scientists Zulma de Gasparini, E. Olivero, R.

Scasso, and C. Rinaldi of the Museum of La Plata. In 1986, they were investigating the Late Cretaceous rocks of James Ross Island, when remains were found that were eventually identified as belonging to an ankylosaur. This was reported in 1988, and in the following year a group of British scientists recorded hypsilophodont remains from the same island. Only two years later the first find was made on mainland Antarctica in December 1990 when David Elliott of Ohio State University found fragments of a large carnivorous dinosaur high in Jurassic beds on Mount Kirkpatrick, 400 miles (644 km) from the South Pole.

For many years, it had been customary to report that dinosaurs have been found in every part of the world except Antarctica. Now even Antarctica is yielding its dinosaur treasures.

Reuniting Gondwanaland

Although the scattered continents and subcontinents of Gondwanaland cannot be physically reunited, the lost supercontinent may be re-created in the scientific imagination through the work of geologists and pale-ontologists. This group of rich and diverse lands, linked by their ancient origin, will repay both the field and the armchair dinosaur hunter in future years.

Here in the southern continents, the excitement of dinosaur hunting is perhaps most alive. After more than twenty years of dedi-cated spare time collection, New Zealander Joan Wiffen still feels the enthusiasm of all dinosaur hunters.

> There is still so much to do, to learn, to study, record. For me, collecting fossils, holding these ancient bones in my hands, studying to find out what they are, how the creatures they repre-sent lived, has enabled me to reach back in time, to touch the past. . . . Such excitement and joy is more than I ever hoped to experience. The tempo of our collecting has probably slowed down a little over the years. . . . But the enthusiasm is still as great, the magic is still there. . . . The car is packed and ready. The ham-mers, chisels, backpacks and rope are in the boot. . . . Who knows what treasures are waiting . . .

AFTERWORD: DINOSAURS TODAY

JUST AS DINOSAURS HAVE COMMON FEATURES WITH THE mythical dragons, so the dinosaur hunter has a lot in common with the mythical dragon hunter. Joseph Campbell describes two variants of the hero's journey. "One is the physical deed, in which the hero performs a courageous act. . . . The other is the spiritual deed, in which the hero learns to experience the supernormal range of human spiritual life and then comes back with a message." Part of the fascination of the dinosaur quest is surely that it offers an opportunity to participate in both kinds of journey.

The hunting of dinosaurs has often been a courageous act, requiring at the least great mental and physical effort, often exposure to harsh climates and topography, and sometimes the real dangers of disease, banditry, and war. Intellectually and spiritually, it requires the uncommon ability to envisage a dream, an idea, a vision of wonder and truth; to follow it with tenacity at the expense of the normal comforts of life; to find and understand hidden knowledge; and to share it with the rest of humankind.

For the individual dinosaur collector and researcher, such motives have, consciously or unconsciously, fueled the patient searches, the long expeditions, and the often tedious research. For some, involvement with dinosaurs has been a small but exciting incident in an academic or other career, for others it is a consuming passion so strong that it dominates the pattern of an entire life. Why else would Charles Sternberg go out fossil hunting in his eighties, or Roy Chapman Andrews hang on in Beijing long after the Mongolian expeditions were over, hoping against hope that the frontier would open again? For some, the quest has led to tragedy. The bitter rivals Cope and Marsh reaped much personal pain along with their triumphs; Mantell became embittered and perhaps committed suicide; Cutler found a stormy but still promising career cut short in an African hut; while Fraas carried back to Germany both the bones with which he launched the quest and the disease which prevented him from returning to Africa as its leader. But for many others, dinosaurs have provided a career so exciting that, once embarked on the voyage, they never considered anything else.

If it is easy to see why individual scientists (increasingly of both sexes) are motivated to make their hero's journey, we must still ask what has been the value to society of the treasure brought back from more than 150 years of dinosaur hunting? First, dinosaur hunting is approachable, user-friendly science, and one of the greatest of the spectator sports. Directly though volunteering in the field and museum, and indirectly through books, film, and television, the man (and woman and child) in the street can participate in the excitements of science in a way that is not possible in many other fields. An expedition and a scientific discovery offer fun and entertainment, but are of more significance than yet another goal or a winning hand of cards. Like the thousands that begged for a place on Andrews's expeditions to Mongolia, there seems to be something to do on an expedition that any of us can aspire to. Moreover a dinosaur is a very tangible discovery, and even if some of its scientific significance escapes the layperson, there is the feeling that anything so large, strange, or old has real importance; that it is in some way symbolic of all the mysteries of the earth and the past.

Scientists and collectors have discovered a lot of dinosaurs, in a great diversity of places. Tons of bones occupy museum storerooms around the world. Humanity can see the products of the most spectacular trophy hunts ever conducted, in exhibits in our big museums, or can find more words to read about dinosaurs than can be read in a dozen lifetimes. Some dinosaurs are so complete that we can count their ribs and feel their skin, while others are still known only by tantalizing fragments. Certainly, it is clear that we haven't found them all (even if we've named more than we've found) and that every new expedition may still answer one question and raise another dozen.

In some ways dinosaurs are almost as well understood as if we could drive out to a game park to watch them, yet in others they are as mysterious as the least understood creatures. Particularly puzzling are the broad questions of physiology and behavior, and the still mysterious disappearance of the dinosaurs. Though these questions have not dominated the pages of this regional book, they are at the back of all paleontologist's minds when they go into the field or open the bone drawer—not just because they are of great scientific interest, but because they will inevitably come up on the next radio talk show.

What use are dinosaurs? They do not have to be any use to us, for they existed long before we came along, and our valuation of them will not affect their lives. But how do we justify the human activity they generate; the amount of money that continues to go into their collection, study and interpretation. First, the study of dinosaurs is real science—it deals with real creatures, which have played a significant role in earth history, and are of enormous scientific interest for their own sake. Second, a knowledge of dinosaurs has a bearing on many related areas of science, such as continental drift; extinction theory; the physiology, anatomy, and ecology of other animals: and the evolution of plants. The study of dinosaurs is never likely to produce the economic benefits or ethical nightmares of another science once seen as equally useless—atomic physics. But for those for whom science has to have a practical "use" beyond the advancement of knowledge, it can certainly be shown that some of the products of dinosaur study can serve more mundane needs, including education; entertainment: and the commercial and economic benefits of publishing, tourism, and other businesses.

The study of dinosaurs satisfies a profound human need to know, to understand. As once living creatures, dinosaurs tell us something about ourselves as well as themselves. At an even deeper level, dinosaurs have a multiplicity of symbolic meanings for us. They are the closest we can get to the dragons of mythology, the "bug eyed monsters" of speculative fiction, the animal that is within every human, the beast that lurks in us all. Even as we gaze at their horns and scales, some of us feel kinship.

Ultimately, perhaps the highest and best use of dinosaurs is to nourish in scientist and layperson alike a sense of wonder, to keep alive in us a sense of humility in the face of an only partially comprehensible universe. In an age where man has walked on the moon, where genes are being mapped and altered, where organic compounds of unbelievable complexity are being studied, dinosaurs remind us vividly that we still do not know everything. It is not an unimportant role. Let us hope that the next 150 years of dinosaur discovery will continue to raise new questions, and that some small boys and girls will still grow up wanting to find out the answers.

SELECTED BIBLIOGRAPHY

This book is based on far more sources than can conveniently be listed here, including biographies, histories of science, many scientific papers and magazine articles, archival sources, and my own experiences and discussions with others. I have tried to summarize here the more accessible published sources that I have found most useful, and those that will help readers wishing to go farther in their own discovery of the dinosaurs. General references are followed by some specific chapter sources.

OVERVIEWS

Camp, L. Sprague de, and C. Crook de Camp. 1986. *The Day of the Dinosaur*. New York: Curtis Books.

Charig, A. 1983. *A New Look at the Dinosaurs*. New York: Facts on File, Inc.

Colbert, E.H. 1983. *Dinosaurs: An Illustrated History*. Maplewood, N.J.: Hammond Inc.

Czerkas, S.M., and S.A. Czerkas. 1990. *Dinosaurs: A Complete World History*. Limpsfield: B. Mitchell.

Lambert, D., and the Diagram Group. 1990. *The Dinosaur Data Book*. New York: Avon Books.

Lessem, D. 1992. *Kings of Creation*. New York: Simon and Schuster.

McGowan, C. 1991. *Dinosaurs, Spitfires, and Sea Dragons*. Cambridge, Mass.: Harvard University Press.

Man, J. 1987. *The Day of the Dinosaur*. London: Excalibur Books.

Norman, D. 1985. *The Illustrated Encyclopedia of Dinosaurs*. New York: Crescent Books.

Preiss, B. and R. Silverberg, eds. 1992. *The Ultimate Dinosaur: Past : Present: Future*. New York: Bantam Books.

Russell, D.A. 1989. *An Odyssey in Time: The Dinosaurs of North America*. Toronto: University of Toronto Press.

Wilford, J.N. 1985. *The Riddle of the Dinosaur*. New York: Knopf.

AUTOBIOGRAPHY

Colbert, E.H. 1989. *Digging into the Past: An Autobiography*. New York: Dembner Books.

BIBLIOGRAPHIES

Chure, D.J., and J.S. McIntosh, eds. 1989. *A Bibliography of the Dinosauria (Exclusive of the Aves) 1677-1986*. Grand Junction, Colo.: Museum of Western Colorado.

Sarjeant, W.A.S., comp. 1980. *Geologists and the History of Geology: An International Bibliography from the Origins to 1978*. 5 vols. New York: Arno Press.

– – –. 1987. *Supplement 1979–1984 and Additions,* 2 vols. Malabar, Fla.: Robert E. Krieger Publishing Company.

HISTORY OF VERTEBRATE PALEONTOLOGY

Buffetaut, E. 1987. *A Short History of Vertebrate Palaeontology*. London: Croom Helm.

Colbert, E.H. 1968. *Men and Dinosaurs: The Search in Field and Laboratory*. New York: E.P. Dutton & Co.

Howard, R.W. 1975. *The Dawnseekers: The First History of American Palaeontology*. New York: Harcourt, Brace, Jovanovich.

Lanham, U. 1973. *The Bone Hunters*. New York: Columbia University Press.

Wendt, H. 1970. *Before the Deluge*. London: Granada Publishing Ltd.

KINDS OF DINOSAURS

Benton, M. 1984. *The Dinosaur Encyclopedia*. New York: Simon & Schuster, Inc.

Dodson, P., et al. 1990. *Encyclopedia of Dinosaurs*. New York: Beekman House.

Glut, D.E. 1982. *The New Dinosaur Dictionary*. Secaucus, N.J.: Citadel Press.

Paul, G.S. 1988. *Predatory Dinosaurs of the World: A Complete Illustrated Guide*. New York: Simon & Schuster, Inc.

PALEONTOLOGY

Halstead, L.B. 1982. *Hunting the Past: Fossils, Rocks, Tracks and Trails. The Search for the Origin of Life*. London: Hamish Hamilton Ltd.

SPECIALIZED STUDIES

Carpenter, K., and P.J. Currie, eds. 1990. *Dinosaur Systematics. Approaches and Perspectives*. New York: Cambridge University Press.

Czerkas, S.M., and E.C. Olson. 1987. *Dinosaurs Past and Present*, 2 vols. Los Angeles: Natural History Museum of Los Angeles County & University of Washington Press.

Jacobs, L.L., ed. 1980. *Aspects of Vertebrate History: Essays in Honor of Edwin Harris Colbert*. Flagstaff: Museum of Northern Arizona Press.

Padian, K., ed. 1986. *The Beginning of the Age of Dinosaurs: Faunal Change across the Triassic-Jurassic Boundary*. New York: Cambridge University Press.

Weishampel, D.B., P. Dodson, and H. Osmolska. 1990. *The Dinosauria*. Berkeley: University of California Press.

TRACKS

Gillette, D.D., and M.G. Lockley, eds. 1989. *Dinosaur Tracks and Traces*. New York: Cambridge University Press.

Lockley, M. 1991. *Tracking Dinosaurs*. New York: Cambridge University Press.

SOURCES BY CHAPTER

1. A World of Dinosaurs

Adams, F.D. 1938. *The Birth and Development of the Geological Sciences*. New York: Dover Publications, Inc.

2. A Distinct Tribe of Saurian Reptiles

Delair, J.B., and W.A.S. Sarjeant. 1975. "The Earliest Discoveries of Dinosaurs," *Isis* 66: 5–25.

Desmond, A.J. 1976. *The Hot-Blooded Dinosaurs*. New York: Dial Press.

– – –. 1982. *Archetypes and Ancestors: Palaeontology in Victorian London 1850–1875*. London: Blond & Briggs.

Edmonds, W. 1979. *The Iguanodon Mystery*. Harmondsworth, Middlesex: Kestrel Books.

3. Elegant Jaws and Ancient Wings

Barthel, K.W., N.H.M. Swinburne, and S.C.Morris. 1990. *Solnhofen: A Study of Mesozoic Palaeontology*. New York: Cambridge University Press.

Currie, P.J. 1991. *The Flying Dinosaurs: The Illustrated Guide to the Evolution of Flight*. Red Deer: Red Deer College Press.

Feduccia, A. 1980. *The Age of Birds*. Cambridge, Mass.: Harvard University Press.

Hecht, M.K., J.H. Ostrom, G. Viohl, and P. Wellnhofer, eds. 1985. *The Beginnings of Birds: Proceedings of the International Archaeopteryx Conference, Eichstatt, 1984*. Eichstatt, Germany: Freunde des Jura-Museums Eichstatt.

4. The Iguanodons of Bernissart

Norman, D.B. 1980. *On the Ornithischian dinosaur Iguanodon bernissartensis of Bernissart (Belgium)*, Memoire 178. Brussels: Institut Royal des Sciences Naturelles de Belgique.

5. From Whale Lizard to Superclaw

Milner, A., and R. Croucher 1987. *"Claws": The Story (So Far) of a Great British Dinosaur Baryonyx walkeri*. London: British Museum (Natural History).

Whybrow, P.J. 1985. "A History of Fossil Collecting and Preparation Techniques," *Curator* 28: 5–26.

6. A Marvelous Abundance of Footprints

Hitchcock, E. 1858. *Ichnology of New England: A Report on the Sandstone of the Connecticut Valley, Especially Its Fossil Footmarks. Made to the Government of the Commonwealth of Massachusetts*. Reprint. Boston: Arno Press 1974.

Lull, Richard Swann. 1953. *Triassic Life of the Connecticut Valley*, Bulletin no. 81. Hartford: State of Connecticut Geological and Natural History Survey.

7. Bones by the Ton

"History of Vertebrate Paleontology in the Rocky Mountain Region," *Earth Sciences History* 9/1 (1990).

Osborn, H.F. 1930. *Fifty-two Years of Research, Observation and Publication, 1877–1929*. New York: Charles Scribner's Sons.

Ostrom, J.H., and J.S. McIntosh, 1966. *Marsh's Dinosaurs: Collections from Como Bluff*. New Haven: Yale University Press.

Shor, E.N. 1971. *Fossils and Flies: The Life of a Compleat Scientist. Samuel Wendell Williston (1851–1918)*. Norman: University of Oklahoma Press.

8. Triceratops and Tyrannosaurus

Bird, R.T. 1985. *Bones for Barnum Brown: Adventures of a Dinosaur Hunter.* Fort Worth: Texas Christian University Press.

Brown, B. 1919. "Hunting Big Game of Other Days: A Boating Expedition in Search of Fossils in Alberta, Canada," *National Geographic Magazine* 35: 40 7–29.

Brown, F.R. 1987. *Let's Call Him Barnum.* New York: Vantage Press.

Inglis, Alex. 1978. *Northern Vagabond: The Life and Career of J.B. Tyrrell — The Man Who Conquered the Canadian North.* Toronto: McClelland & Stewart.

Rainger, R. 1990. "Collectors and Entrepreneurs: Hatcher, Wortman and the Structure of American Vertebrate Paleontology c. 1900," *Earth Sciences History* 9: 14–21.

Russell, L.S. 1966. *Dinosaur Hunting in Western Canada.* Royal Ontario Museum Life Sciences Contribution 70. Toronto.

Sternberg, C.H. 1909. *The Life of a Fossil Hunter.* Reprint. Bloomington: University of Indiana Press. 1990.

–––. 1932. *Hunting Dinosaurs in the Bad Lands of the Red Deer River, Alberta, Canada.* Reprint. Edmonton: NeWest Press, 1985.

Weston, T.C. 1899. *Reminiscences among the Rocks. In Connection with the Geological Survey of Canada.* Toronto: Warwick Bros. & Rutter.

Winslow-Spragge, L. 1962. *The Life of George Mercer Dawson, 1849–1901.* Privately published.

9. The Most Colossal Animal Found Out West

McGinnis, H.J. 1982. *Carnegie's Dinosaurs.* Pittsburgh: Carnegie Museum.

10. Large Duckbills and Small Carnivores

Churcher, C.S., ed. 1976. *Athlon: Essays on Palaeontology in Honour of Loris Shano Russell.* Toronto: Royal Ontario Museum.

Folinsbee, R.E., and D.M. Ross, eds. 1965. *Vertebrate Palaeontology in Alberta: Report of a conference held at the University of Alberta August 29 to September 3, 1963.* Edmonton: University of Alberta.

Rogers, K. 1991. *The Sternberg Fossil Hunters: A Dinosaur Dynasty.* Missoula, Mont. Mountain Press Publishing Company.

Spalding, D., and A. Spalding. 1985. *Dinosaur Provincial Park Learning Resources Manual.* Edmonton, Alberta Recreation and Parks.

11. Little Dinosaurs and Big Trees

Colbert, E.H. 1980. *A Fossil-Hunter's Notebook: My Life with Dinosaurs and Other Friends.* New York: E.P. Dutton.

– – –. 1989. *The Triassic Dinosaur Coelophysis,* Bulletin no. 57. Flagstaff: Museum of Northern Arizona.

Long, R.A., and R. Houk. 1988. *Dawn of the Dinosaurs. The Triassic in Petrified Forest.* Petrified Forest: Petrified Forest Museum Association.

Zimmer, C. 1992. "Ruffled Feathers." *Discover* 13, 5: 44–54.

12. The Good Mother and the Dinosauroid

Alberta: Studies in the Arts and Sciences 1/1 (1988). Special issue on the Tyrrell Museum.

Bakker, R.T. 1986. *The Dinosaur Heresies*. New York: William Morrow & Co.

Currie, P.J. 1981. "The Provincial Museum of Alberta: Dinosaurs in the Public Eye". *Geoscience Canada* 8/1: 33–35.

Gross, R. 1985. *Dinosaur Country: Unearthing the Badlands' Prehistoric Past*. Saskatoon: Western Producer Prairie Books.

Horner, J.R., and J. Gorman. 1988. *Digging Dinosaurs*. New York: Workman Publishing.

Reid, M. 1990. *The Last Great Dinosaurs*. Red Deer: Red Deer College Press.

Russell, D.A., and R. Seguin. 1982. *Reconstructions of a Small Cretaceous Theropod Slenonychosaurus inequalis and a Hypoyhetical Denosauroid,* Syllogeus no.37. Ottawa: National Museum of Natural Sciences.

Russel, D.A., and G. Rice, eds. 1992. K–TEC II: *Cretaceous–Tertiary Extinctions and Possible Terrestrial and Extraterrestrial Causes,* Syllogeus no. 39. Ottawa: National Museum of Natural Sciences.

13. These Must Be Dinosaur Eggs

Andrews, R.C. 1926. *On the Trail of Ancient Man*. New York: G.P. Putnam's Sons.

– – –. 1943. *Under a Lucky Star*. New York: Viking Press.

Perkins, John, and the American Museum of Natural History 1981. *To the Ends of the Earth*. New York: Pantheon Books.

Preston, D.J. 1986. *Dinosaurs in the Attic: An Excursion into the American Museum of Natural History*. New York: Ballantine Books.

14. Dragons' Tombs in the Desert

Kielan-Jaworowska, Z. 1969. *Hunting for Dinosaurs*. Cambridge, Mass.: MIT Press.

15. Dragons of China and Japan

Andersson, J.G. 1973. *Children of the Yellow Earth*. Reprint. Cambridge, Mass.: MIT Press. 1973.

Dong Z., and A.C. Milner. 1988. *Dinosaurs from China*. London: British Museum (Natural History).

16. Astonishing Creature

Alexander, R.M. 1989. *Dynamics of Dinosaurs and Other Extinct Giants*. New York: Columbia University Press.

Parkinson, J. 1930. *The Dinosaur in East Africa*. London: H., F. & G. Witherby.

17. Reunite Gondwanaland

Rich, P.V., and G.F. van Tets, eds. 1985. *Kadimakara: Extinct Vertebrates of Australia*. Princeton: Princeton University Press.

Simpson, G.G. 1988. *Discoverers of the Lost World*. New Haven: Yale University Press.

Wiffen, J. 1991. *Valley of the Dragons: The Story of New Zealand's Dinosaur Woman*. Glenfield: Random Century New Zealand Ltd.

INDEX

As this is a historical work, names of fossils, people, and places generally appear as they were used at the time. Scientific names are in *italics*.

Hastings, Sussex 14, 69
Hatcher, John Bell 120-3, 280-1
Hawkins, Benjamin Waterhouse 67, 91-3
Hayden, Ferdinand Vandiveer 98, 113, 140, 205
Hell Creek, Montana 126
Helopus zdanskyi 242
Hennig, Edwin 258, 260, 262-4
Herrerasaurus 2, 283-4
Hesperornis 205
Hitchcock, Charles Henry 90-1
 Edward 80-9, 93, 94,
 Edward Jr. 89-90
Hokkaido University 250
Holland, William Jacob 138-46
Horner, John (Jack) 195, 197-201, 206, 219
Hot-blooded dinosaurs 34, 39, 41, 162, 170, 186, 189
Howe Quarry 149
Huayangosaurus taibaii 246
Huene, Friedrich von 37-8, 64, 94, 136, 172, 243-4, 276, 281-2, 284, 287
Hulke, John Whitaker 63, 70, 72
Humboldt Museum für Naturkunde 30, 36, 263
Hunterian Museum 21
Huxley, Thomas Henry 29, 34-5, 39, 49, 63, 69, 70, 108, 109, 256
Hylaeosaurus 22, 60-1, 65, 71-2
Hypsilophodon 70, 72-3, 200-1

Iguanodon 3, 15, 17, 20, 22, 44, 48-63, 65-7, 69-70, 73-4, 84-5, 88
 I. bernissartensis 47, 52-3
 I. foxii 70
 I. mantelli 52
India, Geological Survey 276, 280
Indian Statistical Institute 181, 277
 Geology Museum 279
Indosaurus 277
Iren Dabasu 217-8, 248
Irvine Coulee, Alberta 117
Isaac, J.C. 115, 117
Ischisaurus 283
Isle of Wight 64-5, 70-2

James Ross Island 293
Janensch, Werner 258, 261-2, 264
Jarzen, David 189
Jefferson, Thomas 112-3
Jensen, James "Dinosaur Jim" 150-1, 292
 Ron 150

Jiangjunmiaosaurus 249
Johns Hopkins University 186, 201
Johnson, Albert F. 218-9
Jones, Eddie 150
 H.S. "Corky" 158
Judith River 113
Jurassic 1, 9, 26, 62, 65, 68-9, 77, 95, 102, 104, 136-7, 140, 150, 172, 202, 243-7, 249, 253, 256, 261, 270, 278, 282, 285-6, 293
Juvenile dinosaurs 68, 144, 148, 180, 194, 196, 199, 205, 250, 290

Kaisen, Peter C. 111, 218
Kakuru 289
Kansas, State Agricultural College 99, 115
 University 125, 157
Kentrosaurus 262
 K. aethiopicus 262
Kielan-Jaworowska, Zofia 229-34, 236-7
Kindope 261, 267
Kirkpatrick, 292-3
Knight, Charles Robert 223
 Wilbur Clinton 110, 136-7, 139, 187
Kovalevsky, Vladimir 54
Kowalski, Kazimierz 231
Kozlowski, Roman 229
Kritosaurus 160
Kryshtofovitch, Afrikan Nikolaevich 240
K-TEC conference 186
Kulczycki, Julian 230-1
Kurzanov, Sergei Mikhailovich 238

Laelaps 91, 117
 L. aquilunguis 91-2
Lakes, Arthur 97, 99-100, 105-7
Lambe, Lawrence 123, 131-2, 157, 161
Lambeosaurus 3, 132, 158, 167
 L. lambei 157
Lametasaurus indicus 276
Landslide Butte, Montana 201
Langdon, D. 288
Langham, Peter 68
Langston, Wann Jr. 165-6, 192
Laosaurus 104
La Plata Museum 280-2, 293
Laplatasaurus 281
Lausanne, University 37
Leaellynasaura 290
Leakey, Louis Seymour Bazett 264-6
Leeds, Alfred Nicholson 63
 Charles Edward 63
LeFeuvre, Grace (Mrs Loris Russell) 162